D0952225

BLOOD PROFITS

BLOOD
PROFITS

How American Consumers
Unwittingly Fund Terrorists

VANESSA NEUMANN

ST. MARTIN'S PRESS ⚏ NEW YORK

www.stmartins.com

The Library of Congress Cataloging-in-Publication Data is available upon request.

ISBN 978-1-250-08935-9 (hardcover)
ISBN 978-1-250-08936-6 (ebook)

Our books may be purchased in bulk for promotional, educational, or business use. Please contact your local bookseller or the Macmillan Corporate and Premium Sales Department at 1-800-221-7945, extension 5442, or by email at MacmillanSpecialMarkets@macmillan.com.

First Edition: December 2017

10 9 8 7 6 5 4 3 2 1

For Stuart, and the ones, now stilled,
now silent—who sacrificed

CONTENTS

Acknowledgments   ix

From "A Smuggler's Song," by Rudyard Kipling   xi

Introduction   1

1: A Simple Transaction   6

2: Learning About Crime, Terror, and Corruption   27

3: "A Little Fun"   42

4: Filling in the Puzzle   63

5: Sheikh, Colonel, Trafficker, Terrorist   77

6: The War Games Begin   99

7: Khans, Bags, and Triads   119

8: Up in Smoke   136

9: Bad Sport   160

10: Trading in Sickness and Violence   190

11: It's All About the Benjamins   209

12: Crime and Terror Converge   238

13: The Stories We Tell   256

Selected Bibliography   277
Notes   282
Index   297

ACKNOWLEDGMENTS

My earliest formulations of the links between illicit trade and terrorist finance appeared in publications for the Foreign Policy Research Institute.

This book would not have been possible without the valuable insights and contributions of numerous brilliant and talented professionals. I am greatly indebted to my agent, Keith Korman, of Raines & Raines, and my editor, Karen Wolny, of St. Martin's Press. I am indebted also to: Jack Radisch of the Organisation for Economic Development and Co-operation (OECD); Professor Thomas Pogge at Yale University's Global Justice Program (GJP); Dr. Lieutenant Colonel Scott Crino; the Johns Hopkins University Applied Physics Laboratory; Danielle Schwab; "Chris Howard"; Deborah Ayis of the Counter-Terrorism Committee Executive Directorate (CTED) of the United Nations; General David Petraeus; former president of Mexico Felipe Calderón; Jean-Luc Moreau; Ron Noble; and Dr. Mathew Burrows of the Atlantic Council.

From "A Smuggler's Song,"
by Rudyard Kipling

. . . .

Five and twenty ponies,
Trotting through the dark—
Brandy for the Parson, 'Baccy for the Clerk.
Laces for a lady; letters for a spy,
Watch the wall my darling while the Gentlemen go by!

. . . .

If you meet King George's men, dressed in blue and red,
You be careful what you say, and mindful what is said.
If they call you "pretty maid," and chuck you 'neath the chin,
Don't you tell where no one is, nor yet where no one's been!

. . . .

Five and twenty ponies,
Trotting through the dark—
Brandy for the Parson, 'Baccy for the Clerk.
Them that asks no questions isn't told a lie—
Watch the wall my darling while the Gentlemen go by!

Introduction

This book and the events it describes were born of love and anger: love of two countries (the US and Venezuela), freedom, and dignity; anger at repression, corruption, and manipulation. It's in my blood.

My Neumann grandparents were Czech Jews, who lost most of their family to the Nazis and then escaped Soviet oppression with the help of a smuggler who got them to Venezuela, after the US had rejected them. In 1949, Venezuela was under a military dictatorship, but it was still the Promised Land to poor refugees: my grandparents worked hard and prospered, so much so that within ten years their son (my father) was going to boarding school in Millbrook, New York. He eventually married a middle-class American girl he met through her godparents, who worked for Shell Oil in Venezuela. The Neumann family business, Corimon, listed on the New York Stock Exchange in 1993, one of the first South American companies to do so. We and other Venezuelan business leaders set up an MBA program, one not only modeled on Harvard's, but actually under the guidance of Harvard Business

School professor Michael Porter, the guru behind the books *Competitive Strategy* and *Competitive Advantage.*

I was too naïve to realize it then, but change was afoot. While attending Columbia University, I spent my summer holidays working on *The Daily Journal* (our English-language newspaper; much of its staff would move to *The Latin American Herald Tribune*, founded by *The Daily Journal's* former editor) and in Corimon's corporate planning and finance departments. As a Caracas socialite, I was featured in society pages, magazine covers, and even cinema newsreels.

The last Air France Concorde flight from Paris to Caracas was March 23, 1982, just a few months before I moved to the US. Middle-class Venezuelans used to make fun of Americans as poor, and there were frequent shopping flights from Caracas to Miami: fly out in the morning, shop all day, return to Caracas at night. It was the trope in a signature comedy sketch not unlike those one might see on *Saturday Night Live:* hordes of ill-mannered, newly middle-class Venezuelans would wreak havoc in Miami and then end the sketch with: "It's cheap—give me two." Those were the "Days of the 4.30," when Venezuela's currency, the Bolívar, was 4.30 to 1 US dollar. Now that currency is about Bs.F. 2,200,000=US$1,[1] and the channel on which that show aired—started by the Venezuelan branch of the Phelps family, Rockefeller relations—was long ago closed by President Hugo Chávez. It was the channel with the broadest reach in Venezuela. I was there when the change began, but I was too naïve to recognize its implications.

Colonel Chávez burst onto the political scene with fiery revolutionary rhetoric and great charisma during his failed coup in February 1992. In his one minute of national television the government gave him to call down his troops, Chávez announced: "Our cause has not succeeded *por ahora.*" *Por ahora* (for now) became his motto—and remained so more than a decade later when he ruled as president. In that 1992 speech, he expressed both I-will-be-back determination and accountability for what had gone wrong that day. Angry, poor, marginalized Venezuelans were impressed. No Venezuelan leader had taken any responsibility for anything that had gone wrong in decades: not the rising crime, not the rising inequality, not the rising corruption. Hugo Chávez instantly became a revolutionary hero to many: the battle for justice for the oppressed poor now had a hero's face (Chávez) and a slogan (*por ahora*).

After being released from prison for the coup attempt, he prevailed in the 1998 presidential election: he rode a wave of anger and riots all the way to the presidential palace. After Chávez was elected, my grandfather cofounded another newspaper, called *Tal Cual*, which translates roughly as "Just So"—it's how you punctuate a story you are telling in detail ("It happened just so!") or how you express agreement with a story you are hearing. *Tal Cual* was designed to counter *Chavismo*, as the ideology of Hugo Chávez came to be known, and to be distributed in the poorer, pro-*Chavista* areas. The newspaper's cofounder and editor-in-chief, Teodoro Petkoff, was a former Communist guerrilla, which made his rejection of the Chávez regime all the more powerful.

In my doctoral dissertation for Columbia University in the early 2000s, I wrote critically of Hugo Chávez's rise to the presidency of Venezuela and of his subsequent consolidation of power, which he justified in angry and divisive rhetoric. I thought it was a recipe for corruption and a dictatorial trampling of human rights.

I was right. By 2006, I was splitting my time between teaching political philosophy at Hunter College in New York and working for the International Institute of Strategic Studies, a London-based think tank that specializes in analyzing armed conflict. I was examining details of the low-intensity civil war in Colombia and looking at the roles of both the Chávez government in neighboring Venezuela and drug trafficking in empowering Colombia's violent narcoterrorist insurgency (a terrorist insurgency that controls drug production in its territory), the Revolutionary Armed Forces of Colombia, better known by their Spanish acronym, FARC. From my research, I knew the Venezuelan Chávez-led

Bolivarian Revolution was full of crime, corruption, and its own imperialist agenda, but in his first decade as president, Chávez had parlayed socioeconomic resentment into near-invincibility.

His armor was dented, though, in December 2007, when he lost a referendum on the constitutional changes that would have extended his dictatorial powers to rule by decree, suspending civil rights and effectively making him president for life. He quickly turned defiant: "For me, this isn't a defeat. This is *por ahora*."

In 2008 I married into a British family that was both political and journalistic: my father-in-law, Bill Cash, MP, was a renowned Thatcherite Tory (a Conservative Euroskeptic); my husband, William Cash, was a writer and magazine owner. Our wedding reception was in the Speaker's Palace of the Palace of Westminster, the UK Parliament, and was attended by the editor and owner of every single major UK publication, from the *Financial Times* to *The Sun*, except for *The Guardian*.

Not liking the results of the 2007 referendum, President Chávez held another one in 2009—the one that got me on the BBC and launched my political commentary career. When I returned to New York, press interest in Venezuela continued, and I rode the wave. I appeared on Al Jazeera English, continued writing for the British magazine *Standpoint*, and started writing for the US conservative magazine *The Weekly Standard*. Then the Colombian government (which is Conservative, pro-American, and anti-*Chavista*) invited me to come to Colombia, twice.

In 2010 I incorporated as Vanessa Neumann, Inc. My first professional foray into this dark world of illicit trade was in 2011, when I was asked to assist in an anticorruption investigation. A Washington, D.C., investigative firm tapped me specifically because they knew I had unique access into the company in question. The client company (long-standing, legitimate, and huge) had had a substantial portion of its assets seized for the benefit of a rival company (into which I had access) by government officials. The stolen assets were used as collateral for a loan from a foreign bank. Much of the money from the loan was funneled into bank accounts of the government officials in a jurisdiction with strong banking secrecy. It was not an easy case to unravel or to explain, but we won. Since then, anticorruption has been a personal cause.

In 2013, I signed my first long-term client, a global corporation that has big problems with both counterfeiters and competition from businesses owned by huge criminal organizations. I rechristened my company Asymmetrica, to apply the precepts of asymmetric warfare (the ways in which a small and agile power can defeat a larger one) with the stated mission of combating illicit trade for corporate and government clients. This is the story of our experiences.

A Simple Transaction

Jackie loves a bargain, and she's very chic—always on trend. As a banker, she knows a good deal when she sees one, and this was a deal that stopped her in her tracks.[1]

She was on her way out of Bloomingdale's in New York City, where she'd picked up a bottle of her favorite perfume, when she came across the street vendor and his counterfeit luxury handbags. Her eyes scanned the offerings: limited-edition Louis Vuittons decorated by Japanese artist Takashi Murakami (some with cherries, some with blossoms), some D-shaped cross-body Pradas, and quilted Chanels.

"Nice selection," said Jackie.

Her eyes settled on a cream Chanel. The tall, very black man noticed.

"You have good taste," he said in a French African accent.

Jackie picked up the bag and inspected it. The leather was soft and smooth, the stitching good and straight.

"Where are you from?" she asked, opening the bag.

"Senegal."

She looked up. *"Alors, vous parlez francais?"*

"Oui."

The bag didn't have the raised interlocking Cs on the inside, but it was a convincing replica from the outside.

"How much?"

"A hundred fifty dollars."

"That's expensive," she protested. The real thing retails for over $4,300.

"It's good bag," he answered.

"No Cs on the inside," she countered. He probably would not know the difference, but she was showing she did: if she could convince him of its defects, she could get him to lower the price.

He held firm. "It's good price for good bag."

"Eighty," she offered.

"No. One fifty."

"One twenty," Jackie countered.

"Okay."

A little yelp of pleasure escaped her lips as she pulled six twenties from her wallet and handed them to the vendor.

The vendor's name was Amadou, and his family was still in Senegal. He was trying to get them out of poverty, away from Al Qaeda in the Islamic Maghreb and drug traffickers and the separatists in Senegal's Casamance region, where his family lived, a staging point for insurgents doing cross-border attacks into their neighboring homelands, The Gambia and Guinea-Bissau. All of this activity means a lot of men are smuggling weapons through Amadou's village. The armed men are also protecting their Senegalese crops of marijuana, as well as shipments of heroin from Southwest and Southeast Asia and cocaine from South America; the drugs are bound for Europe.

Smugglers brought Amadou to the US, via Mexico, for a cost of $10,000.[2] That was a princely sum for him, but he was told he could work it off and pay over time, and that this would be easy, as he would immediately get a job in America and even have money left over to send home to his family in Senegal.

But the journey was hard, and the reality very different from how the smugglers had sold it to him. He was provided a fake passport and flown to Spain. From there he traveled by boat to Colombia; Cuba, Ecuador, or Argentina were his other options. He stayed working in Colombia for six months to earn a bit more money to pay the smugglers for his onward journey into Mexico and then into the United States.

His debt to the smugglers never seemed to decline. His transporters had become his captors: they took away his passport and charged him for room and board in a building in Queens that warehoused many other illegal aliens they had brought in. The conditions were primitive: the aliens shivered in sleeping bags at night, their cold, huddled bodies covering the bare floor. He thought the people who smuggled him might even be related (either just through business or, more likely, families) to the Chinese smugglers who manufactured and shipped the handbags he was recruited into selling.

The counterfeit bags likely passed through Dubai's Jebel Ali Free Zone area in the United Arab Emirates. Some Dubai customs officials know about the shipments from China and handle them personally, because they are paid bribes by the criminal network's local representative. The corrupt customs officials stamp the paperwork to read that the shipments have been separated into new parcels and add new local company names to make it appear that the shipments originated in Dubai, rather than China, which would be a red flag for US customs agents to check for counterfeits.

To make doubly sure the counterfeits get through, the bags and labels are shipped separately, and the labels are stuck on the bags only after they both arrive at the Queens warehouse. Without the labels, the fake bags don't count as an infringement on intellectual property rights and therefore cannot be seized by law enforcement. The practice of legally shipping in generic items, then having workers, many of them illegal immigrants, stamp, embroider, or attach logos or other identifying details in the retail market is called "finishing."[3]

Jackie's Chanel, like the rest of Amadou's bags, was likely made in Guangzhou, China. China is the primary source economy for counterfeit and pirated goods: it accounts for 63 percent of all counterfeit seizures, with a total value (based on suggested retail price) of $772 million; Hong Kong ranks second with $310 million, or 25 percent.[4]

Or perhaps they were made in Thailand, through child slavery: little children, all under ten years old, sitting on the floor assembling counterfeit leather handbags. They work under brutal conditions: some of them have their legs broken so they cannot stand. In some cases, the lower legs are tied to the thigh bone, so the bones won't mend.[5]

The Chinese criminal network (known as a triad) that owns the factories also ships heroin, crystal meth, and cocaine, sometimes by placing them inside the counterfeit bags. As well as illegal immigrants like Amadou, they also smuggle Asian girls, who then become prostitutes in Paris or Amsterdam or in the "massage parlors" of Camden, New Jersey—or any other city. The triads are well-organized networks of criminals, but they also have deep political connections in China and other countries with a significant Chinese population—all the Chinatowns in the world, for a start.

The profits from trafficking in people and drugs are then laundered through bets on fixed games and casinos the triads also own. A gambler in one country can access an online betting platform located in another country and maybe bet on the results of sporting events taking place in a third country in real time. From the casinos, the money from the winnings is then wired to London or straight to Geneva, where a good banker takes a higher-than-normal fee to "layer the money"—combine it with that of several other clients—into financial products held by trusts, controlled by a law firm in Liechtenstein or Panama. The money is now fully secure and untraceable.

The good Swiss banker will, when requested, transfer millions (or tens of millions) to a company incorporated in the Seychelles, with an office address in Dubai and a bank account in Guernsey. This is the company of an arms dealer, who ships weapons to fighters for the Colombian FARC, Lebanese Hezbollah, Boko Haram and Al Qaeda in the Islamic Maghreb in West Africa, Al Shabaab in Somalia, and Daesh (the Arabic name for ISIS) in Syria and Iraq.

My doorbell rings. It's Jackie.

"Oh my God, *chica*, I have to show you my new amazing buy." She pulls out her new cream-colored Chanel. "Isn't it great?! You can barely tell it from the real thing. You've got a great vendor right here, just a few blocks away. A hundred and twenty dollars, instead of forty-three hundred at retail."

I know that even at those prices the profit margin is as large as for a gram of heroin, but neither Amadou nor his suppliers nor the corrupt customs agents will ever likely see the inside of a prison cell.

My phone beeps with a text message from my boyfriend: he's on his way to Iraq to join the Mosul Offensive, the Iraqi-led, Western-coalition-supported military operation launched in October 2016 to liberate Mosul from Daesh. The city had been in the terrorist group's brutal grip since June 2014, when Daesh stormed across the region at lightning speed. It was then the world realized that Daesh was unlike any terrorist group that had come before. The Iraqi army had fled, dropping their US-supplied weapons, which the terrorists promptly picked up and added to their growing arsenal. At Mosul, Daesh leader Abu Bakr Al Baghdadi announced the establishment of the Islamic Caliphate, imposing a brutal rule that placed women under *niqabs* (the black veil that covers the entire face, leaving only a slit for the eyes) or making them sex slaves, chopping off the hands and heads of the noncompliant and pushing homosexuals off rooftops. My boyfriend, Chris (not his real name), would join the Special Forces in retaking the city. If he were to be captured by Daesh, I might someday be watching a video of his beheading.

I look at the counterfeit Chanel and ponder its true cost.

A WORLD OF FAKES

Everything from baby formula to medicine is counterfeited, with tragic results to consumers, who can be injured or killed. But consumers have little appetite to push for an aggressive crackdown: they like the bargains. The illegal trade is huge. The Organisation for Economic Co-operation and Development (OECD), which writes economic policy recommendations for its thirty-five member states and whose Task Force on Countering Illicit Trade I advise, estimates that in 2013 international trade in counterfeit and pirated goods amounted to 2.5 percent of world trade, worth US$461 billion.[6] In the European Union, it was higher: up to 5 percent of imports.[7]

But some people are suspicious of claims from brand holders about the huge harms to industry. Preeminent among them is Professor David Wall, from the University of Durham. Wall coauthored a report that argued that the real cost to the industry from counterfeiting could be one-fifth of previously calculated figures, and that consumers are rarely duped by black market manufacturers, and in fact welcome the choice offered by fakes. Besides, he argued: "it actually helps the brands, by quickening the fashion cycle and raising brand awareness."[8] Counterfeit luxury goods are therefore a low priority in his view. He thinks an overstretched law enforcement should focus on "stuff that really causes public harm," like "dodgy aircraft parts."

He misunderstands the paradigm: how "pulling the thread" by investigating the consumer goods we buy every day leads to intelligence that impacts major bad guys and gives law enforcement powerful tools to defend our citizens. In the world of the crime-terror pipeline (CTP), money from counterfeit handbags, medicines, and cigarettes ends up buying weapons that kill our soldiers and bombs that terrorize our cities. The 1993 World Trade Center bombing was likely partly financed by the sales of counterfeit T-shirts, according to the International Anti-Counterfeiting Coalition.[9] The former Spanish minister of the interior, Angel Acebes, said that "one of the [Al Qaeda] suspects [in the Madrid bombings of March 11, 2004] arrested was already a well-known counterfeiter."[10] Counterfeit cigarettes fund paramilitary groups in Northern Ireland; counterfeit CDs and other goods fund Hezbollah in the Middle East. Al Qaeda supporters have been found with huge amounts of counterfeit items.

"If you find one Al Qaeda operative with it, it's like finding one roach in your house or one rat in your house," former Interpol secretary-general Ron Noble said. "It should be enough to draw your attention to it."

Counterfeits are tremendously popular. According to Wall's report, every year over two-fifths of all consumers (43 percent) buy counterfeit goods carrying one of the top designer labels, such as Louis Vuitton, Yves Saint Laurent, Burberry, or Gucci. Nearly a third of the sales are over the Internet, 90 percent of which are counterfeit,[11] according to LVMH, the world's premier luxury goods conglomerate.[12] It's not just clothes and accessories—everything we consume can be counterfeited: electronics, medicines and personal care products, eyewear (including contact lenses), toys, and even labels and tags, which as we saw above are often shipped separately. Even food is counterfeited: since the 1990s, fake eggs have been found in China and nearby countries.[13] The yolk, white, and shell are made of gypsum powder, calcium carbonate, and wax. The cost of producing them can be half of what it costs to produce real eggs, especially when prices spike due to a supply crisis like during the avian flu in 2012. Fake eggs were more profitable and common then.

THE CONVERGENCE

All the illegal goods we so easily obtain—cheap cigarettes, crude oil, prostitution, fake Viagra, fake designer bags, and even bootleg DVDs—fund serious bad guys. Either the goods themselves or the money from their sale passes through the hands of Russian mobsters, Muslim jihadists, Mexican cartels, Chinese triads, and Eastern European heads of state. And it is we who hand them that money.

From the jungles of Colombia to the halls of power in Washington and Paris, I have traced the growing collusion among criminals, terrorists, and those engaged in global trade. Terrorists are increasingly going into business: illegal transactions and illicit trade. Where once the money went to buy the weapons, the weapons now secure the money. This is the dark side of globalization: both criminals and terrorists feed off the free trade infrastructure, in which goods can cross borders more easily than ever before. The profits are huge. Thanks to drastic hikes in taxation, contraband cigarettes now have the same profit margin as cocaine, and counterfeit handbags are as profitable as heroin; and the penalties if one is caught are ludicrously light. So why wouldn't terrorists become increasingly involved in trafficking illicit consumer goods? Illicit trade is booming.

Officials are aware of the problem. On my November 2014 trip to the United Arab Emirates, a consultant to the emir of Abu Dhabi said during a private meeting: "We have a branding problem here—especially Dubai and the Jebel Ali Free Trade Zone. When people hear 'Dubai' or 'Jebel Ali,' they think: *illicit trade*. So the UAE is bending over backward to sign every anti-money-laundering and anti-illicit-trade protocol it can. But the reality is, we've got criminals and we've got terrorists, and they're parasitic on the infrastructure we've built."

The official clearly felt squeezed: "They've ruined what we built here, and we don't know what to do. Now terrorists are in the trade business and want to make a lot of money, and the criminals—who used to be easy to deal with, because they just wanted to make a lot of money—now have political objectives. It's a nightmare!" The UAE consultant's comments encapsulate the problem: the terrorists are increasingly behaving like criminal businessmen, moving from grievance to greed, while the criminals are increasingly challenging the government, and the more that criminals and terrorists interact, the more they learn from each other.

The reason is simple: terrorists need the money. The countries that significantly funded terrorist groups in the past (Iran, Libya, Saudi Arabia, Russia) are now giving them substantially less. Meanwhile wealthy and powerful individual donors have had their funding streams monitored and disrupted. Without traditional donations, terrorists have turned to doing business with criminals. It means they share information and learn faster and are more successful than ever before. This is the terrifying reality of the crime-terror pipeline: a convergence of the criminal threat with the terrorist threat—double trouble.

Convergence in the crime-terror pipeline contradicts traditional security thinking that terrorists and criminals don't want to be linked. The argument was: criminals don't want the additional scrutiny and heat that working with terrorists will bring, and terrorists are too ideological to work with profit-driven criminals; criminals move lots of money for a long period of time, while terrorists don't need that much money. But this is not what I have found in my work, investigating smuggled consumer goods and finding the connections with drug smugglers, terrorists, and corrupt government officials. In Colombia, Venezuela, and Lebanon, I learned how cocaine funds Hezbollah, which is also funded by smuggled cigarettes in North and South America. In Panama, I saw how counterfeit sporting goods fund Islamist radicalization programs. In Eastern Europe, Iraq, Syria, and Turkey, we found how "illicit white" (smuggled but not counterfeit) cigarettes fund Russian organized crime linked to the Russian intelligence service and its covert operations in Syria and Ukraine.

While any individual terrorist attack may be cheap (easily costing less than \$10,000), maintaining a terrorist network is not. Operatives living throughout the network (which in some cases span the world) have to be housed, fed, trained, and transported. Terrorist networks also maintain Web sites, newspapers, and television stations, and they often provide social services to the local communities that are their constituencies and sources of support. Such networks cost hundreds of millions of dollars annually.

It is expensive to recruit and indoctrinate terrorist foot soldiers and train them to operate clandestinely. The training has to take place in remote locations that have to be maintained, like the safe houses the operatives will use. Document forgers and human smugglers all have to be paid so the terrorists can cross borders; so do corrupt border guards and intelligence and government officials. They need to have a constant supply of disposable phones and encrypted apps.[14] That's the traditional model of terrorism. The shift to using social media to recruit "lone wolves" (usually disaffected individuals with psychological problems), who acquire their own weapons, act on their own, and label it "jihad," changes the model in ways we will see in depth later.

Seeking the opportunity to earn money, terrorists have to go into illicit trade. They have either to work with transnational organized crime groups or to employ their methods and become criminals themselves. After all, revolutionaries need money: for weapons, for fighters, and to set up paternalistic systems in the territories they conquer so that the conquered will be beholden to them. Hezbollah has done this brilliantly: in Lebanon, Hezbollah is a more reliable provider of food, health care, housing, and even water, trash removal, and electricity for its Shia constituents than the national government.

Daesh has done the same in Raqqa, Syria, where it has the longest history of governance of all its territory. There Daesh indoctrinates for militant Islamism in schools and controls the distribution of water and bread and sends armed patrols to ensure people's attire and behavior is suitably chaste and Muslim.

None of this would be possible without the money. The money comes from wealthy Persian Gulf donors, as is the traditional model, yes, but more important, it is derived from illicit trade: oil smuggling, cigarette smuggling, and human trafficking—sex slaves for their fighters and hostages taken by other groups and sold to Daesh for Daesh to ransom, or behead when the ransom is not paid.

Hezbollah owns the illicit trade in tobacco products in Latin America and is a key trafficker of both heroin and cocaine into the Levant—never mind that drugs are against Muslim Sharia law. The Marxist FARC guerrillas are the original narcoterrorists: the world's biggest cocaine producer and the world's longest-running terrorist insurgency. So, in short: effective terrorists have to become effective criminals, smugglers, and experts at organized crime.

This collusion should not be surprising. Criminals and terrorists have much in common.[15] First, they are both, for the most part, rational actors. Second, they both operate secretly. Third, they use similar tactics, including kidnapping, extortion, and assassination. Although they may have different motives, they pursue the same kinds of interests, in that both criminals and terrorists need to acquire resources and power in order to achieve their objectives.

While the collusion of criminal and terrorist groups has been a fact for decades, their convergence (as my Abu Dhabi friend noted) is accelerating. This acceleration is facilitated by the networks' flattening: their organizations are less hierarchical. They are more horizontal, and interact more peer to peer, with fewer bosses. Also, the different cells in different geographical areas have more autonomy over what they do in their areas: they take fewer orders from overseas commanders. So they can do business without other cells from their own group knowing. From a business perspective, they are moving away from a corporate leadership model to a franchise model. Just as Ray Kroc did not necessarily know what was going on in every single McDonald's restaurant, Treviño

Morales would not know what is going on in every cell of the Zetas. They are "flatter" now, less accountable—and more dangerous.

As both terrorists and traffickers become more horizontally structured, they have begun to rely on each other, and work together to create the crime-terror pipeline that now poses such a major threat to global security. For example, illicit human smuggling networks (which move illegal immigrants, but also offer modern slaves and covert tactical personnel movements) are of increasing importance to terrorists seeking to circumvent US Homeland Security programs.

Ironically, the flattening of terrorist networks is partly caused by the effectiveness of US counterterrorism programs targeting their leaders. Drone strikes and other counterterrorism tactics have significantly degraded and disrupted the command structures of foreign terrorist organizations, engendering a new hybrid threat. The combination of a degradation of command and control and a heightened desire for fast money has helped create the burgeoning relationship between terrorists and criminals in Central America and elsewhere.

In many ways, Al Qaeda's cells have been left to their own devices to function, resulting in greater self-sufficiency when it comes to funding their operations. This makes them much harder to spot, neutralize, and eradicate. The flatter networks are also far more adaptive in their survival tactics and more structurally complex, making it harder for law enforcement to destroy them. Operating as a loosely organized network of cells gives these cells greater organizational flexibility, reduces the risk of law enforcement penetration, provides greater efficiency, and shields the leadership.

This flattening and fracturing is particularly evident in Colombia. When the hierarchical structures of the Medellín and Cali cartels were significantly degraded, the drug traffickers turned to decommissioned FARC terrorists and demobilized paramilitaries, and some of those regrouped as *bacrim*, a Spanish abbreviation of "criminal gangs." These new *bacrim* flourished and became two more modern and powerful cartels: the Norte del Valle cartel and the North Coast cartel.

However, to evade surveillance, capture, and disruption by the Colombian National Police, security services, or the US's Drug Enforcement Administration (DEA), the cartels have moved to splinter into *cartelitos,* or "minicartels."[16] This process of fracturing, movement, reconnection, expansion, and refracturing makes these organizations behave like a vibrant organism, one whose stimuli are money and power.

Their greater collusion means criminals and terrorists are sharing information and tactical experiences. A US congressional committee report concluded that they "are frequenting the same shady bars, the same seedy hotels and the same sweaty brothels in a growing number of areas around the world . . . They are most assuredly talking business and sharing lessons learned."[17] They learn from each other and imitate each other's best practices. Security wonks call it "activity appropriation."

Another reason for the accelerating convergence of criminals and terrorists is that they are flocking to the same fixers and facilitators: the experts in illicit trade. The concept is simple: you want the best at each task, those who can do what you need done, and because of the risk and fierce competition involved in illicit business, there will only be a few excellent service providers at any point in time. Both foreign terrorist organizations and drug traffickers rely heavily on these "shadow facilitators"[18] to operate effectively: arms traffickers, money launderers, human traffickers, document forgers, et cetera. Outsourcing to experts in a particular field is efficient and saves money, and also reduces the risk of getting caught through hiring amateurs. These facilitators and fixers take the regional thugs' business and make it global, infiltrating the distribution chains of legal global trade. It is the document forgers and customs agents who enable the illicit cargo to get on a legally registered tanker owned by a major company; it is the bankers and lawyers who place their clients' criminal profits in well-known banks, and buy apartments in buildings on Park or Fifth Avenue alongside old-money high society or villas on Caribbean islands with banking secrecy.

These shadow facilitators are also the nexus between the networks: wittingly or unwittingly, they often serve to bridge the divide between foreign terrorist organizations and drug trafficking organizations operating in the same permissive environments around the globe. A government official, a banker, or another type of facilitator can be recruited either by corruption or intimidation. The choice is crystallized as *plata o plomo*: "silver [i.e., money] or lead [i.e., a bullet]." The dead bodies of those who chose the latter option are prominently displayed in Mexican cartel territory.

In the places where state governance is weak (either through a lack of resources, a lack of will, or corruption), the shadow facilitators have the ability to move freely within and between both the terrorist and criminal circles, where they often promote meetings, the formation of alliances, and the sharing of lessons learned. Like any effective service providers, they are masters at creating demand for their goods and services, concurrently cashing in on the needs and requirements of the terrorists, the drug traffickers, and other organized criminals. These illicit experts thus accelerate the adaptive behavior process of criminals and terrorists, helping them to react faster, learn more effectively, and quickly develop new strategies to both survive and increase their productivity.

Among the lessons learned by the criminals and the terrorists are the strategies that are most effective for different types of networks. For intelligence and law enforcement to respond effectively, they must accelerate their capacity to confront a rapid evolution of strategies, tactics, and behaviors in networks—much more rapid than has ever been observed before, as criminals and terrorists learn and adopt effective tactics from each other. Mexican smugglers now dig Gaza Strip–style tunnels under the US-Mexico border, while cartels behead opponents and post the videos online.

Other classic criminal tactics have been modified to inspire terror and maintain control over territory.

More straightforward than any of these aspects, however, is the simple basis for collusion: insofar as criminals are highly effective at accomplishing tasks that are necessary to terrorists, terrorist organizations are paying clients of criminal organizations. Their collusion—or, more simply, the terrorist use of criminal services—presents major security threats. Criminal networks can provide terrorists with cross-border transportation and logistics, as well as cover for the clandestine movement of goods and people, including terrorist operatives and their weapons. The profits gleaned from the illicit trafficking that is the business of transnational organized criminals undermine state-imposed financial sanctions on terrorist groups.

EATING THE STATE

The most obvious mutual benefit criminals and terrorists occupying the same space create for each other is the exhaustion of state resources, both financial and judicial. But the causes and the effects of the interaction are subtler and more pernicious. The interaction between terrorists and international criminals with regard to the state has three aspects: (1) they collude against a common enemy (particularly the state's law enforcement security forces); (2) they exploit state weakness, because both groups arise in response to state shortcomings; and (3) they parasitically feed upon each other's externalities.

The violent acts of terrorists cause the mass public to doubt their government's ability to provide protection; criminals (despite occasionally colluding with governments) breaking accepted rules and violating law and order cause citizens to lose confidence in their governing institutions. When the citizens lose faith in their government, they will accept the rule of strongmen and terrorist groups.

Take the classic case of that most famous criminal organization: the Italian Mafia. Through its infiltration of Italy's law enforcement agencies and legislature, the organization has hindered the state's ability to protect its citizens and administer justice—a weakness the Mafia cultivates and exploits by signaling to its constituents that "only we can protect you, so be loyal to us." The Mafia has infiltrated the Italian government and bent it to its will in some places, so that the state sometimes serves the Mafia. Any state whose competence, integrity, or efficiency is questioned by its citizenry is well poised for overthrow by a terrorist group, which will effectively exploit and compound the citizens' doubts.

These gray areas can serve as a springboard to greater legitimacy for the criminal and terrorist organizations, further complicating interdiction as "dirty" and "clean" markets intertwine. Transnational criminals work with banks, governments, mining companies, security firms, and even charities. They launch public relations campaigns whose strategies are designed to gain them legitimacy, weaving moving narratives of community spirit by positioning themselves as champions of disaster victims (such as in the Japanese Yakuza's prompt dispatch of aid to the survivors of the 1995 Kobe earthquake) or as champions of national or cultural identity (whether in Kosovo, Chechnya, or Kurdistan)[19] or of the poor (as did Pablo Escobar in Medellín, Colombia). In these interactions, legitimate and criminal businesses interface and dirty money and goods infiltrate the global financial and trade systems, touching each and every one of us, the consumers.

DIRTY MONEY

The money is huge: an estimated $1.6 trillion was laundered through the global financial system in 2008, one year into the global financial crisis.[20] This is all money seeking a "legitimate" and untraceable home somewhere, as the bankers take their cut and the money flows through the system and back into the hands of criminals and corrupt officials. The illegal economy is full of dark corners arrived at by the tangled pathways of illicit trade.

Illicit money flows into the United States through conduits, including facilitators who allow access to the financial system and to financial institutions that ignore their anti–money laundering obligations. These channels allow kleptocrats, criminals, and in some cases terrorists or their sympathizers to inject billions of dollars of illicit wealth into the stream of licit commerce, corrupting markets, financial institutions, officials, and communities. In the process, they prevent fair and open markets from reaching their full economic potential; in the developing world, they keep communities from building the markets and investment frontiers of tomorrow.

Given that illicit trade (dealing in counterfeit goods; trafficking in drugs, weapons, or people; laundering money) is estimated to account for 8 to 15 percent of world GDP, it is hardly surprising that the licit and illicit economies connect and feed off each other in interesting and dynamic ways. This is termed "the gray economy," and it is not happening in some faraway land; it is happening in London, New York, Dubai, and your local bank.

Compounding these complexities is the rather more mundane reality that illicit business hides amid legitimate business that crosses borders every day, whether via shippers and government agencies (as with guns) or via tourists and immigrants (as with counterfeit pharmaceuticals and cigarettes). Some of this traffic is a result of good business practice: for a truck returning from making a delivery, it is better to come back full rather than empty. Differentiating between clean and dirty commerce is not easy.

THE POWER OF NARRATIVE

The terrorist *cause* is far from dead. Regardless of how badly a terrorist group may have "sold out" to the profit motive, grievance is a good fund-raiser: grievance recruits more angry young men and women every hour of every day. A good grievance is still the best tool to raise donations, recruit fighters, and motivate the diaspora. I have seen how both criminals and terrorists use the classic manipulations of subversive identity politics: to be one of us, you will support our cause; to be a good citizen, you need to be a good supporter of our revolutionary cause—you will fund it, you will advocate it, and you will enjoin others to do so, too.

The leaders manipulate the emotions of their likely supporters by setting up a mythic persona, which the average person who wants to be a good patriot or citizen will do his or her best to resemble. After all, everyone wants to belong to the "cool kids" group. Everyone wants to be respected and admired and to have friends who are also respected and admired. No one wants to be ridiculed or excluded. This natural tendency is the key to manipulation of group identity and to the dynamics that exist among the individuals in that group. One can manipulate not only emotions, but values as well.

Our emotions influence what we value and see as important. Pride, vanity, and resentment are perfect examples: they are temporary emotions, but they can also be someone's main character feature, so that his or her emotional predisposition is to be proud, vain, or resentful. "If I'm proud, I will value respect or independence or both. If I'm vain, I will value praise and attention. If I'm resentful, I will value stories of perceived rivals brought low."[21] This is how life narratives are told—or manipulated. Manipulate how people see themselves and their life stories, and you can manipulate the people. After all, this is how parents raise children to have appropriate and proportionate responses to the world around them, teaching them "This warrants sympathy," "This should make you proud," et cetera.

In the context of terror, the shortest route to pride is making others fear you. Fear is power.

What is happening in the world today is less about religion and ideology than it is about power. If you strip away the terrorist rhetoric on religion, the scenario is the same as always: thugs inspiring fear to consolidate their power. Religion is their excuse, fear their method.

Terrorists and the Mexican cartels operate much the same way: they control territory, kill their enemies, and videotape beheadings to intimidate those who would challenge them. The Mexican cartels also use religious insignia to mark their territory and legitimize their power. The violence we see across our television screens at night is at least as much about getting and keeping power as it is about Christians or Jews or Muslims.

People will support the powerful; they want to be part of the power structure, not excluded from or by it. In the Middle East, this is called "Strong Horse" politics. (Osama bin Laden famously said: "When people see a strong horse and a weak horse, by nature, they will like the strong horse."[22]) The Middle East is a region defined over centuries by violent power struggles between factions, and America has less blame to bear than is generally attributed to it either by liberals or by the Middle Eastern warring factions manipulating narratives in their quest for power.[23] I saw in Lebanon how Sunni and Shia, rulers and rebels, all claim they want America out—even as they ask for money, weapons, and military intervention to fight their cause against the other side, whom they have been fighting since the eighth century.

Beyond that hypocrisy, America, as the world's strongest military force, is a natural target for a group (Sunni or Shia) who wants to earn credibility and publicity, to be known as the one who can get things done—and therefore attract more fighters and more money, and ultimately more power. By attacking America and claiming to rout it from the region, a violent extremist group can earn a loyal following. It is a branding exercise.

The extent to which the violent extremists need America as a whipping boy was highlighted by the beheadings of James Foley and Steven Sotloff by Daesh. Up until that point, America was not paying attention to Daesh, was exiting rapidly from Iraq, and had no interest in doing anything more in Syria than provide a few weapons. Like a spoiled child frustrated that it can't get the attention it wants, the group beheaded two Americans and posted the videos. That worked: the videos of two beheaded Americans posted on social media was enough to get the US military to reverse course and go back into Iraq.

The Middle East (whether North Africa, the Levant, or the Persian Gulf) is not a region with a culture or a history of liberal democracy. A fellow CNN en Español panelist (an Iranian living in Israel) was brave enough to make this point on air: the problems of the Middle East lie in the Middle East. A history of oppressive rule by a corrupt elite is at the heart of the region's cycle of violence—a process witnessed firsthand by many who have worked in the region. The people don't trust their politicians; they trust only their revolutionaries.

The growth of militant Islamism is a historical consequence of the region's experimentation with secular political Islam (as in Turkey, Egypt, and Libya) practiced under autocratic presidents-for-life who banned other political parties. As corrupt dictators banned rival political parties and stifled dissent, the only space left for group gatherings expressing alternate views became the mosque. As anger and frustration grew, they became increasingly couched in religion. So religion took up the role of revolution and tapped into an old paradigmatic persona: the good revolutionary Muslim.

The persona of the honorable religious fighter is not unique to Muslims; Christians have their version of it too—and not just in the Middle East during the Crusades, but in the New World, since the Conquest. In 1481, Pope Sixtus IV issued a papal bull entitled *Aeterni Regis* (*King Eternal*) that argued that pagan natives' right to self-rule was overridden by papal responsibility for their souls. Thus, conquering non-Christian lands was a moral duty to the conquered: Europeans were told to conquer them to save their heathen souls. But they were told it would save European souls as well. The Conquerors then effectively became "holy warriors," purifying themselves and their community in the fight.

The religious semiotics were so prevalent that upon landing in Venezuela, Christopher Columbus wrote in his diaries that he had found the Garden of Eden. The myth of the noble savage has persisted and become transmuted over time to a more modern persona:[24] the savior of Latin American culture, the good revolutionary, the anti-imperialist defender of the native against the foreign or white oligarchic ravager. I saw how effective this was in the country of my birth, Venezuela. Hugo Chávez, who attempted a coup, won an election on a wave of class (and ethnically tinged) discontent and rewrote the constitution to centralize power. Now Venezuela is a violent and corrupt dictatorship, economically imploding while its people starve. It is also a key component in a broad and powerful crime-terror pipeline.

2

Learning About Crime, Terror, and Corruption

It was in my birthplace of Venezuela that I first learned about the vast expanding tentacles of crime-terror pipelines. The 2008 seizure of the laptop of Raúl Reyes, a commander of the Colombian narcoterrorist insurgency FARC—taken during a 2008 raid on his camp just across the Colombian border in Ecuador—confirmed what I and many others had long suspected: that the regime of Venezuela's president, Hugo Chávez, was giving material support to the drug trafficking and terrorist operations of neighboring Colombia's FARC insurgency.

The files, reviewed by the think tank with which I had worked a couple of years earlier—the International Institute of Strategic Studies, a specialist in wars and military matters—revealed that Chávez's supporters, the *Chavistas,* were making huge personal profits by trafficking in drugs, giving safe haven to terrorists, and facilitating terrorists' access to very deadly weapons, including "MANPADs," which can be foisted by one man on his shoulder, then fire a missile capable of bringing down an airliner. The files detailed how *Chavistas* were shipping Colombian cocaine they got from the FARC on to the Mexican drug cartels (fueling slaughter in Central America and across the US Southwest border) and to the Lebanese Hezbollah terrorist group, an Iranian proxy so well armed it fought Israel to a tie in the 2006 war. All of these activities continue in 2017, and Lebanese Hezbollah is responsible for very lethal terrorist attacks both in Latin America (killing *Chavistas'* fellow Latinos) and against the US in the Middle East: 241 US Marines were killed when Hezbollah bombed their barracks in Beirut in 1983; 29 were killed and 242 injured in the March 1992 bombing of the Israeli Embassy in Buenos Aires; 85 were killed and hundreds more injured again in Buenos Aires in July 1994 at the Argentine-Israeli Mutual Association.

Furthermore, my government's narcoterrorism and corruption was couched as some socialist liberation from US-led imperialist oppression: this "anti-Yankee" and "anti-oligarchy" narrative was the excuse the government was using to rewrite the constitution and centralize power under a charismatic populist president, ensuring that those in power could stay in power—making money and spreading slaughter around the world—for years to come, if not indefinitely. On top of it all, while I saw it for what it was (a cynical kleptocratic crime-terror pipeline), a lot of the rest of the world thought this Bolivarian Revolution was a great idea—even as late as 2009.

PRESS AND POLITICS

"We have learned some things about your background," said *The Guardian* newspaper editor on the phone.

"What things about my background exactly?" I retorted.

"Well, that you come from a wealthy Venezuelan family, so you would obviously be opposed to Hugo Chávez."

It was early February 2009, and I had called the editorial desk and asked them for comment on an op-ed by their deputy editor, Seumas Milne, now UK Labour Party spin doctor, praising Venezuelan president Hugo Chávez in the typical style of liberals who had not previously been able to find Venezuela on a map, but wanted to believe in some mojito-sipping version of Lawrence of Arabia—never mind that he was dismantling government institutions and centralizing power around his cult of personality.

International celebrities were piling in fast: actor Sean Penn, who'd been an avid and vociferous supporter since he'd first traveled to Venezuela to meet Chávez in 2007 (since then Penn has interviewed and defended criminal despot *"El Chapo"* Guzmán and seemingly wants to shape US drug policy); film director Oliver Stone, who went on to make a cinematic hagiography called *South of the Border;* actor and director Danny Glover, who received $18 million to make a film (which he has yet to deliver) about the life of Haitian revolutionary Toussaint Louverture; documentarian Michael Moore, who met Chávez at the Venice Film Festival in 2009 and posted pictures on social media of them together and praised him as a fellow enemy of President Bush; model Naomi Campbell, renowned for her temper, who'd been to Caracas, waved to the people from Miraflores presidential palace, and called Chávez her "Rebel Angel."

I was disgusted. Celebrities and *The Guardian* were using their media power to anoint a putschist populist, and some celebrities even benefited financially themselves, through projects directly financed by corruption or by hitching onto the geopolitical enfant terrible du jour to renew their media brands. Besides that, to my mind they were playing with the lives of millions of my compatriots.

"So are you saying that I, a native-born Venezuelan, am not entitled to my opinion? Is *The Guardian* going on record that its editorial line is that the voice of a native is to be silenced if it does not fit the newspaper's editorial definition of the correct socioeconomic background or political stance, in favor of a foreigner who has never been there?"

"No, that's not what we're saying," he persisted. "But isn't it true that he is taking the oil wealth away from the oligarchy and giving it to the poor?"

"No, it's the foreigners, including you Brits, who exploited

Venezuela's oil wealth from 1918 until 1976, when it was nationalized by the Venezuelan government. It was never in private hands. I've actually written about this in other British publications."

I got my editorial in *The Guardian,* though not until it had been put through some aggressive editing. But the games were just beginning.

Only a few days later, Venezuela held a referendum that abolished presidential term limits. Up until then, terms were five years and nonconsecutive: a president would have to take a term off before running again. The 55 percent yes versus 45 percent no results came in on the day I was flying from London back to New York for good, initiating my divorce from my English husband. I was checking in at the American Airlines counter at Heathrow Airport when I got the call.

"I'm Colin Pereira, a producer on *BBC Newsnight.* Would you like to come on the show tonight to discuss the referendum in Venezuela? You would be on opposite the Venezuelan ambassador to the UK."

I was surprised they had reached out to me, but then I was probably the only Venezuelan in the British public eye. In 1999, the British tabloids had nicknamed me "the Cracker from Caracas" ("cracker" in Britain means "hot chick," not "racist" as it does in the US) when they revealed I was dating Mick Jagger, whom I had known since childhood, as he was our neighbor on a Caribbean island. The celebrity frisson launched a lot of interest in my life, just at the time I was pursuing my doctorate in political philosophy at Columbia University. The departmental secretary was none too pleased with the incoming calls. Over time, I steered the press attention into opportunities to write for newspapers and magazines. My first forays were about what it was like to be a Latin American living in London society; then I turned to writing about politics, Venezuela, and justice—which was, after all, what my dissertation was about.

My brush with British tabloid quasi-celebrity was not the only reason I understood the power of the media. I had already been on both sides of the journalistic fence—predator and prey—as both a journalist and a fixture of society pages. I knew how the media shapes political discourse. I also knew *BBC Newsnight* wouldn't ask me twice.

"Yes, I'll do it."

My dog had already been checked into the cargo hold, and I could barely walk due to a horse-riding accident I'd suffered a couple of days before that had never been treated. The pain was excruciating, but I just wanted to get home to New York. It turned out later I had a compression fracture in one of the vertebrae: it was crushed by the impact of landing on my head and my spine collapsing like a closed accordion. I was lucky to be alive, never mind walk, pain or not. I called my mother to go pick up my dog for me when the plane landed at JFK, then I took my suitcase and turned back to my London flat to change for the television interview.

In the studio, I sat pin-straight, my high heels belying the pain. Under the white, hot lights, my heart thumped in my ears. The Venezuelan ambassador and I were quite friendly, despite being on opposing political sides. Since I was the best-known Venezuelan in the UK, Ambassador Samuel Moncada had come to my engagement party in London, and I respected him: he was a true believer in reducing inequality and in greater political inclusion. I just didn't like his boss, President Chávez, and he was okay with that. In our earpieces, the producers egged us on to argue vigorously for the cameras, and we did.

"The people have spoken. The Bolivarian Revolution has taken hold. People are tired of the inequality. The days of the old oligarchy are over. Now power is really devolving to the people."

"No, it isn't," I countered. "This 'democratization' is really a centralization of power: the poor get handouts of food and medicine directly from the executive branch on condition that they sign an oath of fealty. They get paid to wear red T-shirts at the rallies.

He bribed them for their vote—and by the way, Chávez also personally controls the people who count the votes. Furthermore, in the ten years Chávez has been in power, poverty has grown along both dimensions: there are more poor, and the poor are poorer. The Gini coefficient of income inequality is bigger now than it was when the Chávez supporters railed against the system, supported a man who has no respect for democratic institutions (which we know, because he made his name attempting a military coup), and signed away their rights to a populist despot. The Venezuelan people will regret this."

To the producers' surprise, though, when the cameras stopped rolling, we hugged Latin style and chatted amiably before wishing each other a good evening. In retrospect, of course, I was right—the Venezuelan people did come to regret their choice. The well-meaning Ambassador Moncada was briefly Venezuela's foreign minister in 2017. Prior to that, Moncada served as ambassador to the Organization of American States in Washington, D.C., and railed against foreign intervention in Venezuela, whose ruling elite operates as a drug cartel and where the citizens are starving.

MEDELLÍN: THE LAND OF PABLO ESCOBAR AND NARRATIVE OPERATIONS

In April 2009, my spine mostly healed, I was on my first tour of Colombia to see the changes under President Alvaro Uribe and his then-minister of defense (and now Colombian president), Juan Manuel Santos. Since 1948, Colombia had been racked by Conservative-versus-Liberal violence, known as *"La Violencia."* Since 1964, the violence had been explicitly leftist guerrilla versus right-wing paramilitary; it's the year FARC was founded and basically took over the violence. FARC is a Marxist-Leninist revolutionary guerrilla organization whose stated aim is agrarian reform and the overthrow of a political system dominated by an oligarchy of *latifundistas* (owners of *latifundios,* huge rural estates). There were other guerrilla organizations (including the number-two group, ELN, the Ejército de Liberación Nacional), creating an alphabet soup of insurgencies.

In response, the landowners set up their own right-wing paramilitaries, which coalesced as the United Colombian Self-Defense Forces. (Their Spanish acronym is AUC.) The civil war was on, and it has raged until now, as President Juan Manuel Santos struggles to pass a peace deal. In the 1970s and 1980s, the Colombian drug cartels sprung up, of which Cali and Medellín were the most powerful. They fought each other and used the other various insurgent and paramilitary groups and rival cartels in temporary and shifting alliances. They all trafficked drugs, set off bombs, assassinated leaders, kidnapped civilians. I arrived in 2009 to see the progress then-president Uribe was making in fighting them all. Several other political commentators and I were shipped in under the aegis of the newly set up national branding office; their motto was: "Colombia: the only danger is not wanting to leave." Not exactly Madison Avenue's greatest brainchild, but certainly to the point.

It was then that I heard my first *narcocorrido,* a song that glorifies the exploits of the drug cartels, in the popular Bogotá restaurant Andrés Carne de Res. The huge steakhouse looked like a nightclub, and pumped out local dance music. As I stood in line for the bathroom, listening to the sounds of people in the stalls snorting what undoubtedly was very pure cocaine, I could hear lyrics about how the Colombian drug capos ran drugs into Venezuela with the protection of their friend, President Hugo Chávez. Not only did it gall me as a native Venezuelan, but I wondered if the people snorting their lines were aware of the contradiction between their drug consumption and their railing against the conflict those drugs had funded, which had been tearing their country apart for half a century. Not to be a pedant, I kept my opinions to myself.

Narcocultura, the criminal culture of the drug cartels, has hit the mainstream in all drug-producing countries (the "White

Triangle" of Peru, Bolivia, and Colombia) and in the transshipment countries of Central America and Mexico—and even across the US border. It is part of the information operations waged by these criminal groups. The *narcocorridos* are sung by popular groups that are closely affiliated with the cartels; the groups are often in the cartels' direct employment, serving as their own latter-day troubadours. The ones most explicit about their patrons' marvelous exploits—Secret Airstrip, Coca Growers of Putumayo, and The Snitch—were *corridos prohibidos:* the radio stations refused to play them, lest the broadcasters get caught in the ego-driven crossfire of rival cartels. They were right to be afraid: later, in August 2010, drug-funded terrorists set off a car bomb at the headquarters of Radio Caracol.

The highlight of our tour of the wonders of the Uribe administration's brutal-yet-effective tactics against narcoterrorist insurgents was a tour of Medellín: the original "Cartel Land," famed for Pablo Escobar, the head of the Medellín cartel during the cocaine craze of the 1980s. Cocaine made the terrorists powerful, but it all started when they were mere service providers to the Cali and Medellín capos, including Pablo Escobar. Escobar is still regarded as the "King of Cocaine" and is the wealthiest criminal in history, with an estimated net worth of $30 billion at the time of his death in 1993 in a violent shoot-out in Medellín by the combined forces of his enemies: *Los Pepes,* an ultraviolent group based on the Spanish acronym for "people persecuted by Pablo Escobar"; the Colombian military; US Special Forces; and the US Drug Enforcement Administration. His death is considered to mark the end of the Golden Age of the Colombian drug cartels and the start of the Golden Age of the narcoterrorists.

The beginning of the end for Escobar was his brazen terrorist attack on a national airliner: he ordered the blowing up of Avianca flight 203, bound from Bogotá to Cali, on November 27, 1989, killing all 107 people on board. Hours later, a man called Radio Caracol saying *Los Extraditables* ("The Extraditables") were behind the bombing,[1] referring to the list of drug capos that the United States wanted extradited from Colombia for trial and imprisonment.

Pablo Escobar was at the top of that list; the *Extraditables* were protesting the Colombian government's signing of the extradition treaty with the US, as the capos knew they could influence Colombia's law enforcement apparatus, but not the Americans'. So they couched their protest in a manner that got a lot of popular support: as a violation of national sovereignty. The narrative of the imperialist ravager of the native resonates deeply in Latin America. Why not use it to get the people to support the cartel's power play? It worked for Hugo Chávez in Venezuela and for the FARC narcoterrorists in Colombia. Why not for the Medellín cartel?

In short, the criminal group was using another terrorist recruitment tactic: the manipulation of a group identity's grievance narrative—the narrative in this case being the Colombian people's humiliation by the imperialist and manipulative United States. It had millions of supporters across Colombia. But the purpose of the narcos' use of this grievance narrative was clear: to retain the power they had over the citizens they exploited so they could continue making money with their criminal activity and keep operating in an environment in which they were given latitude by a government they already had on its back foot.

When we arrived in Medellín, the animals from Pablo Escobar's zoo had long ago escaped and his home (we were told) was in decay. No, we could not go visit it; no, it was not a tourist attraction. What was on display were all the wondrous new libraries, the aquarium, and the cable car that linked the slums to downtown, part of the program to integrate the urban poor to the mainstream economy and to the educational system.

The mayor of Medellín was a left-wing hippie intellectual, a mathematics professor who both understood the need for redressing economic marginalization—a prime recruitment angle for both insurgent and criminal groups that Colombia had long been battling—and had a very metrics-based approach to economic development programs. It all sounded and looked great, but it didn't work as well as advertised: there has been some regression as the criminal gangs (*bacrim*) have returned to their old drug trafficking antics. But the violence is still less than it was in the old days, when both the cartels and the terrorist insurgents were setting off bombs. Lest the locals forget the bad old days: an exploded sculpture of a bird by world-renowned Medellín artist Fernando Botero stands in the central square as a reminder.

FLYING HOME

The H1N1 avian flu pandemic was in full swing in Colombia by the time my 2009 trip was over. All the passengers and airport security at Bogotá's El Dorado Airport were wearing surgical masks when I boarded my flight to Caracas to visit my brother. My face was hot from the mask and my head was full of frustration that the country I had grown up viewing as the troublesome neighbor was getting its act together and emerging from violence, while my birthplace fell apart.

The entrenchment of the dictatorial regime that has riven Venezuela and threatens to destabilize the entire Western Hemisphere was made possible by the world's consumption of Venezuela's oil. In the US, it is American consumers filling their cars at Citgo gasoline stations that have funded them: Citgo is wholly owned by the Venezuelan government's oil company, PDVSA (Petroleum of Venezuela). The *Chavista* regime used the oil wealth to buy regional influence and line its own pockets—and later, to buy the guns that would shoot protesters demanding canceled elections and food.

"It's incredible," I said to my brother when I arrived at his Caracas apartment. "Medellín. Medellín! The poster child for drug and terrorist violence, what was once one of the most dangerous cities on earth, is now better than Caracas. Where did we go wrong?"

He shrugged his shoulders.

I wanted some answers, so I began asking questions of anyone who would meet with me and be trusted not to rat me out to the Venezuelan government for being overly inquisitive. Not to embroil my brother, I turned to three childhood friends, one of whom had dated my cousin, the other two who were now involved in the political opposition.

THE REVOLUTION'S TRUSTY STEEDS

Maria Elena, my cousin's childhood sweetheart, called me up.

"Want to go to the show-jumping competition at the country club today?" We were both riding enthusiasts, and our families have been multigenerational members of the Caracas Country Club—the "old school," as we call it; the "oligarchy," as the *Chavistas* call it.

"I'd love that! What fun!"

We arrived suitably underdressed in jeans. While Latinos have a reputation for flamboyance, it's a hallmark of the upper class to act and dress in the understated manner of the American WASPs of the US Northeast—minus the pastel ginghams, of course. We waved to the guard as he lifted the gate without asking Maria Elena's membership number, parked under a shady tree near the stables, and went straight to the stalls to pet some of the horses: gleaming, muscular bodies, legs wrapped in bandages that coordinated well with the horse's chestnut, bay, or gray coloring.

The stables of the Caracas Country Club are built into the foothills of the Ávila Mountains, the trailing off of the Andes that separate Caracas from the Caribbean and give it its perfect year-round weather. Cascading stepped fields separate the stables from the bar, and the bar from the outdoor stadium competition ring. As we watched the show-jumping from our bleachers, a little ripple emerged among the audience as a dark-skinned, broad man with a scar on his face approached. One by one people rose to greet him. He didn't look like your usual Caracas Country Club member.

"He's a *Chavista*," Maria Elena explained. "Alejandro Andrade, a military commander very close to Chávez. The story is that they were childhood friends and Chávez nearly took out his eye in a game of baseball. Chávez rewarded his loyalty. He is the wealthiest new member of the country club and owns at least ten horses, all champions, bought on the international market. Welcome to the Bolivarian Revolution."

"I thought they hated all we stood for and that the Caracas Country Club was the very symbol of our evil," I quipped.

"Oh, my dear. They want to be us. And what are we to do? If we don't let them in and play nice, they really will destroy us. Besides, they're the only ones who can afford the club dues anymore."

In the lobby of the main clubhouse entrance, there used to be a list of members who were delinquent in their payments and how much they owed. The list got to be so long the club had to take it down. I had heard of these changes and accommodations taking place in African countries. I had never imagined I would see it happen in my own.

So I started pulling the thread a bit, as we say in my business, to find out the underlying story of how this had come to pass. I sought out two of the more vociferous analysts and critics of the changes Venezuela was undergoing.

My first stop was Diego Arria, a former governor and UN ambassador and a failed Venezuelan presidential candidate, about whom more than one colorful story of how he had made his money swirled. I knew him very well: I had grown up with his stepchildren. He was all over traditional and social media, well ahead of the curve, opining on the finer points of Venezuelan constitutional law and how the *Chavistas* were subverting them. As we chatted, we sipped coffee, brought in on a silver tray by his uniformed maid amid the dark colonial furniture of his home just across from one of the holes of the Caracas Country Club golf course.

He was exceedingly well informed and made compelling arguments, but I did wonder whether he was the most credible voice for this message. If the *Chavistas* had risen on a sea of anger about inequality and elitism, Arria perhaps might not be the best messenger for a more inclusive alternative.

I kept looking.

Next, I went to speak to Teodoro Petkoff, a former Communist guerrilla who was the editor and cofounder of *Tal Cual*, the anti-*Chavista* paper he had started with my grandfather Hans.

"You have to understand, everyone is guilty in this," said Petkoff. "This was foreseeable. The forces of the MBR-200 [the military-founded political party that backed Hugo Chávez] were well known to many, but either they accommodated them or discredited them. Chávez's forces were trained in guerrilla tactics to combat the Communists; that the military should turn in their sympathies [away from liberal democratic capitalism and toward Cuban-style communism] was surprising, but they had more in common with their [Communist] enemies than their elite commanders. The *Caracazo* of 1989 was the turning point."

When enraged commuters and students flipped over the little *por puesto* buses (jitneys) that transport most urban workers, then set them on fire (after their owners had doubled fares and refused student discounts in response to a hike in gasoline prices), riots spread across nineteen cities for a week, riots that were termed "the *Caracazo*." The military was called in to protect private property from the looters streaming down from the hillside slums.

By the time the riots ended on March 5, medical personnel estimated that 1,000 to 1,500 people had been killed; the government gave an official body count of 287.[2] The class wars had begun, and soon all the country's problems were viewed through the lens of a white (*mantuano*) elite dominating and withholding financial and other resources from a brown-skinned (*mestizo*) majority.

Among the soldiers who participated in what was (not entirely inaccurately) perceived as a massacre of the poor to protect the property of the wealthy was a little-known cabal that called itself the MBR-200, the Spanish acronym for the Bolivarian Revolutionary Movement 200, named in honor of the two hundredth birthday of its iconic inspiration, Latin American liberator Simón Bolívar, and founded under a tree where the liberator once napped. MBR-200's leader, Col. Hugo Chávez, was at home sick with the measles, but he realized that the *Caracazo* would be the trampoline for the revolutionary change he had been wanting, and that he could ride the wave of anger and racially underpinned class warfare all the way to the presidential palace.

Since he was a soldier and not a politician, he planned to do it by force. Three years later, Colonel Chávez, citing the brutal massacres of the *Caracazo,* attempted a coup, but he was captured and ordered by the Venezuelan government of President Carlos Andrés Pérez to call down his troops on February 4, 1992, on one minute of television airtime. He was then summarily rushed off to prison, turning him into a martyr—one who would in 1998 win the presidency and install the *Chavista* regime under the banner of the Bolivarian Revolution.

THE WOMEN WITH ELECTORAL POWER

While in Caracas in 2009, I also went to speak to Maria Corina Machado, a presidential candidate to whom I am distantly related, about what was likely the opposition's worst mistake: abstaining from the 2005 National Assembly elections, claiming they would be "rigged." Instead of stopping the election, the boycott simply handed the entire National Assembly to the regime's candidates— to the country's eternal regret, as they rubber-stamped one power after another for the president and stacked the Supreme Court with their own party.

Prior to talking to Maria Corina, I had spent hours in the offices of Smartmatic, the makers of the disputed voting machines. The company's communications director, Samira Saba, explained at length that the required fingerprints were for identification purposes only, that the regime would not be able to access records to identify and punish those who had voted against it, and that the firm's machines could not be hacked. Ms. Saba said the company's technology was standard and that its machines were used in elections all over the world. Smartmatic even provided biometric technology to the UK, the country with the highest rate of video surveillance on the planet. If it was good enough for the Brits, why not the Venezuelans? she asked.

But suspicion ran deep, and there was little about the regime's intimidating behavior that would help counter it. Indeed, the government openly announced that those who voted against the regime would lose their government jobs and benefits.

"Do you think that boycott was a mistake?" I asked Maria Corina.

"In retrospect, probably."

In Colombia, the FARC Marxist insurgency had worked popular anger of the rural poor into a revolutionary cause. Across the border in Venezuela, so had Chávez, but he won a presidential election, where bucking the system was his brand—not unlike Trump's win in the 2016 US presidential election. All of them rallied supporters by positioning themselves as defenders of the politically and economically forgotten against a corrupt and elitist system. What is remarkable about Venezuela is how, far from fighting corruption, it became one of the most corrupt, violent, and dictatorial countries on earth—and the world's main transit point for cocaine. Meanwhile, people die of a lack of food and medicine, hundreds of political opponents are imprisoned, and the country is broke, despite sitting on the world's largest oil reserves. The process of parsing out how this happened led me to understand the links among corruption, organized crime, and terrorism: the crime-terror pipeline.

"A Little Fun"

When I returned to Colombia in January 2010, I was the only journalist to accompany an international delegation that was there to study the country's peacekeeping program, one that would reintegrate paramilitary fighters into society, a process known in security circles as DDR: demobilization, disarmament, and reintegration. Colombia needed it to work. Its conflict with the FARC is the last remaining guerrilla war in the Western Hemisphere. It has killed nearly a quarter of a million people and created five million refugees within Colombia itself—"internally displaced" is the official term. By numbers of refugees, Colombia's conflict is in third place behind Syria and Sudan.

Violence begets violence in a self-feeding cycle: violence creates poverty, which creates more violence. Massive displacement and land grabs only exacerbated rural poverty (estimated at 43 percent),[1] which drove more poor to take up arms, if only for the salary and the uniforms. Violence nearly collapsed the country.

Around the turn of the millennium, the US Defense Intelligence Agency wrote a report in which it stated that it was concerned that the FARC would overthrow the Colombian government and turn the country into a "narco-state." Since that report, the US has poured more than US$10 billion into a counternarcotics program, known as "Plan Colombia," to help prop up the Colombian government. There was also a less-well-chronicled counterinsurgency program called Plan Patriota, which came later: getting into counterinsurgency was a less popular proposition for US lawmakers, who were keen on avoiding another Vietnam quagmire.

So when I was invited to meet former fighters and victims in 2010, Colombia was a security legend in the Western Hemisphere. I was honored and readily accepted. My friends, however, thought I was crazy.

This was the plan: to demonstrate the effectiveness of their demobilization efforts, the Colombians would move sixty high-level military and political leaders from twenty countries and the United Nations and transport them daily across combat zones that the Colombian military had only recently retaken from either the guerrilla insurgents or the right-wing paramilitaries. The insurgents and FARC terrorists were still very much around and would have spies reporting on our identities and movements. These groups were in protracted negotiations with the government.

We would make tempting targets for them, especially the FARC, who did not yet have a deal but was being bombed into near-extinction. If the FARC wanted to strengthen its negotiating hand, seizing a busload, planeload, or hotel full of sixty foreigners from twenty countries and the UN would do the trick. If its fighters kidnapped us (or killed us), they would have the attention not only of the Colombian government, but of the twenty other governments and the UN as well. These other countries and the UN, in turn, would bring their diplomatic weight to bear on Colombia. Security was tight, to say the least—just how tight, I would only find out while already in Colombia. I was a writer, without any military or security training.

The reintegration of former fighters into civilian society is a complicated three-step process, and all countries that want to end a civil war go through it. The first step is demobilization: get the fighters to quit the fighting groups, insurgent or paramilitary as the case may be. For this, you usually need the very big stick of killing them in large numbers: they need to be persuaded that they will not win militarily, will die, and are losing popular support for their cause, so they are better off reaching a peace deal. The demobilization occurs when a peace deal is reached that sets the terms for what happens to the fighters if they demobilize (quit the groups), outlining the rules by which they must abide to receive government benefits.

In 2010, the Colombian government had reached a peace deal only with the paramilitaries, the United Colombian Self-Defense forces (AUC), based on a deal struck in 2005, the Justice and Peace Law, which was amended in 2006 to emphasize societal reintegration. The government had not reached a peace deal with any of the insurgencies, of which the FARC was the most powerful.

The second step is disarmament: the fighters have to turn in their weapons to the government or UN peacekeepers, depending on the deal. The third step is reintegration: the former fighters must become productive members of society. This is the most complicated part. Many fighters joined when they were children, and fighting is the only skill they have. So the government has to send them back to school, give them job training, help them find jobs, get them psychologists to deal with their trauma and anger, and teach them to be good spouses, parents, and citizens. Colombia even gave the former paramilitaries life insurance policies. The populace is not always very happy about the reintegration packages—with former drug traffickers, kidnappers, extortionists, and terrorists getting better education and welfare than law-abiding citizens ever got.

"Colombia's is the Rolls-Royce of programs. That's why we're all here," said a keen American as we joined the rest of the participants boarding a bus from our hotel to Bogotá's El Dorado Airport for our first risky transfer. It was also the first time all the delegates got to meet each other: we had arrived in Bogotá from our disparate points of origin the night before. The weeklong trip would be my immersion in the aftermath of political violence funded by the illicit trade in narcotics and other smuggled goods. I was about to see the real price of cocaine and other forms of illicit trade, inscribed on the bodies of children with missing limbs and millions of refugees.

From Bogotá we flew 150 miles west to the town of Armenia, the capital of Quindío Department, in the Andes region. Armenia is a medium-sized city located between Bogotá, Medellín, and Cali, the three biggest cities in Colombia; it is in the heart of the Colombian coffee-growing axis. In the elevations where coffee grows, so grow coca and poppy plants, for cocaine and heroin.

The area surrounding towns like Armenia can be extremely dangerous due to the presence of terrorists and criminals, including armed gangs, resulting in kidnappings, killings, and explosions. The reintegration occurs in such disputed territories, so we were there to see how the government was moving former fighters into the coffee-picking business, away from the drug trafficking and killing business. Though we didn't see any trouble, seven years later, in 2017, the US State Department was still posting travel warnings for the area.[2]

Despite the government's best efforts, there was no doubt we were moving around amid a significant threat. In Armenia, our buses were joined by police escorts: two police officers on each of about three motorcycles were all we could see from the windows. When we arrived at our country hotel, I saw the full security detail: on either side of the imposing gates were about twenty grim and earnest soldiers, clutching what I mistook for M-16s. Their eyes followed us steadily, and when someone tried to photograph them, they turned their backs to the camera. Wherever we moved, police, Special Forces, sharpshooters, and helicopters hovered over us constantly, a steady reminder of what peace-building without a comprehensive peace accord means.

On our hour-long open-backed-jeep journey to La Linda, a hilltop village that had long been in the crossfire, Alejandro Eder, leader of the reintegration effort and therefore our de facto tour guide through the reintegration projects scattered across the country, told me that the area had been encircled and cleared by soldiers for three days prior to our arrival. In addition to the armed convoy, the Black Hawk helicopters, and the soldiers dotting the landscape, "there are many others you cannot see," he said in a tone he intended to be reassuring.

Almost twenty relatives of Alejandro Eder had been kidnapped over the years. His family is well known, very wealthy, and, as sugar producers, big landowners, or *latifundistas,* ideal targets for the Marxist guerrillas arguing for agrarian reform and against an oligarchic system. Fearing for his safety in Colombia, his family sent him to the US to get a first-rate education. To hear him speak English, you would take him for American. But his love of country got the better of him: he gave up a lucrative banking job in New York to return home and help build a more peaceful and prosperous Colombia.

Though Colombia wants to emerge from the right-versus-left fighting that has shredded the country continuously since 1948, it has enacted only piecemeal laws to enable demobilization.

The Justice and Peace Law has been widely criticized by Human Rights Watch and other NGOs as inadequate punishment for the paramilitaries. But it was specifically designed to give demobilized fighters who have committed crimes against humanity and members of a "recognized armed group at the margins of the law" reduced sentences in exchange for full disclosure and reparations to the affected families. (The demobilized fighters serve five or eight years instead of cumulative sentences that could easily run more than forty.)

It's Colombia's version of South Africa's Truth and Reconciliation Commission, and by early 2010 it had uncovered knowledge of 257,089 registered victims, 32,909 specific crimes—of which

14,612 had been confessed to—and 2,182 exhumed graves. In 2009 the government had approved reparations of $100 million, plus $500 million in aid budgeted for the internally displaced, the refugees within Colombia. The demobilization process also greatly increased intelligence about the armed groups, enabling the government to combat them more effectively. Murders have dropped from 30,000 in 2002 (when Alvaro Uribe was elected president) to 16,000 in 2009, and kidnappings from 3,000 to 213 over the same period.

Now, in 2017, the Colombian government is trying to come to a similar deal with the left-wing FARC and ELN terrorist groups. The intelligence it gained in all those Justice and Peace Law deals with the right-wing paramilitaries helped it bomb the left-wing terrorists nearly to oblivion and bring them to the negotiating table today. Such are the Graham Greene–esque contradictions of Colombia: a revolution alongside a state, forgiveness with prosecution, peace-building without peace accords, and a peace process driven by the US-backed military prowess of the government.

A thin, pale, kind of spy plane known as "The Cross" will hover above guerrilla jungle camps and guide in soldiers or Black Hawk helicopters. After the battle comes the psychology: leaflets, banners, and booming messages encouraging the embattled guerrillas to quit. Even Ingrid Betancourt, the French-Colombian politician who spent six and a half years as an FARC hostage, was pressed into service within twenty-four hours of her rescue: "I am Ingrid Betancourt and I am free. Cross the bridge and come join me in freedom. Life is better out here. Give up your weapons now."

The idea is to chip away at unpaid and unhappy foot soldiers so there won't be much of an enemy to resist the military onslaught. Colombian authorities say they had three strategic priorities to reduce violence: "Demobilize, capture, kill." Now paramilitaries and the occasional former FARC fighter pick coffee beans alongside the villagers they once terrorized to produce *El Café de la Reconciliación* ("Reconciliation Coffee"), which is then packaged, sold, and marketed by Colombia's powerful Coffee Growers Federation, which owns the Juan Valdéz brand.

"We're tired of the violence. We just want it to end," said the weather-worn coffee farmer clinging to the back of our jeep as it headed up the dirt road from the small Risaralda town of Santuario ("Sanctuary") to a cliff promontory called La Linda ("The Pretty One"). La Linda was a FARC stronghold from 1999 until 2003, when it was taken over by a paramilitary front known as the "Heroes and Martyrs of Guática" of the Central Bolivar Bloc of the AUC, the umbrella organization for the right-wing paramilitaries. The Heroes and Martyrs of Guática then demobilized at La Linda in December 2005 under the Justice and Peace Law. In 2009 the government funded a playing field and a schoolhouse in La Linda in exchange for the community's accepting the former fighters back into their fold, living and building the school alongside their former torturers.

One woman told me her community in La Linda had taken in a FARC fighter who had killed her son and a paramilitary who had killed her husband. She knew their names; they were her neighbors now. I asked how she felt; she didn't want to answer with the government representatives within earshot. I kept asking until I got an answer: not thrilled, but patiently tolerant.

Our self-appointed guide (the jeep clinger) referred to the right-wing paramilitary (the United Colombian Self-Defense, or AUC) as *los muchachos* ("the boys"), still afraid to call them paramilitaries. When the paramilitaries occupied the town, relatives of the locals were delivered in body bags or hacked to pieces by chainsaws in the town square—starting from the ankles and working up, so the victim lived (and screamed) as long as possible. This was a common (and effective) paramilitary tactic: after witnessing it, villagers fell into line and did not challenge their occupiers.

Our local guide had witnessed the chainsaw executions, yet spoke of the paramilitaries as cleansing the village of the FARC and of their brutally imposed curfews (anyone out at night was killed) as being for the villagers' protection. Might, apparently, made right. After all, there was no government entity there to protect them, so at least they had order and security under the paramilitaries. It's a pattern of criminal acceptance I have seen repeated elsewhere since then.

By global standards, Colombia's peace process is privileged. Because Colombia's warring revolutionary and counterrevolutionary forces have fought alongside an active state infrastructure, the peace and reintegration process is run by the state itself rather than an outside mediator like the United Nations or NATO. It is tougher than it sounds, though. Peace-building in Colombia is a form of territorial conquest: the government uses its slowly developed military might to force the surrender by opposing fighters into the state structure, not some UN-mediated power-sharing agreement as in Northern Ireland or Liberia. The extent of US military assistance and training was evident at the agricultural commune integrating former guerrillas in VallenPaz in Cauca on the southwest coast. The soldiers guarding us had "US" stamped on their vests and radios. Their guns, though, were Israeli.

"We used to use American M-16s," a soldier told me, "but they're too unreliable and take too much cleaning if you're using them in the bush. We can't afford the time. So we carry these Israeli Galils; they're much sturdier. They're all encased in metal, though—they weigh two and a half times what an M-16 weighs." Likewise the Urban Counter-Terrorist branch of the Special Forces that guarded us in Bogotá: they carried Israeli TAR-21 snub-nosed semiautomatics.

While Colombia's armed factions are busy slaughtering each other, sometimes with foreign and domestic state sponsors, every single one of these groups has also been involved in criminal activity: drug trafficking, kidnapping, torture, extortions, and assassinations, to name but a few of their favorite things. None of this protracted and brutal violence would be possible without

First World demand for narcotics. This point was made poignantly to me by a farmer the Colombian government was retraining to grow coffee rather than coca. The government was giving him subsidies for equipment, training in small business management and efficient agricultural processes, and facilitated access to local, regional, and international markets under the Juan Valdéz brand.

"We are poor. I have to feed my family," he said to me. "Coca grows fast; I can harvest it two to three times a year. I can sell coca for more money than coffee. So I make five or six times more money growing coca to feed my family. I'm just growing something people want. These groups fighting—killing—are fighting for money coming out of the United States. The guns, the land mines, they come out of the United States. This is a gringo problem," he said, using the slang (and slightly derogatory) term for Americans, "not a Colombian one."

This assertion seemed rather glib a day later when I spoke with a ten-year-old farm girl lucky to have prosthetic legs who was serving us fruit juices as we talked to more child soldiers demobilized from the paramilitaries. She hobbled over, careful not to spill the cups on her wooden tray, with a big smile on her face.

"*¿Qué te pasó?*" ("What happened to you?")

"*Minas. En mi finca. Tengo suerte.*" ("Mines. On my farm. I'm lucky.")

"*Gracias,*" I said as I took the cup off the tray and gave her a big smile.

Despite her youth and disability, she was remarkably dignified, so I didn't want to embarrass her by making too big a fuss. She didn't expand on whether she was lucky to be alive or lucky to have prosthetic legs. Probably both. Because of the narcotics cultivation and the long-running conflict, Colombia is second in the world in land mine victims, after Afghanistan, with the government reporting 11, 408 deaths and injuries since 1990.[3] Try talking, too, about how none of this is a Colombian problem to the civilians and former fighters (both left-wing terrorists and right-wing para-

militaries) who have seen loved ones chopped to pieces by ma-
chete or chain saw to conserve ammunition.

Two generations have been lost to this conflict, all funded by
narcotics. That little gram bought in New York or London to be
snorted in clubs or at private parties results in these kids being
raped by fighters, kidnapped for ransom (and then likely raped),
or blown up: two generations devastated by a foreigner's appetite
for "a little fun." The US has tried to implement aid and crop re-
placement programs in other drug-producing countries in the
world, mainly Afghanistan, encouraging peasants to plant crops
other than those that generate narcotics. Neither the program in
Colombia nor Afghanistan has been deemed successful: the numbers simply don't add up.

PIPELINES OF ILLICIT GOODS

The FARC, however, is not a fully integrated drug cartel as we
generally understand the term: an organization effective at cross-
border transactions. Nor is it involved in the most profitable
downstream segment of the drug trade: the retail sale. It is when
the user in the US or Europe buys from the dealer that the biggest
profit is made. The FARC's drug funding comes mostly from its
involvement in the upstream, domestic supply chain: it controls
the coca fields in twenty-three of the country's thirty-two departments (states), which helps its members "recruit fresh troops and
impose their own laws and taxes."[4]

The FARC started collecting a "war tax" on drug crops in 1982,
when cocaine use became prevalent and its trafficking profitable. FARC charged 10 percent of the per-kilogram price[5] of coca
base, the raw form of cocaine (which is actually greenish, after being
processed—the mashed-up coca leaves are mixed with kerosene—
in water-accessible riverside huts in the jungle). FARC also collected
fees for every drug flight leaving from areas it controlled and taxed
marijuana and opium (for heroin) farmers. It still does, though

getting out of the drug business is one of the conditions of the peace deal FARC is now negotiating with President Santos.

Like the jihadis with whom I would later become familiar, the FARC, which was supposed to be a revolutionary group fighting for greater justice, also crafted a convenient narrative for its criminality and involvement in illicit trade: that with little government presence or support, the peasants lacked alternatives to making a living. True, growing coca is far more profitable than growing other crops, but it was also not in the FARC's or the paramilitaries' interest to give the peasants much choice: much of the fighting between the two sides was for control of the fields and the trafficking routes.

To increase their profits from the drug trade, the armed groups have attempted to move more into the midstream supply chain: smuggling. To do so, they have forged alliances with several of the criminal gangs (*bacrim*), mainly composed of demobilized fighters returning to their old tricks. The *Urabeños* is the most famous and powerful of the *bacrim*. In September 2017, however, their leader, Dairo Antonio Usuaga (*alias* "Otoniel") offered to surrender and demobilize, in a manner similar to the FARC. That is no coincidence: the groups are linked. The *bacrim* pay the FARC's famous taxes to move product through territory the FARC controls. Otherwise, the *bacrim* can pay the FARC directly in weapons, ammunition, and other supplies. The alliances also entail intelligence sharing; for which the FARC will provide shelter and training[6] in military tactics to the neophyte *bacrim* members. That is a concrete example of a convergent threat when criminal and terrorist groups work together.

These alliances, based on money and self-interest, are fleeting, also due to money and self-interest. The FARC has sought to cut out the *bacrim* middlemen and further vertically integrate its drug business by selling cocaine directly to the Mexican drug cartels. FARC's profit per kilogram triples if it can get the cocaine cross-border to pickup points on the Colombian coast or into neighboring Venezuela, Panama, or Ecuador, rather than selling the green paste product from laboratories inside Colombia.[7] Depending on the estimate, each fighter costs the FARC between $6,000 and $12,000[8] a year to maintain. If the FARC can cover costs by selling drugs, it stays fighting. So cutting out the drug profits will stop the violence, the terrorism, and the insurgency: cutting the consumption of the illicit product, taking the money out of the illicit trade, is an effective counterterrorism and counterinsurgency tactic.

In his speech before the UN General Assembly in September 2013, Colombian president Juan Manuel Santos asserted that drug trafficking "has been the main funding source for violence and terrorism in my country . . . Without the grim influence of drug trafficking—which fuels the fire of our war—I'm sure it would have already ended."[9]

Perhaps, but that is not the whole story; narcotics are not the only source of revenue here: both the terrorist insurgencies and the cartels have a long involvement in smuggling consumer products. Before Pablo Escobar entered the cocaine trade, he smuggled cigarettes and electronics. The FARC are now also involved in smuggling cigarettes that come in from the Tri-Border Area at the intersection of Brazil-Argentina-Paraguay via free trade zones in the Caribbean and Panama. According to current estimates, drugs account for only 25 to 50 percent of the FARC's income. So without its involvement in narcotics, the FARC would be weakened, but still well funded.[10]

Extortion has also long been FARC policy and a huge additional source of revenue. In 2000, the FARC issued "Law 002," which stated that every Colombian with a net worth over $1 million was obligated to pay a "war tax" to it. Dutch-born FARC fighter Tanja Nijmeier has detailed[11] how, as a member of the FARC's fierce RUAN (Red Urbana Antonio Nariño, or the Antonio Nariño Urban Network), she would get the details of whom to extort (names, addresses, relatives, pattern of life, and details of their finances and private lives), would call them at home, and, if they refused to pay, she would ensure they "entered into action" by bombing them. The FARC would call and ask again for their "war tax," a practice that only ended in July 2016, when FARC leader Timoleón Jiménez (alias "Timochenko") called off the practice by ordering his underlings to "stop the collection of taxes on all legal economic activity."[12] Those "taxed" ran the gamut from small farmers and shopkeepers to multinational corporations.

Illegal mining and the attendant extortion of mining companies are also a major source of income for the FARC and other groups. They impose taxes on illegal gold mines in the Antioquia, Córdoba, and Chocó departments[13] in northwest Colombia. They are also involved in the mining of tungsten, tantalum, and coltan, which are used in consumer electronics such as cell phones. These are known as "conflict minerals," and their regulation was suggested by the OECD *Guidance on Conflict Minerals* that targets the chokepoints in the supply chain: the smelters from which the major corporations (including Apple) buy their raw materials.

In the US, the Dodd-Frank Act has adopted the OECD guidance, so these corporations have to file reports with the Securities and Exchange Commission attesting that they are sourcing their materials from approved suppliers where the minerals came from. The practice, first started with the "blood diamonds" that funded the civil war in Sierra Leone, is drawn from banks' well-established anti-money-laundering protocols.

When Colombia experiences a boom in oil and mining exploration, that increases the probability and profitability of extorting mining and energy companies. Terrorists, too, run with the bulls of capital markets. Illegal mining and extortion offer significant advantages for the FARC compared with drugs: they attract less attention from law enforcement, and the penalties are much lighter—those caught don't face extradition to the US the way drug traffickers do, for a start.

Oil companies have been favorites. Pipelines are easy to poke holes in to steal oil to smuggle or, more simply, blow up and set aflame when the company refuses the up-front tax. In 2013, the FARC had carried out more than 163 attacks on pipelines by the end of November, causing the loss of thirty thousand barrels of oil a day—about 3 percent of Colombia's production that year.[14] Oil pipelines are an ideal target because they are difficult to protect and attacking them inflicts significant economic damage on the state and on "imperialist" foreign investment.

Sometimes the FARC and others would extort the oil companies and their personnel more directly. Kidnapping oil company executives and their families was a very good revenue earner: "K&R" (kidnap and ransom) insurance premiums have traditionally been very high for national senior executives of foreign companies operating in Colombia. Key infrastructure in general, though, is a pretty sweet target: electrical plants have been attacked, cutting off electricity to three hundred thousand people in October 2013.[15] At the time, the Colombian government's peace talks with the FARC were stalled, so the disruptions of oil and electricity supplies were an easy, cheap, and effective way of reminding the government of the FARC's power and keeping it negotiating.

Official figures of kidnappings vary due to a variety of factors: people who were thought kidnapped were not, people were freed and did not notify the authorities, or the authorities might be sure someone had been kidnapped but the organization holding the victim might not be the group that originally took him— everywhere in the world, criminal organizations kidnap people and then sell them to terrorist groups, and more recently, foreigners kidnapped in the Middle East have been sold to ISIS. The average of the best estimates indicates that in the early 2000s, the FARC held between 2,500 and 3,900 civilian hostages, not counting military, police, or contractors. The FARC even built special camps in the heart of the jungle to hold them all.

Fortunately, kidnappings have declined significantly since the FARC officially gave up the practice in 2012 as a precondition to the opening of peace talks with the government. When I was there in 2009 and 2010, kidnappings were still such a phenomenon that there was a special radio program for hostages on the national radio broadcaster, Caracol (whose offices were once bombed). Obtaining a little radio was a major prize in Colombia's internment camps for hostages, deep in the jungle. The kidnapped gathered around the crackling radio in the predawn hours every Sunday to listen to Radio Caracol's *Voices of Kidnap* to hear if one of their relatives came on delivering a message of love to them. A typical broadcast would go something like this:

On cue starts the jingle with a driving beat not heard since the 1980s with a high little singsong: "The Voices of Kidnap on Caracol / are messages of life and liberty." The voice on the radio speaks in a clear Colombian accent. "This is your host, Herbin Hoyos, speaking to all the kidnapped, wherever they may be in the jungles of Colombia. We are speaking to each and every one of you. We are here with you as we are every Sunday night, from midnight to six in the morning, telling you to keep hoping: you will be freed. We will continue broadcasting until the last captive is freed from the jungles of Colombia.

"Kidnapping has been a weapon of war either to extort money or achieve political ends since at least fifteen hundred years before Christ. We know it was used in ancient Egypt and Greece; we read about it in the *Iliad* and the Bible; we know the young Julius Caesar was kidnapped. Now this sad tradition continues in our own country, in our own war. I have with me here tonight someone that was just recently freed after thirteen years in captivity.

"Camila Arango was taken by the paramilitary *autodefensas* [Colombian Self-Defense Forces, AUC] from her own farm in Caquetá. After thirteen years, Camila, you are now on the other end of the radio. What is the message of hope you wish to share with your friends, your fellow captives who are listening out there in the jungle?"

A soft crinkling of paper is heard over the radio. "I just wrote down what I want to say." Her voice is soft and tentative. "As you hear my voice now, you must have hope. So often I doubted my ability to go on, but my being here today is proof that you must, that miracles do happen, that your friends and family still love you, still pray for you, still work for your safe return. I want to express my gratitude to my fellow kidnapped who were with me in the jungle and took care of me and helped me go on. I am still with you, tonight, over the radio, but also every day, as I carry you in my heart and in my prayers and will work for your release, too."

She pauses, then resumes her staccato delivery.

"I am grateful also to my family who daily waited for me, and to Almighty God. Continue praying to Him, my kidnapped friends; He will protect you. Especially to little Ofelia Ramírez, fourteen years old, taken on her way to school in Bogotá. She joined us the last six months of my captivity. Ofelia, do not be afraid, my child, do not be afraid. God is with you, in you, you must find joy in Him and you will be free."

THE BUSINESS OF HUNTING TERRORISTS

I know from my own work that nothing releases the purse strings and unleashes the hounds of state like terrorism. Hunting terrorists is a business of its own. Those agencies that kill the most terrorists get the most funding. In Colombia, this dynamic put pressure on the Colombian military to produce results to justify all the funding and assistance it received, both from its own government and the US. This resulted in a scandal known as the "False Positives."

Poor civilian boys who were reported missing by their mothers in Soacha, just south of Bogotá, were found three days later in a different part of the country dressed in fatigues and shot dead by the military, who identified them as left-wing guerrillas (like the FARC and ELN) killed in combat. The mothers and other family members insisted this was impossible, that they were not members of armed groups. The government prosecuted nearly five hundred soldiers involved in the kidnaps and murders. But some Colombians remained dissatisfied, claiming the prosecutions were too slow and that the prison terms too often became time served while awaiting trial, leaving the kidnappings and murders to go legally unpunished.

"But the legal process is working in this [the Soacha] case [of False Positives]. It is the government itself that made the events at Soacha public, so we are not hiding anything," insisted Carlos Franco as we chatted at the Colombian Embassy in London a few days after my 2010 trip. Franco was the very embodiment of redemption through reintegration: this blue-eyed, middle-aged man with wild wavy hair sitting in a pinstriped blue suit was once a commander of the leftist EPL (Popular Liberation Army, in Spanish) guerrillas, one of the many left-wing insurgencies that are similar to, but competed with, the FARC; when I interviewed him in 2010, he was the director of the Presidential Program for Human Rights, coordinating the tasks of the various government departments and shaping Colombian policy on human rights. He felt they had advanced greatly during the Uribe administration, mainly through strengthened state institutions.

"So the most important thing today," said Franco back in 2010, "is that the state now feels responsible for guaranteeing the rights of the people. I think that's very important—all rights, be they of labor union members or a businessman who should not be kidnapped or political opposition to the government. The second thing is that all the policies are considered in the light of human rights. Our security policy is designed to guarantee rights and it's enacted respecting people's rights."

Perhaps. But I know many Colombians who would beg to differ. Drug money—from the insurgents, paramilitaries, and cartels—has infiltrated Colombian politics. Former Colombian president Ernesto Samper had his US visa canceled after it was alleged his 1994 presidential campaign had received US$6 million from the

Cali cartel. In 2014, a top adviser to President Santos resigned amid allegations he accepted US$12 million from top drug lords, though no criminal charges have been filed.

In terms of human rights violations in its fight against the FARC, the Colombian government has been criticized for its use of violent proxies. It used the right-wing paramilitaries of the AUC to commit atrocities against both the left-wing guerrillas and their civilian supporters that the government did not want to commit itself. This became known as the "Parapolitical Scandal" and revealed that the paramilitaries had political ties reaching deep into the Uribe administration. This is why, some skeptics allege, the paramilitaries were the first to get a reintegration deal.

On November 9, 2006, the Colombian Supreme Court ordered the arrest of three congressmen for their alleged role in establishing paramilitary groups in the Department of Sucre on the Caribbean coast. Foreign Minister Maria Consuelo Araujo resigned at the time of the investigation into her brother's and father's connections to the paramilitaries and their involvement in the kidnapping of Álvaro Araujo's opponent in a Senate election. In December 2007, Congressman Erik Morris was sentenced to six years in prison for his ties to the paramilitaries, making him the first member of Congress sentenced in the scandal.

Along with corruption charges, there have been allegations that the Colombian military passed on intelligence to the AUC paramilitaries to support their battles against the FARC, committing at-arm's-length massacres the government could not sanction directly. In February 2008, the former head of Colombia's Department of Administrative Security (DAS), Jorge Noguera, was formally charged with collaborating with paramilitaries, including giving paramilitaries the names of union activists, some of whom they then murdered.[16]

In April 2008, Mario Uribe, a former senator and a second cousin and close ally of former president Alvaro Uribe, was arrested for colluding with the paramilitaries. On February 21, 2011,

Mario Uribe was convicted of aggravated conspiracy to commit a crime and sentenced to seven and a half years in prison. The US State Department reported that of Colombia's 2006–2010 Congress, 128 former representatives (out of the total of 268) were accused of having paramilitary ties. Of those representatives newly elected to the 2010–2014 Congress, 13 who were reelected were under investigation by the Supreme Court.

Though many facts of the scandal remain sketchy, Colombia's judicial institutions appear to be working better than those in most of the rest of Latin America (and nearly any country with continued armed conflict): the Parapolitical Scandal has resulted in numerous prosecutions, and Colombia claims that its reintegration process will prosecute more fighters than in all previous such efforts put together, including the Nuremberg trials.

Nevertheless, in his London office in 2010, Franco was realistic about the challenges of what he termed "a process of reintegration in the midst of confrontation." He quoted former Israeli prime minister Shimon Peres, a man who arguably knew a thing or two about war and peace and terrorism.

"He said that you have to negotiate as if there were no war and make war as if there were no peace negotiations. It's really two faces of the same coin. A lot of pacifists think they're mutually exclusive, or they make the assessment that this government has chosen war. This government has not chosen war; this government has confronted the circumstances with which it was faced. This is not a decision made by the Colombian government; this is a decision made by the guerrillas."

GRIEVANCE TO GREED

The FARC, ELN, and other left-wing guerrilla terrorists always maintained their revolutionary credentials, insisting that overthrowing the government to bring greater social justice was their goal. Claiming to represent the lower, peasant, and agrarian class of Colombia, the FARC still oppose many of the country's globalization and privatization efforts, which it sees as growing imperialism in a country under the influence of the US and multinational corporations. In 1982, the FARC adopted the suffix "-EP," meaning *Ejército del Pueblo* (the People's Army). The FARC-EP is designated a terrorist group by the governments of Colombia, the United States, Canada, Chile, New Zealand, and the European Union.

Aside from giving them the means to manipulate their supporters, the narrative of their revolutionary cause has also given the FARC and ELN the means to manipulate the peace negotiations. As a result, the FARC will get a much more lenient deal than the paramilitaries did under the 2005 Justice and Peace Law. Though the revolutionary grievance of social inequality and agrarian reform has been the "just cause" of Colombia's left-wing guerrillas, they evolved into an international criminal organization (so did the right-wing paramilitaries, by the way): while the illicit trade in narcotics, oil, and minerals bought weapons for the revolution, the illicit trade became good business. In the end, the weapons were there to guard the money—and the narrative of the revolution became a good fund-raising and community relations tool—including in the peace negotiations.

None of this would be possible if it were not for the appetite of consumers—in this case, the appetite for narcotics, gold, smuggled oil, and raw materials for technology (the "conflict minerals" that go into cell phones). Domestically, it would not be possible without the local support of poor constituencies who are persuaded by a Robin Hood or revolutionary narrative that these armed groups are fighting for the benefit of the poor—when they are both perpetuating and exploiting people's poverty and desperation.

It is important that as informed citizens and consumers, we are aware of these dynamics and refuse to be duped by them. We must also hold governments accountable for corruption that gives safe haven to these groups and demand that they meet their contract with their people to provide security, an education, and job opportunities, so that their constituents are not marginalized and can lead dignified, peaceful, and law-abiding lives. As consumers, we need to stop making choices that devastate the lives of others, just so we can have a little fun.

4

Filling in the Puzzle

In Colombia, I had seen the devastation wrought by protracted violence and was starting to understand the roles in that violence played by illicit goods smuggling, cross-border support for that smuggling (Venezuelan *Chavistas* supporting the FARC), the use of proxy groups (the Colombian government using the paramilitaries to viciously kill FARC members and their supporters), government corruption, and the use of narrative to manipulate constituent support. From 2010 into 2011, I started to expand my analysis of the dynamics moving the key players in Latin America. I talked to anyone I could find: former presidents and presidential candidates, bankers, academics, expats, soldiers, entrepreneurs, journalists. I wrote for the US conservative magazine *The Weekly Standard* and for *Diplomat*, a London-based magazine where I was still editor-at-large, on Colombia's peace process and elections, as well as the elections in Brazil and Argentina. What I started to understand was how foreigners with their own agendas (including terrorists) infiltrate the politics of resource-rich countries such as Venezuela, by using corruption, their diaspora network, and dark money.

One bit of research that opened my eyes was for my article on the geopolitical games surrounding Bolivia's lithium supply. Lithium is a key material in making rechargeable batteries for laptops and cell phones and enabling the energy storage capacity of solar panels. The negotiations to secure the supply of the "oil of the twenty-first century" saw a *Chavista*-sympathizing, pro-coca, "anti-imperialist" president of Bolivia, Evo Morales, being courted by American investment funds, French billionaires, and Chinese officials. Clearly, where there is an energy supply, ideology becomes optional.

In Venezuela, ideology is bent around the pillars of power. The anti-American, "anti-imperialist" regime under Hugo Chávez put several Venezuelans of Middle Eastern descent into senior positions, affecting national interests and security and handing Iran and its terrorist proxy in Lebanon, Lebanese Hezbollah, a potential plug-in for dark money and influence. A few of the ideological sympathizers from the Lebanese or Syrian diaspora whom Chávez appointed include Fadi Kabboul, appointed the executive director of planning (corporate strategy) for Venezuela's government-owned oil company, PDVSA; Aref Richany Jiménez, elevated to the presidency of Venezuelan Military Industries Company (known as CAVIM); and Radwan Sabbagh, placed in charge of the state-owned mining concern, Ferrominera. Venezuela not only has oil, gold, iron, and aluminum, it also has uranium—which is obviously of interest to those involved in Iran's nuclear program. The United States was not amused.

TRADE AND TERRORISM

On June 18, 2008, the US Treasury Department's Office of Foreign Asset Control (OFAC) "designated" two Venezuela-based supporters of Hezbollah, Ghazi Nasr Al-Din and Fawzi Kan'an, along with two travel agencies owned and controlled by Kan'an. An OFAC designation is basically a sanction: assets are frozen and no bank can transact business with the designated entity. No entity whose bank has an office in the US or operates in a country whose currency is dollarized can do business with a designated entity.

The OFAC statement accused Ghazi Nasr Al-Din of using his position as a Venezuelan diplomat (as chargé d'affaires at the Venezuelan Embassy in Damascus, Syria, and subsequently the director of political affairs at the Venezuelan Embassy in Lebanon) and as the president of a Caracas-based Shia Islamic Center to provide financial support to Lebanese Hezbollah. Nasr Al-Din met with senior Hezbollah officials in Lebanon to discuss operational issues, facilitated the travel of Hezbollah members to and from Venezuela, and provided donors with specific information on Hezbollah bank accounts. In late January 2006, Nasr Al-Din facilitated the travel of two Hezbollah representatives from the Lebanese Parliament to Caracas to solicit donations for Hezbollah and to announce the opening of a Hezbollah-sponsored community center and office in Venezuela. The previous year, Nasr Al-Din arranged the travel of Hezbollah members to attend a training course in Iran.

Fawzi Kan'an owned two Venezuela-based travel agencies that were sanctioned by OFAC: Biblos Travel Agency (Biblos is a resort city north of Beirut), to which he couriered funds, and Hilal Travel Agency, which Kan'an formed in April 2001, for facilitating travel for Hezbollah members, even traveling with them to Iran for training. Travel agencies, I have since learned, are a classic ploy in transnational criminal and terrorist groups: not only do travel agencies provide the paperwork and logistics for the movement of people and cargo (often illicit, like weapons and drugs), but the invoicing mechanisms are excellent for laundering money and evading currency exchange or banking controls.

Nasr Al-Din set up Hezbollah cells in Venezuela and was directly supervised by Iran's religious leadership. In the central Venezuelan city of Barquisimeto, he ran the Bolivarian Circles: a militant armed group that is sympathetic to the causes of the *Chavista*

Bolivarian Revolution and the Marxist narcoterrorist insurgency, the FARC. Nasr Al-Din was directly supervised by Mohsen Rabbani,[1] an imam alleged to be personally responsible for the two terrorist bombings in Buenos Aires, in 1992 and 1994. Nasr Al-Din was also responsible for the recruitment and training of Latin American boys in Venezuela and in Qom, Iran.

Qom is legendary to those who work Middle Eastern security: it is the most holy city of the Shia sect of Islam; it is also the operational base of the Quds Force, the group responsible for the "black ops" of spreading Iranian power around the globe through proxies and allies. The Iranian Revolutionary Guard Corps' (IRGC) Quds Force is "like taking the CIA, Special Forces, and the State Department and rolling them into one."[2] One of my Venezuelan sources detailed specific entry points and locations that Quds Force operatives of the IRGC were using to come into Venezuela.

Despite having an Interpol red notice on him that was supposed to stop his travel, Imam Mohsen Rabbani traveled from Qom to Brazil in September 2010 and to Venezuela in March 2011. The Brazilians have said that when he entered Brazil, he went to Venezuela first. Only government complicity could have enabled such free movement for a suspected terrorist agitator. In other words, Venezuelan government officials have been turning poor young Venezuelan boys into jihadis for the benefit of Iran, while in exchange the *Chavistas* use Iranian and Hezbollah skills in asymmetric warfare[3] to keep themselves in power.

This is rather stunning in a country as heavily Catholic as Venezuela. However, in western Venezuela, along the border with Colombia, there is a concentration, albeit a small minority, of Middle Eastern descendants, who mix with FARC sympathizers and drug traffickers. But turning young poor boys into trained terrorist operatives for a militant Islamist group takes an effective strategy of active radicalization. Their poverty and societal marginalization have to be amplified into anger and converted to a revolutionary anti-American, anticapitalist ideology. They have to be taught radical Islam and the guerrilla insurgency tactics of asymmetric warfare, overlaid with jihadism.

So far, there has not been much jihadism coming out of Venezuela, but its *Chavista* rulers were obviously very keen to leverage jihadist tactics in their own quest to maintain power. Venezuelan president Hugo Chávez himself ensured that all the military were trained in and carried a pocket-sized copy of *Peripheral War and Revolutionary Islam: Origins, Rules and Ethics of Asymmetric Warfare*, by Jorge Verstrynge. An unclassified Pentagon report to the US Congress[4] in 2009 expressed concern about the large presence of the Quds Force in Venezuela and what it might mean for regional security. US defense secretary Robert Gates accused Iran of engaging in "subversive activity" in Latin America. No kidding.

Iran's elite IRGC is the branch of the Iranian military charged with protecting and advancing the Islamic Revolution. In Iran, trade and terrorism mix in particularly complex ways. According to a former US national intelligence officer for Asia, about 25 percent of Iran's corporate enterprises are controlled by the IRGC. The super-elite Quds Force (those of the "black ops") has set up subsidiary businesses in Venezuela across the manufacturing, energy, military, and financial sectors, with companies in mining, banking, tractors and bicycles, munitions, and even nuclear technology.

The Quds Force are all over Venezuela. The guards around an alleged "tractor factory" in Bolívar State in central Venezuela are Quds and speak Farsi (the language of Iran), not Spanish. The factory has not been known to ever produce a single tractor, but it is suspected of being an Iranian weapons factory. A November 2008 seizure at sea lends credence to this suspicion: Turkish customs officials in the port of Mersin stopped and inspected an Iranian shipment to Venezuela and found bomb-making materials mislabeled as tractor parts.

Many IRGC companies have set up subsidiaries in Venezuela (Iran's fellow OPEC member) in collaboration with or using the services of Venezuela's national oil company, PDVSA, and its affiliates. By using PDVSA, one of the world's largest state-owned oil companies, the IRGC gains access not just to Venezuela's banking system but, through it, to international financial markets, including its US subsidiary, Citgo. Citgo Petroleum Corporation refines PDVSA's oil and commercializes gasoline, lubricants, and petrochemicals in the United States. In December 2016, 49 percent of Citgo was mortgaged to Russia's Rosneft; if PDVSA defaults, the Russians will take over key pipelines and refineries in the US— and do so while sidestepping the usual US regulations for foreign investment in strategically important sectors, under the aegis of CFIUS—the Committee on Foreign Investment in the United States. That Russia backs Iranian interests is evident in Syria, where they back Iran's man, fellow Shia Bashar al-Assad, while he slaughters his citizens. If the Russians end up owning Citgo, they will be using US-based assets (gasoline, refineries, and pipelines) to support themselves and Iran and al-Assad in Syria.

As would be expected of two major oil producers, Iran's and Venezuela's oil companies also cross-invested in each other: Iran invested in the Orinoco Belt, while PDVSA announced plans to invest $780 million in the South Pars gas field in southern Iran, a project referred to in Venezuelan documentation as "PetroPars." Furthermore, Toseh Saderat Iran Bank set up a subsidiary in Venezuela: the International Development Bank (Banco Internacional de Desarrollo—BID). Every single one of the BID's directors is an Iranian with Iranian government credentials. That would indicate that the BID is likely a pass-through for Iran to launder money and avoid sanctions.[5]

The business relationship between Iran and Venezuela is also ideological. The late Venezuelan president Hugo Chávez and former Iranian president Mahmoud Ahmadinejad signed accords, gave each other gifts, and called each other brothers in the struggle against the "Evil Empire" (the US). Ahmadinejad was one of the recipients of a copy of the sword of Latin American liberator

Simón Bolívar, after whom the *Chavista* Bolivarian Revolution is named and after whom Chávez renamed the Republic of Venezuela the Bolivarian Republic of Venezuela. Replicas of the Sword of Bolívar have also been given to Vladimir Putin and Moammar Qaddafi.

The alleged original Sword of Bolívar has been claimed by the Colombian Marxist guerrilla terrorist groups FARC and M-19, as well as by the late drug kingpin Pablo Escobar. In Latin America, it is the ultimate symbol of resistance: first to Spain, and then to the US and transnational corporations. The Sword of Bolívar's alleged peregrinations through the hands of numerous soi-disant revolutionaries is proof positive that semiotics are still very important in Latin American politics.

The fears of both *Chavismo* and Iranian nefarious intent are lent great credence by *"Aeroterror"* ("Terror Air"), the commonly used slang term for the weekly flights of Iran Air and Venezuelan national carrier Conviasa that hopscotch among Caracas, Tehran, and Damascus. The flights are always full, yet the passengers do not go through immigration and the cargo does not go through customs. They simply pass through their special gate area in Venezuela's Simón Bolívar International Airport. Venezuelans and Venezuela watchers all think the flights transport terrorist operatives (some of those boys heading to Qom, Iran), as well as drugs, cash, and weapons, back and forth among the three cities—hence the epithet *"Aeroterror."*

Connect this government-protected covert route with the visa and trade pacts with other members of ALBA[6] (the Spanish acronym for the Bolivarian Alliance for the Peoples of Our America), and it means terrorists can be transiting regionally with almost no way to track them—a concern Gen. Douglas Fraser, former head of the US Southern Command (which has responsibility for military action south of Mexico), expressed publicly on April 5, 2011.[7]

Stories spread of government involvement in drug trafficking and the provision of Venezuelan identity cards to known Middle Eastern terrorists. The growing routes linking South American cocaine to Middle Eastern terrorists run primarily from Colombia through Venezuela. The United Nations Office on Drugs and Crime (UNODC) 2011 *World Drug Report* named the Bolivarian Republic of Venezuela as the most prominent transshipment point for cocaine bound for Europe, with the cocaine coming mainly from Colombia,[8] primarily from the FARC and ELN terrorist groups.

I spoke to many people who would have a unique insight, including former military officers, to understand how this could have happened. The left-wing alliance of Colombian drug traffickers and Middle Eastern terrorists of various types had been around for decades, but the election of Hugo Chávez put key personnel in the cabinet and elevated them in the military.

Venezuela's vice president and former minister of the interior and justice is Tareck Zaidan El Aissami Maddah, a Venezuelan of Syrian descent. He was sanctioned as a drug kingpin in February 2017 by the US Treasury Department. His father, Carlos El Aissami, was the head of the Ba'ath Party in Venezuela and praised Osama bin Laden as "the great Mujahideen leader" after 9/11 and called himself (in a press conference) "a Taliban." His great-uncle Shibli El Aissami was assistant to the secretary-general of the Ba'ath Party in Iraq under Saddam Hussein. The original Ba'athists were the Syrians; when two warring factions split, one of the factions crossed the border into Iraq. Tareck El Aissami grew up in the border region between Venezuela and Colombia, where he mingled not only with a greater Middle Eastern diaspora, but with Colombia's FARC Marxist guerrillas.

As minister of the interior and justice, El Aissami created the National Bolivarian Police (PNB is the Spanish acronym) in 2009 and oversaw large seizures of narcotics and the capture of various drug capos, including Diego Pérez Henao (aka "Rastrojo"), Ramón Antonio del Rosario Fuentes (alias "Toño Leña"), and Maximiliano Bonilla Orozco (aka "El Valenciano," "Daniel Barrera," and

"El Loco Barrera"). Many international security analysts (including myself) suspected that the seizures were to disrupt a cartel that rivaled the Cartel of the Suns, so named for the sun insignia on the military uniforms of the cocaine trafficking generals. The Cartel of the Suns was led by Venezuela's director of military intelligence, Gen. Hugo Carvajal. The cartel is not linked to the military; it *is* the military.

The administration of President Hugo Chávez found such common cause with Middle Eastern terrorist groups inimical to "the Empire" (aka the United States) and its "Zionist" friends, that thousands of foreign terrorists (Al Qaeda, Hezbollah, and Spain's ETA) were given national identity cards, allowing them full access to the benefits of Venezuelan citizenship—and making them effectively invisible to US intelligence services.

In 2003, Gen. Marcos Ferreira, who had been in charge of Venezuela's Department of Immigration and Foreigners (until he decided to support the 2002 coup against Chávez), said that he had been personally asked by Ramón Rodríguez Chacín (who served as both deputy head of DISIP—Venezuela's intelligence service, now renamed SEBIN—and interior minister under Chávez) to allow the illegal entry of Colombians into Venezuela thirty-five times and that the national intelligence service itself regularly fast-tracked terrorists, including Hezbollah and Al Qaeda. The newly minted Venezuelan citizens during Ferreira's tenure included 2,520 Colombians and 279 Middle Easterners simply identified as "Syrians" on their applications. And that was during only the first three years of a regime that radicalized dramatically after that point.

The man who replaced Gen. Marcos Ferreira as head of Venezuela's Department of Immigration and Foreigners was Hugo Cabezas, who has well-chronicled ties with guerrilla movements at the University of the Andes. Evidence has surfaced that during this time both men illegally issued Venezuelan passports and identity documents to members of Hezbollah and Hamas. Cabezas is also a founding member of Utopia, an armed group that has connections with the Bolivarian Liberation Forces. Reports that Venezuela has provided Hezbollah operatives with Venezuelan national identity cards are so rife that they were raised during the July 27, 2010, Senate hearing for the recently nominated US ambassador to Venezuela, Larry Palmer. When Palmer answered that he believed the reports, Chávez refused to accept him as ambassador. In February 2017, CNN did an investigation, called *Passports to Terror*, on the sale of Venezuelan passports by the Venezuelan Embassy in Baghdad to known terrorists.

Some of the best insights on the interconnections among drug traffickers, terrorists, marginalized diasporas, and government officials have come from Walid Makled, who was arrested on August 19, 2010, in Cúcuta, a town on the Venezuelan-Colombian border. A Venezuelan of Syrian descent known variously as "El Turco" ("The Turk") or "El Arabe" ("The Arab"), Makled is allegedly responsible for smuggling ten tons of cocaine a month into the US and Europe—a full 10 percent of the world's supply and 60 percent of Europe's—which would make him Venezuela's latter-day Pablo Escobar. His massive infrastructure and distribution network make this entirely plausible—and make it entirely *im*plausible that the Venezuelan government did not know about it.

Makled owned Venezuela's biggest airline, Aeropostal, and huge warehouses in Venezuela's biggest port, Puerto Cabello, and bought enormous quantities of urea (used in cocaine processing) from a government-owned chemical company. He got control of Venezuela's biggest port through one of Chávez's inner-circle military cohorts, Luis Felipe Acosta Carles, whom Makled met in the city of Valencia, where both men lived. Makled's position in *Chavismo* was sealed when (by his own words) he gave two million dollars to General Acosta Carles to support Chávez during the attempted recall referendum in 2004, which Chávez won. Chávez then supported Acosta Carles's run for governor shortly afterward, which he won. As a reward, Governor Carles granted

Makled the administration of the most important port in the country: Puerto Cabello. From there, Makled and his cohorts— "the Makleds"—are alleged to have run drugs through the port and supplied weapons to the FARC in exchange for cocaine, which they then purportedly smuggled to Central America and West Africa.[9]

After his arrest and incarceration in the Colombian prison La Picota, Makled gave numerous interviews to various media outlets. When asked on camera by a Univisión television reporter whether he had any connection to the FARC, he answered: "That is what I would say to the American prosecutor." His cryptic answer was intended to tread the thin line between not being killed by the people whose secrets he held and withholding a negotiating chip for the US prosecutor.

Asked directly whether he knew of Hezbollah operations in Venezuela, he answered: "In Venezuela? Of course! That which I understand is that they work in Venezuela. [Hezbollah] make money and all of that money they send to the Middle East."

In Walid Makled's ongoing trial in Caracas, it was revealed that all of the documentation and cover that Makled needed for his criminal enterprise was supplied by a high-ranking *Chavista* who often received orders directly from Chávez himself: Eladio Aponte Aponte, a Venezuelan Supreme Court justice. In an attempt at preemptive damage control, the *Chavista*-controlled Venezuelan National Assembly relieved the justice of his duties and began the process to convict him—whereupon he fled to Costa Rica and was picked up by the US Drug Enforcement Agency and flown to Washington, D.C., where he began singing like a canary.

Aponte's was the highest-level defection from the Chávez regime at that time. Among Aponte's juicy revelations to US authorities were that President Hugo Chávez would call him to tell him how to convict political rivals and that Generals Hugo Carvajal (former director of military intelligence) and Henry Rangel Silva (the interior minister), both designated as drug kingpins by the

US Treasury Department, would call him to tell him to secure and provide legal cover for multiton cocaine shipments from the FARC through Venezuela.

Ayman Joumaa, a Sunni Muslim of the Medellín cartel with deep ties to Shiites in the Hezbollah strongholds of southern Lebanon, was identified as a key broker in the triangulated relationship among *Chavistas*, drug cartels, and terrorist groups. His indictment charged him with "coordinating shipments of Colombian cocaine to Los Zetas in Mexico for sale in the United States, and laundering the proceeds."[10] According to the FBI,[11] the "proceeds" Joumaa laundered amounted to $200 million a month. That was what US intelligence officials previously thought Iran gave to Hezbollah *a year*. In short, vast swaths of the Venezuelan government have become important nodes in an international crime-terror pipeline.

THE REBELLION

The relationships in what Chávez called "the International Rebellion"[12] arose in the immediate aftermath of the collapse of the Soviet Union—the point in history that is also the starting point of the convergence of groups into the crime-terror pipeline. When the Soviet Union collapsed, so did its financial support of Cuba and other Marxist fighting groups. Cubans refer to this time as "the Special Period," presumably special for the starvation that ensued. Cubans who lived through it will tell you how devastating it was for them.

The 1990 São Paulo Forum was attended by prominent (even right-wing) Venezuelan political leaders and international terrorists. The roster included not only then-Venezuelan president Carlos Andrés Pérez (against whom Chávez would attempt a coup in 1992), but also Alí Rodríguez, then-president of the Venezuelan government-owned oil company, PDVSA; Pablo Medina, a left-wing Venezuelan politician who initially supported Chávez, but later moved to the opposition; as well as Fidel Castro, Moammar Qaddafi, and leaders of several Latin American Marxist terrorist groups—Colombia's Revolutionary Armed Forces (FARC), Uruguay's Tupamaros (who were by then already fomenting a powerful cell in Venezuela, centered in the 23 de Enero neighborhood of Caracas), and Peru's Shining Path (*Sendero Luminoso*).

These alliances have deepened and become institutionalized as the Bolivarian Continental Coordinator, the office that coordinates all the Latin American leftist armed groups. They held their first congress in Caracas in 2005 and appointed leadership: Dominican politician Narciso Isa Conde was made president and Amilcar Figueroa (aka "Tino") was made a board member, as were FARC commander Manuel Marulanda Vélez, along with Cuban president Fidel Castro, Venezuelan president Hugo Chávez, and Nicaraguan president Daniel Ortega. FARC commanders Alfonso Cano and Iván Marquéz were made honorary presidents. Their stated mission: to achieve and impose the Bolivarian (Marxist-Leninist) ideology throughout Latin America.

At its congress in Quito in February 2008, the Bolivarian Continental Coordinator rebranded itself the Bolivarian Continental Movement, and Isa Conde outlined a goal of "articulation of revolutionary diversities from a common strategy capable of confronting and defeating the imperialist strategy and definitively emancipating our America."[13] In other words: it is anti-US. The congress that constituted the new Bolivarian Continental Movement met in Caracas on December 7, 2009. It moved the organization from being just an association of left-wing movements to becoming in and of itself a movement founded by the FARC, and one that supports violent insurgency to bring about societal changes.

Unsurprisingly, the opening greeting was a video message from one of the group's honorary presidents: FARC commander Alfonso Cano. According to a well-placed Venezuelan military source of mine, the Bolivarian Continental Movement is headquartered in the Venezuelan state of Barinas—the same state that is effectively a Chávez family fiefdom, with their sprawling family estate, *La Chavera*, and total control of local politics.

I WAS SPENDING December 31, 2011, into 2012 with family on the West Coast when I got an email that my piece for the Foreign Policy Research Institute, "The New Nexus of Narcoterrorism: Hezbollah and Venezuela," my second article on the subject, had been picked up by the ABC News Web site, then by a Spanish-language news Web site called *La Patilla*, and from there by a Venezuelan government Web site, which edited it liberally. The pro-*Chavista* Web site described me as "a highly paid lobbyist" (not true) advocating the assassination of President Chávez—a false accusation, but certainly a very serious crime in any country. It also gave the address of the Foreign Policy Research Institute, where the article claimed I kept an office.

"You need to cancel your trip," read the email from the same former assistant secretary of defense and former national intelligence officer who would later advise me on my trip to Beirut. I called my brother in Caracas and explained why I would be missing his daughter's christening three weeks hence.

Both my anger and my curiosity were piqued. If the Venezuelan government felt threatened by my writing about its relationship with Hezbollah, I knew I should keep digging. Four months later, I touched down at Beirut's Rafic Hariri International Airport.

Sheikh, Colonel, Trafficker, Terrorist

Determined to pull the thread on the relationship between Venezuela's *Chavista* regime and the Iranian-backed terrorist group Lebanese Hezbollah, I contacted a friend who would know a lot about them: Lee Smith, my editor at the US conservative magazine *The Weekly Standard*, for whom I had written several articles. Lee had lived in Beirut, spoke some Arabic, and wrote a lot about the Levant's various power players, including Hezbollah. He had friends in Beirut and, as a journalist, moved around freely there, meeting with political and military leaders from various factions. After the September 11, 2001, attacks on the Twin Towers, whose flaming ruins he saw clearly from his Brooklyn home, Lee had left the US and gone to the Middle East to figure out how this had happened. He alternately lived in Lebanon, Egypt, and Israel to see what he could learn.

In early 2012, I told Lee that the next time he went to Lebanon, I wanted to plan my trip to coincide with his, so he could be my guide. He would be going in early May 2012 and told me to meet him there. No one had asked me to go; no one was covering my expenses. But what I would learn about the vast intercontinental tentacles of crime-terror pipelines, how terrorist groups gain constituencies, and how Americans are viewed in the Middle East would be the turning point in my career.

Once my travel plans were set, I told a friend and colleague in New York of my intention to go to Beirut. He was a well-connected former US assistant secretary of defense. A few days later he told me to stop by at the end of a dinner he was hosting at a private club: the others at the dinner knew Lebanon quite well and would be able to give me a few pointers and contacts.

As they lingered over after-dinner drinks in the back of the basement dining room, I sat down with my friend and two other men: a gray-haired American and a Central Asian. They recommended I speak to a moderate Shia sheikh and an Alawite from a famous and powerful political family. The Alawite was living in exile in Europe, but would be really well informed as to regional networks and connections. I emailed him and called him from New York. He was well mannered, but not as helpful as I had hoped. I waited until I landed in Beirut to contact the moderate Shia sheikh.

"What passport should I use?" was my first question to Lee before I took off from JFK Airport in New York for my trip to Beirut.

"The American."

"Doesn't Hezbollah control the airport? Don't they hate Americans?"

"Yes, but they will respect it. They won't mess with an American at the airport."

Perhaps not at the airport, but maybe later.

Hezbollah is a transliteration from the Arabic for "Party of God." They are both a terrorist group and a political party—in Lebanon, they function as a state within a state, with phenomenal intelligence and covert operatives. They proclaim themselves the armed resistance of Shia Muslims, whose heartland is Iran and who suffer a strong sense of marginalization by their Sunni Muslim brethren, whose homeland is the wealthy and powerful Saudi

Arabia, the Keeper of the Two Mosques, Mecca and Medina. Hezbollah is the front line of the Sunni-versus-Shia civil war that tears apart the Middle East. There are endless complexities and nuances, but in simple and broad brushstrokes, Hezbollah oppose Daesh.

THE COLONEL AND THE SHEIKH

A day after I landed, Lee invited me to the christening of the child of some friends of his. They were Maronite Catholics. The Maronite Church was founded on Mount Lebanon in the fourth century by Saint Maron and it spread across the Levant, including what is modern-day Syria and Jordan. When the Muslims conquered Syria (634–638 AD), the Maronites fled to Lebanon and bound themselves to the Byzantine Empire. They adapted in the face of growing persecution by Muslims, until the Egyptian Mamluks destroyed their forts and monasteries in 1289–1291. In other words, they were Christian allies in the Crusades. Today, they have European allegiances, practice a form of Catholicism, and mostly speak French. They feel rather marginalized by growing Islamic influence (both Sunni and Shia) in Lebanon.

In the large garden, children played while more than forty adults sat at a long lunch table overflowing with Lebanese *mezze*, the selection of small dishes typical of cuisine in the Near East, the Balkans, and parts of Central Asia.

"Who? Who told you to speak to him?" said my host when I asked him about the sheikh whose name I had been given after dinner in New York.

I didn't answer.

"Let me guess . . ." He looked back at me. "No wonder the Americans have no idea what is going on in this country." He paused. "He's not even a real sheikh, you know. He's a farce."

Maybe so, but he was clearly a man non-Muslims knew quite well and who generated some strong responses. And that interested me. When we left the christening, I called the sheikh and gave Lee Smith's cell phone number for him to call me back.

The next day, Lee and I were standing on a sidewalk when his phone rang. It was the sheikh.

"Hello, sir, thank you for calling me back. I was referred to you by our mutual friend . . ."

He spoke no English.

"*Bonjour, monsieur. Merci de m'appeller. Notre ami . . .*"

He spoke no French.

I spoke no Arabic.

I handed the phone to Lee, who did speak Arabic. The sheikh told Lee where and when I should meet him: in one hour at the Habtoor Grand Hotel in Sin El Fil.

"You know this place?" I asked Lee.

"Sure. It's the business district, just a couple of miles that way."

I was soon in the back of a taxi with Lee leaning through the driver's window, giving the driver the address. Lee would not be going with me, having his own interview to do; we would meet up again at the end of the day. I traveled alone in the back of a taxi, with no Arabic and no idea where I was going. When I arrived, I paid the fare on the meter and got out at a very large but run-down Western hotel, clutching my Moleskine notebook and a pen.

I scoped out the lobby and I peered at the arriving cars, then realized I hadn't asked the sheikh what he looked like and hadn't told him what I looked like or what I was wearing. How would we know each other? I waited outside, where the cars pulled up: if I made myself obvious, he would find me. A very old Mercedes pulled up with a man behind the wheel wearing a *thawb* (a white robe-dress men wear in the Persian Gulf) and the red-and-white *keffi-yeh* of a Gulfie sheikh—rather different from the Europeanized Muslims of the Gemmayzeh neighborhood where I was staying.

"Vanessa?"

"Yes."

"Get in."

I hesitated. I hadn't anticipated this.

"Get in," he repeated.

I got in and shut the door. He pulled away.

"We go my house."

"Your house?"

"Yes."

He drove through streets that got increasingly narrower, through neighborhoods that were more remote and poorer. I didn't think many foreigners made it into these parts of Beirut. *This sort of thing usually ends badly, in a YouTube video,* I thought.

We pulled up at one of a series of low, narrow, and plain concrete buildings with small doors, like the sort I knew from Caracas slums; he certainly seemed to live simply. After parking on the street, he opened the building's front door, beckoning me in. It was dark inside; all that was visible was a stairwell leading up.

Again, I hesitated.

Then I proceeded.

My heart thumped.

No one would know where to find me. How would I escape if I got into trouble? We arrived at an apartment, and he beckoned me to the sofa. He gently raised his palm to me, indicating that I should wait. He made a call on his cell phone in Arabic, not a word of which I could understand. When he hung up, he explained.

"Friend. Colonel. Coming. Speak English."

"Okay," I answered, and waited.

After about twenty minutes, a man in military uniform arrived. He introduced himself as a colonel; he said he would be our interpreter. He was terse, forthright, and physically strong, as befit a military man, but how much he was translating the cleric's ideas and how much he was espousing his own would never be known—an unreliable narrator, indeed.

I asked the sheikh, via the colonel, whether he/they had ever seen drugs or money coming in from South America, Venezuela in particular.

"Money comes in from Venezuela. So much money. A roomful of cash," affirmed the colonel, sweeping his arms out in a gesture of large size. "I've seen it."

He was likely boasting about his reach, his importance, his involvement in dark international matters. It was impossible for me to assess his honesty on the spot, without corroboration. But I figured that if he was feeling talkative, I'd keep asking. How about the Colombian cocaine? What did he know about that?

"Hezbollah has always had a relationship with the Colombian FARC," the colonel said. "But the election of Hugo Chávez in Venezuela helped Hezbollah a lot. The drugs that had been flown in little planes are now in industrial airliners and military planes with government protection."

It was inevitable that South American cocaine traffickers and narcoterrorists would become of increasing importance to Hezbollah and other groups.[1] While intelligence officials believe that Hezbollah used to receive as much as $200 million annually from its primary patron, Iran, and additional money from Syria, both these sources have largely dried up due to the onerous sanctions imposed on the former and the turmoil in the latter.

The colonel then proceeded to explain how far Hezbollah's tentacles spread and how they are a full Iranian proxy. Hezbollah, he explained, have a close relationship with North Korea, and the Al Mahdi Army in Iraq (with one million fighters under the command of Shia cleric Moqtada Al Sadr) is also trained and supported by Hezbollah. The Iranian Revolutionary Guard Corps is actually a part of the Lebanese army, he said.

Lebanon is interesting, I said, because it is a microcosm of the broader Middle East: a petri dish of proxy struggles. If you can figure out who is fighting whom and who is aligning with whom in Lebanon, you can probably expand to figure out those patterns in the broader Middle East. There are so many proxy interests, however, that I could not see how there would ever be peace either in Lebanon or the Middle East, I said. The colonel agreed.

He identified four major interests that are obstacles to regional peace: Syria and Iran (which could be considered almost as one, he said), Israel, and then Americans and the West. They each use the presence of their enemies to justify their own agendas, he claimed. "Iran wants Israel in the region because it justifies its nukes. Israel wants a strong Hezbollah in Lebanon because it justifies US support. But Israel and Syria understand each other: the border between them is quiet."

As proof that Syria would never attack Israel, he offered two examples. First, Syrians shoot Lebanese farmers, but not Israelis. Second, Hezbollah's chief of international operations, Imad Mughniyah, was killed in 2008 by a car bomb in Syria, only two hundred meters from the presidential palace. Mughniyah had been implicated in some of Hezbollah's most spectacular terrorist attacks, including those against the US Embassy in Beirut and the Israeli Embassy in Argentina.[2] The Syrians never retaliated against Israel for the killings in their country. It still was not clear to me why the anecdotes were evidence that Syria would never attack Israel, but the colonel seemed to be hinting at dark hidden networks that cross borders and align interests of groups that claim to be enemies but are not as adversarial as they appear. That would hardly be a surprise in the tangled web of the Levant, where the US is often perceived as naïve.

The United States, he said, also unwittingly ends up funneling aid to the terrorist group, including US money earmarked to teach English. The prime example is that of a USAID program in Lebanon's Beqaa Valley—a Hezbollah stronghold (and also where the colonel was born)—which it co-implemented with the DC-based development organization Creative Associates International. The project, which ran from 1998 through 2003, was for the Organization for Social and Agricultural Development in the Beqaa Valley. Hezbollah took the credit for all the local development, increasing their support among the very grateful local population. They even directly received some of the funds, the colonel claimed.

"So what are America's options?" I asked.

"The only solution," he said, "is to back neutral partners in Iraq, Bahrain, et cetera." He named six "moderate" Shia he thought America should back. The Free Shia movement that Sheikh Mohammed (whom I was supposedly interviewing through the colonel) represented was intended to remove the obstacles that Hezbollah imposed on the Shia community—namely, that they must support violent extremism.

"It is a big lie that Hezbollah and Iran impose control in the Shia world and they are isolated from the others," insisted the colonel. He went on to highlight some differences: "The Shia in Iraq and Afghanistan like the US; the Shia in Lebanon don't like the US," he explained.

As evidence, he cited the fact that the president of Iraq gave US president George W. Bush the sword of Imam Ali, the son-in-law of the Prophet Muhammad, whom Shias consider the founder of their sect. It's hardly a surprise, if you know your history. Iraqi president Saddam Hussein was a Sunni, and repressed the Shias. He was also the archenemy of Iran: the Iran-Iraq War lasted from 1980 through 1988 and killed nearly a million people.

When the US invaded Iraq in 2003 and eliminated Saddam's loyalists in the Ba'ath Party (a process called "de-Ba'athification"), it put in power a leader who was from the Shia sect Saddam had oppressed. That instantly turned Iran's archenemy, Iraq, into Iran's ally and puppet. Iraq's ousted Sunnis then sought revenge, unleashing the brutal insurgency that would eventually result in the rise of Daesh, which Americans call ISIS. But there was no Daesh yet when I was speaking to the sheikh and the colonel in Beirut. It was May 2012, the Arab Spring was in full bloom, and Americans still thought that was generally a good thing.

The Lebanese colonel could not resist a little dig: "British officers are smarter than Americans: they never speak, always ask."

It is a bit of a global sport to make fun of the US: it is the biggest kid on the global block, so an obvious target if one wants to earn some quick street cred. I got the feeling he was also gauging my reaction, poking me to see how American I considered myself. I had told him I was Venezuelan, but he also knew I lived in New York. He could have been probing my reaction to see whether I was employed by the US government. He must have been disappointed by my flat demeanor.

Bringing the conversation back to what I was there to learn, I asked about Hezbollah and Chávez.

"Hezbollah will control any president with the same ideology. If Chávez goes, they will just create another Chávez. Venezuela needs its own 'Spring,'" he offered.

When the interview with the cleric, or the colonel, concluded, the colonel took me for lunch in the area around the Beirut-Rafic Hariri International Airport, named after the late Lebanese prime minister whom Hezbollah assassinated as his motorcade drove past a popular hotel in central Beirut—by blowing him up, along with most of his security detail, with 2,200 pounds of TNT. It is not only the airport that is under Hezbollah control, but also the area around it.

BEIRUT OR TEHRAN?

There were posters of "martyred" Hezbollah fighters and billboards featuring icons of Islamist militancy as well as anti-American and anti-Israeli slogans. The billboards commemorated not just Hezbollah's supreme commander, Hassan Nasrallah, but also Iran's Ayatollah Khamenei. There were not very many women in the streets; those who were wore *burqas,* the full head and body robes that cover a woman head to toe in conservative Muslim communities. I took an Hermès scarf from my handbag and wrapped it around my head like a *hijab,* the head scarf moderate Muslim women wear even with jeans.

Is this what Tehran feels like?

"Here," he said, tossing his gun in my lap. "If they attack, you protect us."

Right.

He feigned fear of Hezbollah, but during the interview, I had come to suspect he was one of them. There was no way of knowing whether the answers he was giving me were truly translations of the cleric's responses, but I suspected there was little of the cleric in what he said. Everything about him suggested he was not entirely honest about his adversarial relationship with Hezbollah—not least because he came from Baalbek, in Lebanon's Beqaa Valley, east of the Litani River. Baalbek, a UNESCO World Heritage Site that was the ancient Greek city of Heliopolis ("City of the Sun"), is Hezbollah's heartland.

Whatever uncertainties I had were resolved upon arriving at the restaurant. As the plates of *mezze* came to the table, so did inquiring Hezbollah leadership.

"Don't look!" the colonel said. "There are real Hezbollah moneymen at the other table."

One of them approached us, giving the traditional Muslim greeting: right hand to left shoulder, arm across the chest, and a head movement somewhere between a nod and a bow.

"*Al hayer.*" A Muslim man never touches a woman who is not his wife. "Where are you from?"

I opened my mouth to speak.

"She is from Yugoslavia," interrupted the colonel. "Yes, you are from Yugoslavia." He looked right into my eyes.

Two weeks later, back in New York, I dined in the great hall of the University Club with the former assistant secretary of defense who had given me the references, and I related the anecdote.

"He said you are Yugoslav because it is the only way you can look as European as you do and still be a Muslim. This Hezbollah colonel probably saved your life."

Hezbollah is an Iranian Revolutionary Guard Corps proxy, as

evidenced by its flag and first-edition training manuals: the Hez-bollah and IRGC have almost identical insignia, and Hezbollah's first manuals were in Farsi (the language of Iran), not Arabic (the language of Lebanon and other countries in the Levant and Middle East).

Hezbollah's true loyalties are on display in their deployment in Syria to fight to keep Assad in power. Hezbollah, which is sup-posed to be a resistance group to defend Lebanese independence from foreign interference, is incongruously defending Lebanon's oppressor: Syria.

Syria militarily occupied Lebanon from 1976 through 2005, first under Hafez al-Assad and then by his son, the current tyrant murdering his people en masse, Bashar al-Assad, who was "elected" president in 2000. Bashar al-Assad is considered responsible for the assassination of Lebanese prime minister Rafic Hariri. My Lebanese colonel told me that he himself trained in Syria—that all the Lebanese military trained in Syria. It is what you might call a complicated relationship, as so much is in the Middle East.

Neighboring Syria is ruled by the Assad family, which is Ala-wite, a subsect of Shia Muslim. The Shia owe their allegiance to their "homeland" of Iran (the Sunnis owe their allegiance to their "homeland" of Saudi Arabia). Syria has been backed by Russia since 1944, when the two countries established strong diplomatic relations. In 1946, the USSR backed Syrian independence from France, sealing their relationship.

Syria then became an important piece in the Soviet Union's Cold War chessboard, especially when in 1971 Syria gave the Soviet naval fleet its only Mediterranean naval base, in the coastal town of Tartus. On October 8, 1980 (a year after the Is-lamic Revolution), the USSR signed a Treaty of Friendship and Cooperation with Syria, with Hafez al-Assad. The treaty remains in force, which is why Syria uses military hardware and Russia backs the Assad regime in Syria's civil war, sending refugees flooding over the border into Lebanon. One in six residents in Lebanon today is a Syrian refugee.[3]

AT THE RALLY

As part of our efforts to figure out who were the current major players, what was going on, and what various audiences thought about it, Lee took me to the offices of his friends at the online English-language publication *Now Lebanon*. I told them I had worked as a journalist in Venezuela, the US, and the UK.

They asked me on Lee's last day: "Would you like to come with us to the Hezbollah rally tomorrow?"

"Yes! Of course!"

All I had to do was email the Hezbollah press office a scan of my Venezuelan passport and *Now Lebanon* would assert that I was a well-published journalist (entirely true) who was working with them (not entirely true).

I tried to hide my nerves behind a big smile as the Hezbollah personnel inspected my passport and looked for my name in their computer. I was certain that with a quick Google search they would find my articles on Venezuela and Hezbollah narcoterrorism and I would be killed on the spot. I sat demurely and kept smiling. Surprisingly, the Hezbollah soldiers beckoned me over, handed me a press pass, and put me through airport-style security looking for weapons or explosives. They let us keep our cameras and escorted us to the media enclosure, close to the stage and next to where the VIPs would enter.

In the press enclosure, men and women, most in Western dress and all with visible press badges, commingled, clutching notebooks or cameras. Right in front of us were the VIPs—all men. The rest of the crowd of tens of thousands was segregated: men to one side, and on the other women under *hijabs,* holding up photos of their "martyred" sons, soldiers for Hezbollah. From some of the buildings hung banners in Arabic script.

"What do they say?" I asked my hostess and colleague, who had secured my press credentials for me to attend the rally.

"They say: 'The promise has come true.' It's a play on a common reference to Hezbollah, which refers to itself as 'the true promise.' So Hezbollah has kept its promise to the people."

Men in turbans streamed past us one by one, from left to right. It was remarkable to be so close to these dignitaries. Each one, as he entered the enclosed area, was greeted by a fawning and be-suited usher dressed like a postmodern monk in an all-black suit that eschewed any decoration. The usher-monks escorted the arrivals along the length of the enormous stage, where operatic singers belted out passages from the Koran or the *hadith*,[4] alternating with speakers who proclaimed the might and glory of Hezbollah and the perfidy of Israel. At the far end of the stage, the VIPs gathered as equals. We, the members of the press, had been strategically placed to witness the proceedings.

The music rose and became up-tempo, and tens of thousands of supporters behind the press enclosure became frenzied. Images of the euphoric mass of people were projected on the giant screen above the stage: on one side, young men punched the air; on the other, old women raised huge photographs of their "martyred" sons. The uniform production value of the photographs indicated they had been supplied by Hezbollah. The camera panned over the square: posters of Hezbollah supreme leader Hassan Nasrallah clung to the sides of buildings, watched over by scouts in windows and rooftops. Fanatics clogged every square inch of street that might be an exit from the square. If events took a bad turn, there would be no escape for us.

Taking a deep breath, we turned our attention back to our notes and peered through our video camera. The little red recording light blinked. Was that Hezbollah supreme commander Sayyid Hassan Nasrallah himself? Impossible—he never left his bunker, they said: too many assassination attempts. But with all of Hezbollah's senior leadership there, sure . . . *possible*. Stroking the diamond cross dangling from my neck and concealed under my clothes, I checked the skies for incoming CIA or Israeli missiles.

On the stage an operatic singer led the crowd in signing a song to Hassan Nasrallah: "I would sacrifice my soul to you, Hezbollah." In the first row, beside the Hezbollah grandees, sat Ziad Rahbani, a renowned Communist and musician who was an icon during Lebanese's civil war in the 1980s. The next presenter onstage started chanting verses of the Koran, with a play on words on the day when the promise comes true—presumably that day, May 11, 2012. The rally celebrated Hezbollah's reconstruction of Dahieh, the Beirut suburb that is their stronghold and that took heavy bombing from Israel in the 2006 war. The 2006 war that destroyed Dahieh started when Hezbollah fired rockets into Israeli border towns and kidnapped two Israeli soldiers. Because Iran so amply supplied Hezbollah, the group is widely viewed as the first proxy war between Iran and Israel.

Israel did not win.

The Iranian-supplied weapons were on prominent display in the beautifully produced film playing on the screen. In it, camouflaged special operators called in airstrikes and mobile launchers spat out multiple rockets in response. Somber music played as the film revealed the death and destruction the Israeli rockets wrought in densely populated Dahieh: buildings collapsed on the bodies of children; distraught mothers wailed for their dead babies.

Then came the film's glorious conclusion: Hezbollah rebuilds Dahieh for its people. Buildings rose, children went back to school, and seemingly everyone waved Hezbollah flags in gratitude. Gratitude. Joy. Euphoria. Ecstasy. Until Daesh appeared, Hezbollah were the masters of asymmetric warfare—warfare of the hearts and minds. The danger of such messaging is that people become reliant on handouts from one party—in this case, Hezbollah—eroding national identity, which is always tenuous at best in Lebanon anyway. This propagates division and the manipulation of the people in favor of proxy interests.

Hassan Jeishy, the managing director of the Waad construction company, talked on stage about how difficult life had become under the oppression of the international community, which blocked funding to companies, especially Jihad al-Binah, the Hezbollah construction company sanctioned by the US Treasury Department. But Hezbollah and Waad prevailed nonetheless, he claimed.

In reality, the Lebanese government contributed 33 percent of the $400 million for the reconstruction, and the rest of the money came from the Gulf States (which are overwhelmingly Sunni, the rival Islamic sect), on the basis that this was a Muslim country attacked by Israel. Regardless, Hassan Jeishy thanked Iran, local businesses, and NGOs—but not the Gulf States of Qatar, Saudi Arabia, and Kuwait that actually sent the money. Regarding the government, he acknowledged that it had played a role, but said that it had also hindered the reconstruction's happening sooner. Jeishy was reinforcing the Hezbollah narrative that would strengthen the group's support and grow its constituency; he was not telling the truth.

The fifty thousand or so live spectators became even more frenzied as the face of Hassan Nasrallah appeared on the screen and he began his speech to his people.

"Today is Fatima's birthday," he said, invoking the name of the daughter of the Prophet Muhammad, whose husband was Imam Ali, the first imam of the Shia sect. "Today is as important a victory as July twenty-second, when Hezbollah defeated Israel. That was a victory of war; this is a victory of reconstruction."

"Time to go," whispered my colleague. "We'll get the transcript in the morning."

Escorted out of our enclosure and through the crowd by a guard, we came across a formal grouping of five- to seven-year-old children in military uniform. As I raised a camera to take their photo, a Hezbollah guard lunged at me, yelling: *"Americaaahnn! Americaaahnn!"*

I thought fast. *"No, yo no soy Americana. Soy de Venezuela. Amo Hezbollah."*

No, I am not American. I am from Venezuela. I love Hezbollah.
"Where's the car?"

"The car is this way," my colleague said, pointing down the street, past the security checkpoints, as she lifted her phone to her ear to call the driver and make sure he would be at the agreed pickup spot.

In Lebanon, I was informed by Ali Al-Amine, editor of a publication whose English name is *Southern Affairs*, that Hezbollah has eighty thousand employees, making it the size of Intel, BP, Verizon Wireless, or 3M. To be clear, the armed forces are only a small fraction of these eighty thousand; most of them are medical personnel, teachers, store owners, et cetera—all sorts of people are on the Hezbollah payroll. Lebanese Hezbollah is often called a state-within-a-state, because it has its own charities, hospitals, schools, food, water and electricity distribution systems, trash collection, and of, course, propaganda machine—not least of which is Al-Manar, its television station, which broadcasts twenty-four hours a day, all over the world. And now it has Hispan TV, broadcasting in Farsi to a growing number of Latin American countries, mainly the Bolivarian ones: Venezuela, Ecuador, Bolivia. Hezbollah challenges the Lebanese government for the loyalty of its constituents, making itself both an opponent and a necessary partner for a national government that is weak and riven by confessionalism, a political system of power sharing though which political office is distributed according to different religions or ethnic groups. Northern Ireland has a similar system. While praised as constitutional power sharing, it generates (often unsavory) competition among the different ethnic or religious groups in power.

THE CASE OF THE LEBANESE CANADIAN BANK

The 2011 case of the Lebanese Canadian Bank (LBC) had exposed the inner workings of Hezbollah's illicit trade network from South

America to the US to West Africa and into the Levant. The bank was the hub of an intricate money-laundering mechanism that laundered money from Colombia's FARC and the Mexican drug cartel Los Zetas by mixing it with money from the sales of used cars, purchased by Hezbollah reps in the US and exported to West Africa. The result was hundreds of millions of dollars churning through the bank accounts of West African Shiite businessmen, who traded in everything from diamonds to cosmetics to frozen chicken, as fronts for Hezbollah.[5]

It seems the car sales might have served two purposes: they allowed for the combining of criminal and legitimate money, but possibly also provided the means for smuggling contraband (including bulk cash) inside the cars themselves. The whole scheme was uncovered by pulling the thread on Lebanese Hezbollah senior personnel's direct involvement with the South American cocaine trade. Ayman Joumaa, the Lebanese-Colombian indicted for money laundering, is charged with buying used cars in the US, shipping them to West Africa, where they were sold, and flying the cash into money exchange houses in Beirut and then into the LCB, which was previously a subsidiary of the Royal Bank of Canada Middle East.

But the cash was too much even for a booming trade in used cars. Investigators concluded that cash from the car sales was being "layered" with the proceeds of drug sales in Europe. Then some of the money returned to the US to buy more used cars.

For Hezbollah, money laundering and military strategy were combined in Lebanon's richest real estate deal: Christian Lebanese jeweler Robert Mouawad sold 740 acres of land overlooking the Mediterranean for $240 million to a Shia Muslim diamond dealer, Nazem Said Ahmad—but the real money behind the deal, the development corporation's major investor, was a relative of a Hezbollah commander, Ali Tajeddine. Real estate and diamonds are both great ways to store and transfer value, but in this case the land acquisition extends Hezbollah's presence into a religiously diverse region that is not predominantly Muslim. The investor who bought the land (Tajeddine's relative) personally received money through companies known to be Hezbollah fronts and from dealers of conflict diamonds.

The Lebanese Canadian Bank was punished with a USA Patriot Act Section 311 designation, which initially cut the bank off from the global banking system—until it was purchased by the Société Generale Bank of Lebanon (SGBL). According to the Center for a New American Security: "SGBL apparently has not provided full access to the former LCB records, nor has it proved that it has closed Hezbollah bank accounts or verifiably stopped Hezbollah money laundering and Iran sanctions evasion schemes."[6]

At the center of the LCB money-laundering network sat Ayman Joumaa, a Sunni Muslim of the Medellín cartel with deep ties to Shiites in the Hezbollah strongholds of southern Lebanon. When money is involved, ideology goes out the window. A friend of my grandmother's used to say: "Money doesn't care who owns it." I have learned in my work that people don't care with whom they do business, as long as the money flows. My clients often struggle to understand when I explain the tangled networks to them: enemies do business together. Joumaa is accused of coordinating shipments of Colombian cocaine to the ultraviolent Los Zetas cartel in Mexico for sale in the United States, and of laundering the proceeds. According to his indictment, he single-handedly laundered $200 million a month for Hezbollah.

SMUGGLING DRUGS FROM THE BEQAA VALLEY
TO AMERICA: A TRUE STORY

I arrived at the Winter Garden of the World Financial Center in early December 2015 to meet a socially connected but notorious former drug trafficker who in the late 1970s smuggled hashish from Lebanon's Beqaa Valley (the Hezbollah stronghold) into the United States: Richard Stratton. I figured if I wanted to understand the drug smuggling business connecting through Lebanon, I should ask an expert. In 1977–1978 Stratton vertically integrated his hashish trade.

Prior to that, he had been smuggling small quantities in suitcases, and then in sailboats. But then, in a midnight raid at his lodgings in Beirut, Stratton had been taken to meet a judge at his home. The judge informed him of the stiff sentences Stratton could be facing, before turning and introducing him to the head of customs, who told Stratton that Stratton would now be working with him.

From that point on, with government complicity in this criminal activity that essentially made the corrupt politicians a key component of the drug trafficking network, Stratton's loads grew, and were soon being shipped on commercial airliners into Boston Logan and New York John F. Kennedy airports. He also continued to send loads by sailboats into Montauk, New York. As the commercial smuggling grew, he took a bonded warehouse in New Jersey and acquired a trucking company to enable his distribution through the college campuses and hippie communities of the Northeast.

The loads from Beirut needed cover. Stratton used dates. He went to Baghdad to buy the dates, and then arranged for them to be shipped overland from Baghdad to Beirut, where they were stored. He then went to Baalbek, in Lebanon's Beqaa Valley, and bought 7.5 metric tons (16,534.7 pounds) of the best hashish available: *zahra* (loosely, "beautiful flower" in Arabic) and double *zahra*. He began competing with Afghani hash, which was of inferior quality.

Stratton blames Lebanese warlord families for ruining the US market for Lebanese hash by importing product of lower price but lesser quality. Those networks could export in much greater bulk than Stratton could manage. When the US market became less favorable, Stratton kept his importation lines into the US and started moving his product overland into Canada. This is what is known in illicit trade as the balloon effect: when a network is squeezed in one location, it shifts distribution to another.

An American named Pierre, who lived in Florida, was the "Wizard of ID": he provided all the passports, driver's licenses, and other documents Stratton and his network of smugglers needed. He was what we call in the security business a "key facilitator."

The head of the hashish growers' organization in the Beqaa was a man named Abu Ali. Stratton says he met Abu Ali's son in Texas, where he was an American soldier with ASIA (Army Support Intelligence Activity) at Fort Hood; the group gathered highly compartmentalized military intelligence. Stratton says that he once came home to find his garage filled with US military-grade weapons that were being moved from Houston to Beirut for the civil war in support of Bachir Gemayel, who commanded the Lebanese Forces militia and was a senior leader of the right-wing Christian Phalange Party, which the CIA was reputed to have backed in the Lebanese civil war.

In 1982, Gemayel was indeed elected president of Lebanon, but he died before he could take office, when a bomb planted by a Syrian agent blasted Phalange headquarters. According to Stratton, it was rumored that the US Drug Enforcement Administration and CIA were doing controlled shipments of heroin from the Jafar family in Baalbek to Detroit. Controlled shipments are standard in complex intelligence operations: an undercover intelligence operative becomes part of the criminal network and gives it drugs or money in order to trace the movements and find out who is involved, because the only way to map the network is to flow through it.

Khalid Jafar died in the explosion of the Pan Am Flight 103 over Lockerbie, Scotland. Jafar was a frequent passenger on that route, accompanying the drug shipments. But something went wrong the day Pan Am 103 exploded over Lockerbie: one of the drug suitcases was replaced with a bomb.

MONSAR AL-KASSAR AND PAN AM 103

The families of the victims of Pan Am 103 hired a private investigative firm called Interfor, headed by an Israeli ex-Mossad operative, Juval Aviv. The Interfor Report, as it has come to be known, poses a number of theories. One of them is that the bomb was planted by Hezbollah or other groups who were targeting the five Beirut station CIA operatives they had learned were on the flight. The CIA allegedly had the flights under surveillance because of shipments of interest from the Soviet-controlled Eastern Bloc via Pan Am through Frankfurt, Berlin, and Moscow.[7]

The report claims the route was controlled by Monser al-Kassar, who was married to Syrian president Hafez al-Assad's sister. Al-Kassar was a major trafficker of weapons and drugs, and also an asset of Iranian intelligence. It is suspected that the Beirut station of the CIA was trying to use al-Kassar to free the American hostages in Iran, as well as to get weapons for the Nicaraguan Contras: in other words, he was involved in the Iran-Contra affair.

Monser al-Kassar was a Syrian-born arms smuggler who rose to prominence via his work with Eastern European intelligence agencies in the early 1980s and sold arms to Bosnia, Croatia, and Somalia in violation of UN sanctions. He was arrested in 1992 in Spain for his involvement in the *Achille Lauro* hijacking.[8] Arms dealers like al-Kassar and Viktor Bout (who supplied weapons to wars on every continent of the world at one time) were key nodes linking criminals to terrorists in a global network. Bout was a well-known weapons supplier to the Colombian FARC, too.

The investigations and prosecutions of two key facilitators in the crime-terror pipeline illustrate both the threat convergence and the political aspirations of the actors. Bout and al-Kassar were lured by the promise of multimillion-dollar sales of arms to the FARC to achieve political objectives in line with their personal views. For al-Kassar, it was going after the Colombian army; for

Bout, it was going after American advisers to the Colombian government and military.

The crime-terror pipeline links not only crime and terrorism, but insurgency as well. Terrorists are funded by crime and criminals with political agendas: both are facilitated by government corruption. Both groups are also used by governments (or government agencies) as proxies to achieve defined objectives. Once again, both are significantly funded by US consumption of narcotics. All the while, the violence spreads like a virus across oceans and continents, to be inscribed on the bodies of the dead, the maimed, the tortured, the enslaved, and the refugee.

The War Games Begin

My trip to Lebanon put me on the map in a way I did not expect. In the summer of 2012, I'd been home only a couple of weeks when I got an email from US Army's Asymmetric Warfare Group inviting me to participate in a "vulnerability assessment exercise" (a war game, they were honest enough to call it) on the Levant. I did not know it yet, but it was my turning point: I would learn how the US military thinks about groups like Lebanese Hezbollah and the crime-terror pipeline of which those groups are a part. Then I would see these pipelines at work in Central America: the violence from drugs pushing people toward the US and terrorist groups exploiting those flows, while state governments are increasingly overwhelmed. At the end of the line is the American consumer, citizen, and taxpayer, buying the drugs or profiting from modern slavery while the smuggling networks bring violence to our neighborhoods.

The Asymmetric Warfare Group is a unit of highly trained warriors who are also strategic thinkers. Their job is to identify vulnerabilities in the systems of opponents that we can exploit to our advantage, and to identify our own weaknesses and come up with quick solutions, whether they have to do with military hardware, personnel, or tactics. The best way to describe it is as the ultimate game of chess: a group representing the US and its allies sits in one room (the blue cell), the opponent group in another (the red cell), and other groups like the UN or NGOs in another (the gray cell). There can be other cells, depending on game design. Each cell devises secret strategies and takes actions, of which it informs only a roaming moderator with a laptop that runs the algorithms of the game. After each round, everyone sees who did what to whom and then each cell has to decide what to do next. The Asymmetric Warfare Group brings in civilian consultants to these games, and I was asked to participate in the next one.

I arrived at the sprawling military base in a suit and, in my rented car, drove up to the security gate. They checked my passport and inspected my car before waving me through and directing me to the building where the war game would be played. I didn't know what to expect. After getting my name badge, I moved into a giant conference room, where big tables arranged into rectangles designated different groups: red cell, blue cell, gray cell. I was part of the gray cell; I was told that was an honor—it's where the subject matter experts (SMEs, pronounced *smees*) are and is the cell with the most flexibility in the game; it can change roles.

Dr. Lt. Col. Scott Crino, a Special Ops helicopter pilot with a PhD in systems engineering and movie-star good looks, explained the basics of asymmetric war gaming: identify your opponent's center of gravity, its critical capabilities, its critical vulnerabilities, and exploit them.

Then someone else stood up and explained the gray cell's role: "We're here to find less kinetic solutions."

Kinetic?

"SEALs wanna kick down the door; Deltas wanna put a bullet in their brain; but CIA is telling us not to kill them until they can interrogate them—they can't give us information if they're dead. You're to identify friendly tactics that are less kinetic."

In fact, there was nothing "friendly" about the tactics. I was a long way from teaching political theory; I was now neck-deep in the real tactics of dismantling networks of bad guys, taking away their sources of funding and community support. I stepped outside for a cigarette at the next break. By the end of the four-day game, I was scheming, disrupting, and interdicting with the best of them, and loving it. I took to asymmetric war gaming naturally: it turns out I am highly competitive and tend to think strategically to form coalitions and solutions that are not typical.

I'd had another round of war gaming on another military base by the time I got my invitation to perfect and disseminate its practice in Latin America. The DC think tank Center for a Secure Free Society (where my friend Joe Humire works) was hosting a four-day forum led by Professor Max Manwaring, a guru in the techniques of asymmetric warfare. The intent was to fight fire with fire: gangs and drug traffickers in Guatemala use the techniques of asymmetric warfare, so the security services needed to do the same to counter them.

FOURTH-GENERATION WARFARE: ASYMMETRIC OR "TOTAL WAR"

In military theory, there are widely considered to be four generations of warfare. The first three generations are variations of tactics in state-on-state conflicts; the fourth is messier, encompassing state and nonstate actors, like those we observe in crime-terror pipelines and in insurgencies.

The first generation is traditional column warfare, a gruesome affair of attrition: tightly ordered columns of soldiers face a similarly armed enemy. The one with the most survivors wins the battle. As military and weapons technology improved, this type of warfare was abandoned by the major world powers by the second half of the nineteenth century.

Second-generation warfare still used an adherence to strict

discipline in formation and uniform, but included some maneuverability and indirect fire to break stalemates. World War I is a classic example: long-range muskets with greater accuracy meant that face-to-face column-formation combat was too lethal, so it was abandoned in favor of trenches and snipers.

Third-generation warfare seeks to bypass the enemy's front lines, infiltrate, and attack the rear forward, cutting off supply and communications lines, disrupting command and control, and taking over cities and their surrounding territory one by one. The German blitzkrieg introduced the concept, but the Americans used similar tactics during their 2003 invasion of Iraq. Again, the tactics shifted alongside technological advancement: the cavalry morphed from an emphasis on heavy armor to one on greater speed. The development of the helicopter allowed insertions in hostile territory, and advanced missile technology allowed forces to bypass enemy defenses and strike at targets from great distances.

This marked the turn to a new military organization that is a bit flatter (less hierarchical), with more adaptive cells. For third-generation warfare tactics to work, higher-ranking officers place greater trust in junior officers commanding subunits, who are entrusted to achieve their objectives without micromanagement from higher-ranking commanders in headquarters.

Asymmetric warfare is the fourth generation of warfare: "4GW," in military shorthand. It is the strategy of a successful insurgency: a smaller and militarily weaker group defeating a larger and better-equipped enemy by using alternate tools. The alternate tools include guerrilla warfare, terrorist attacks, and influence operations (IO: propaganda). The insurgents can use their smaller size to be nimble and stealthy and to hide among the people, making them difficult to target and eradicate. Influence operations include leaks, blogs, memes, fake news, social media, and using proxies to hold seminars and disseminate information that plays on people's fears and prejudices—basically what we saw unfold in the 2016 US presidential election. When all the tools of 4GW are mobilized effectively simultaneously, the result is a superinsurgency—"total war."

Officially, 4GW is conflict where at least one of the participants is not a nation-state but a violent nonstate actor. The term "fourth-generation warfare" was coined by a team of American security analysts to signify the erosion of the state's role in combat forces and the ability of the military to be the sole determinant of whether a war is won or lost: more guns will not win you the war. Fourth-generation war blurs the lines among combatants, civilians, and politics. Fourth-generation wars are typically low-intensity conflicts that are long term, involve actors across networks that are generally nonhierarchical, as they are in the networks of crime-terror pipelines, and use insurgent and guerrilla tactics, as well as terrorism and psychological warfare through media manipulation. The use of noncombatants greatly complicates tactical planning for the state's armed forces, which is exactly one of the objectives, as 4GW is an attack on the enemy's culture.

The strategies and tactics of fourth-generation warfare are often used in unconventional warfare, which features battles involving terrorists, cartels, and gangs. These fights can play out as unconventional *non*state war or as unconventional *intra*state war.[1] In *non*state war, these various violent nonstate actors battle each other within countries and across borders, for control of what analysts like to term "ungoverned or weakly governed spaces." Unconventional *intra*state war features direct and indirect battles between the state apparatus and the violent nonstate actors: gangs, cartels, insurgents, paramilitaries, and terrorists. The enemy of the state's goal in unconventional intrastate war (such as we see when governments battle cartels and insurgents) is to control or radically change the government, making it more compliant to the will and operations of the various nonstate actors. From a strategic level, these long conflicts are unconventional because the battle space is complicated. "[There are] no formal declarations or terminations of war; no easily identified human foe to attack and defeat; no specific geographical territory to attack and hold; no single credible government or political actor with which to deal; and no guarantee that any agreement between or among contending actors will be honored."[2] It is warfare where there is nowhere to run and nowhere to hide. "There are no front lines, no visible distinctions between civilian and irregular forces personnel, and no sanctuaries."[3]

The goal is to move the opponent's "center of gravity" and force the opponent to make choices and react according to rules determined by the insurgents. The center of gravity is the core activity that gives an opponent its power. For a drug cartel, the center of gravity is the ability to make, move, and sell drugs. The critical capabilities for that center of gravity are: secure supply of raw materials, control of border crossings and transportation (including vessels), access to retail networks, means to move money, the retaining of loyal personnel, and a permissive environment with local support. Each of these capabilities has vulnerabilities that can be exploited to bring down the opponent—in this example, the cartel.

Asymmetric warfare works. The mujahideen booted the Soviets out of Afghanistan; the US withdrew from Vietnam in disgrace. It took decades for both the Soviets and the Americans to heal the psychic wounds of their losses in those fourth-generation conflicts.

Its application by terrorist groups such as Al Qaeda and Daesh has modified the policy agenda and the politics themselves of Western countries. For example, up until the 2004 Madrid train bombings, perpetrated by Al Qaeda, Spain had been an ally of the US in operations in Iraq and the Global War on Terror (GWOT). Just three days after the Madrid train bombings, Spain held its regularly scheduled parliamentary elections. The conservative, pro-US government of Prime Minister José Maria Aznar was roundly defeated by the anti-US and anti–Iraq War socialists, and José Luis Rodriguez Zapatero became prime minister. Spain withdrew its thirteen hundred troops from Iraq and its security cooperation from the US.[4] A well-timed terrorist attack had fractured an American-led coalition, weakening the US. Playing on the fears of citizens against their politicians is a classic asymmetric play.

Guatemala is a hotbed of asymmetric warfare activity. It started with Central America's pro-Communist revolutions and civil wars that started in the late 1970s and escalated through the 1980s. Guatemala borders Mexico; it is the northernmost country of Central America's Northern Triangle: Guatemala, El Salvador, and Honduras. The entire Northern Triangle is racked by a confluence of violence from gangs and drug traffickers, with whom the gangs sometimes collude and sometimes compete. Honduras is the main entry point for cocaine—from Colombia via Venezuela—into Central America. From there it goes overland into Mexico and across the border into the US. There are many routes, but that is one of the bigger ones, and the resulting money for violence overwhelms the security forces of those three small countries. These were also the countries of origin for the wave of unaccompanied children that swamped the US border in 2014, prompting the Obama administration to declare a humanitarian crisis.

The gangs that are the Northern Triangle's main nonstate violent actors grew out of civil wars that shook the region in the 1980s and that have developed into a major transnational threat. Dr. Max Manwaring has argued that the gangs have evolved across generations on an instability continuum. The first generation of gangs (basically gangsters and brigands) were focused on protecting and controlling markets through violent competition: the most violent gang won the local territory. The second generation continued using violence as an instrument of control, but branched out from local markets and linked with transnational criminal organizations. In that partnership, their violence turned toward a more ambitious target: the police and other law enforcement and security organizations they sought to incapacitate or corrupt. In the third generation, the gangs became involved in or encouraged "ethnic feuds and riots, genocide, population dislocations, and terrorism."[5] This was the environment into which Joe Humire and I and others landed in Guatemala City in late August 2012, to participate in a forum led by Dr. Max Manwaring.

LANDING IN GUATEMALA

From La Aurora International Airport, our little minibus drove the delegation through the streets of Guatemala City, winding amid the patchwork urban landscape that is so typical and familiar to those of us who have spent time in the poorer parts of the Western Hemisphere. We arrived at our American-style hotel: medium-sized and beige throughout.

In the far corner of the lobby stood a man who easily betrayed himself as American Special Ops: blond, tall, preternaturally muscular, his arms crossed and his eyes obscured by black wraparound Oakley sunglasses. The corner is the preferred vantage point for special operators and spooks: no one can come up behind you and you can discreetly survey the room. I figured he was there as part of Operation Martillo, the fourteen-nation program against transnational organized crime that targets transshipment points, particularly through Central America and the Caribbean.[6] As I walked past him, I resisted the urge to greet my fellow American with a warm hello. Nor did he flinch a single muscle, though his eyes undoubtedly tracked my movements.

To board our minibus again the following morning, I had to hop over red rivulets spreading like fingers by the impulsion of the hose, the rivulets coalescing as they entered the gutter. The sidewalk was being rinsed of the blood from the previous night's shooting. Around 1 a.m., there had been a shoot-out just outside the hotel's front entrance—cause: unknown, but a fight over drug supplies and distribution territory was a good guess.

Its proximity to Mexico makes Guatemala a major staging area for drugs (particularly cocaine, but also heroin), which concerns the CIA,[7] as does money laundering, corruption, and the displacement of at least 258,500 people, first by internal ethnic conflict and now by cartel and gang violence. US law enforcement agencies estimate that about 84 percent of the cocaine entering the United States passes through Central America and Mexico.[8]

As we rounded the corner, we saw one indication of the problem: lots of weapons, openly for sale, not just in the storefront of the gun shop but on the sidewalk. Our mood lightened as the gates opened to our venue: the libertarian Universidad Francisco Marroquín, where we would be discussing the best asymmetric strategies to counter the regional threats of gangs and cartels behaving like insurgencies.

Central American states have been weakened by civil wars, poverty, gangs, and drug traffickers, and now an increasing number of terrorists are adding to the toxic mix of asymmetric threats in Central America's Northern Triangle and Mexico. Major foreign terrorist organizations have come calling in Central America, renowned for its movements of migrants and drugs stretching back through a long history of brutal civil wars. Long-established drug trade networks have become very good at what they do, especially human smuggling, document forging, arms trafficking, and money laundering. Terrorists need all these skills.

Because security has tightened at airports, with advanced screening of passenger lists provided before takeoff of a flight to the US, overland routes from Canada and Mexico are preferred. If you are a terrorist organization looking to move personnel and materials, such as weapons and bomb parts, what better option could there be than drug smuggling networks? They already hire talented people to create fake passports and fake bills of lading; they already have corrupt US customs agents on the payroll who will wave a load through. The all-important US customs agent can be corrupted with a difficult and clear choice: *"plata o plomo"*—silver or lead. He will either accept the bribe and provide a better life for his wife and kids, or the smuggler will find out where he lives, where his kids go to school, and threaten them.

Experts now believe the Southwest border poses the greatest threat from terrorist networks. The strategic alliance between terrorist and criminal organizations in Central America, encompassed by an exchange of narcotics and weapons, and human smuggling operations that exist south of the US-Mexico border, increases the likelihood that terrorist operatives would be smuggled in through this route. A primary cause is the greatly heightened security for air travel post-9/11.

As part of a strategy to constrain the international travel of terrorists, the 9/11 Commission recommended that a computer system be developed that would identify foreign travelers and check them against terrorist and criminal databases. This recommendation was realized in January 2004, when the United States Visitor and Immigrant Status Indicator Technology (US-VISIT) system began deployment at US ports of entry. US-VISIT scans the fingerprints of foreign visitors and checks them against numerous criminal and intelligence databases that include enemy combatants captured on the battlefield. Besides US-VISIT, there is also much greater scrutiny of individuals seeking a visa to travel to the United States.

Now immigration and customs enforcement (ICE) special agents work side by side with State Department employees at strategic foreign posts, helping them screen these applicants to weed out criminals and terrorists before they board a plane to the US. This is known as "exporting the border." Sophisticated terror networks like Al Qaeda and Hezbollah are well aware of this practice and account for it in their operational plans; they are surely considering alternative methods of travel in order to increase their chances of success.

Illicit human smuggling networks (so prevalent across the US-Mexico border) are of increasing importance to terrorists seeking to circumvent effective US homeland security programs. Many experts believe the same thing is happening with Al Qaeda. As both terrorist and drug trafficking organizations become more horizontally structured, they have begun to rely on each other and work together to create the crime-terror pipeline that poses such a major convergent threat to the national interest.

The US-Mexico border is very porous; well-established human smuggling routes have brought thousands of people a year into the United States, and those running the operations have become highly skilled at what they do. A 2012 report by the United Nations titled *The Globalization of Crime* estimated that Mexican smugglers raked in $6.6 billion annually[9] from the three million Latin Americans they took across the southern US border each year. According to Mexico's National Institute of Migration, six out of ten migrants paid traffickers to help them cross the US border.

Once inside the US border, the smuggled migrants sometimes become enslaved, as the criminal networks layer their profits. They not only charge the migrants for the passage, they then use them as slave labor in other businesses from which they derive profit: prostitution, sweatshops, massage parlors, karaoke bars— and construction. Many of the services we use are provided by people into whose eyes we rarely gaze, people whom the criminals see as commodities, paid for by our money. If one day we had to flee our countries or our brutal employer or spouse, we might end up like them: modern slaves. A third layer of criminal profit is added if those businesses are money-laundering operations: businesses that are fronts to disguise the illicit profits from the sales of narcotics, for example.

In the 1990s, I watched huge empty buildings go up all over Caracas after Venezuela and Colombia signed a free trade agreement and the US clamped down on banking transactions between Colombia and the US to stop the flow of money to and from

Colombia's cartels. The cartels used the Venezuelan banking system instead, as a pass-through to the US system. The banks then funded construction that was not needed in order to launder the Colombian drug money. It worked until sixteen banks caught in the net failed, wreaking havoc in the Venezuelan financial system.

The layering of smuggling people with networks involved in narcotics produces network connectivity in other ways, too. When Chinese triads smuggle Chinese migrants into Mexico's Pacific Coast, they pass through areas that are under the control of the Juárez and Gulf cartels, while those entering Mexico from Central America use routes controlled by Los Zetas. The Chinese triads therefore developed a greater collaboration with the Juárez, Gulf, and Los Zetas cartels,[10] reflected in the greater sourcing of precursor chemicals for narcotics from China and, on the return trip, greater distribution back into China of the products of these cartels.

SMUGGLING AS THE NODE IN THE CRIME-TERROR PIPELINE

The interactions among gangs, transnational criminals, and terrorists are complex and ever-changing. Gangs have shifting alliances with a broad array of players, including insurgents, warlords, terrorists, transnational criminals, and, importantly, governments (that use them to maintain some level of plausible deniability regarding aggressive illicit or covert actions) as well as "any other state or non-state actor that might require the services of a mercenary gang organization or surrogate to coerce radical change in policy and or government."[11] In other words, a foreign government, terrorist group, cartel, or major business interest could hire a gang to commit acts of violence that appear random or "gang-related" but are really used to cause a mayor to resign, stop an investigation, change the outcome of an election by frightening the voters, or other political outcomes.

The major cartels are "the big four" (Juárez, Gulf, Sinaloa, and

Tijuana, all of whom operate in the north), but there are signs of a fourth generation in the instability continuum of gangs: Los Zetas have become a cartel in their own right, and have launched an aggressive expansion strategy into areas as far south as Guatemala, Honduras, and El Salvador—overlapping traditional gang territory, particularly of the Mara Salvatruchas, with whom they are now in business.

The complex relation of gangs and other criminal organizations to the state is illustrated by their geographic distributions and differences, in response to local conditions of both market and governance. For instance, the gang situation is markedly different in the north, along the US-Mexico border, than it is in the south, along the Guatemala-Belize border. Nevertheless, there is a clear and formidable gang presence throughout Mexico, where gangs intimidate and kill everyone from entertainers to journalists to teachers to bureaucrats to candidates for political office to current political officeholders, and anyone else who may not be sympathetic to their causes or are an obstacle to their control.[12]

Simultaneously and overlapping this territory, the Central American Mara Salvatrucha 13 and Mara Salvatrucha 18 gangs (commonly referred to as "the Maras") have made significant inroads into Mexican territory and appear to be working as mercenaries for, and sometimes competing effectively against, Mexican criminal organizations and gangs. In the south along the Belize-Guatemala borders, the Maras have gained control of illegal immigrants and drug trafficking movement north through Mexico into the United States. Between the northern and southern borders, an ad hoc mix of up to fifteen thousand members of the various Mexican gangs and Central American Maras are reported to be operating in more than twenty of Mexico's thirty states.

Additionally, members and former members of the elite Guatemalan Special Forces (*Kaibiles*) are being recruited as mercenaries by the Zetas. Former foot soldiers recruit foot soldiers of their own:[13] Los Zetas were originally Mexican Special Forces who were recruited by the Sinaloa cartel before forming their own cartel.

The history of the Mara Salvatrucha gang illuminates the impact of geopolitical pressures and diaspora movements on the spread of violence and criminality. "Mara Salvatrucha," commonly referred to as MS-13, means "Salvadoran gang" and was formed in Los Angeles in the 1980s by refugees from war-torn El Salvador. The gang is believed to have between fifteen hundred and three thousand members, most of whom are between the ages of sixteen and eighteen. The "13" is believed by experts to come from the thirteenth letter of the alphabet: M, for "Mara."

The gang network spread across the United States as the immigrants migrated in search of work. Aside from their own traditional criminal activity, they are now also the enforcers of and distributors for the illicit trafficking of foreign terrorist organizations. MS-13 is made up of cliques (*clicas*) with names such as the Sailors, Normandy, Peajes, Uniones, and Fultons, and work through a partnership called *La Hermandad* (The Brotherhood) across the District of Columbia, Maryland, and Virginia. Evidence points to these Mexican drug cartels using American gangs as their foot soldiers. There are thirty thousand gangs in America, with a million gang members in them,[14] and everyone is making money.

The US Drug Enforcement Administration estimates that $322 billion is generated annually by the global drug trade.[15] With such a large amount of money at stake, it is no surprise that there is a giant illicit business straddling the US-Mexico border, over which seven major cartels and some forty subsidiary groups (all with a significant presence in the United States) fight. There are over 280 US cities in which organized crime activity is dominated by a Mexican cartel; and the cartels have associates in more than a thousand American cities.[16] The important synergies between terrorists and criminals drive them to overcome their different ideological and financial goals and to collaborate through Central America and across the US Southwest border.

FLATTENING TO ADAPT

Mexican drug trafficking organizations have followed the same playbook as jihadis since 2001. They have morphed from hierarchical structures, topped by hard-to-capture kingpins and bound by familial ties, into loose and adaptable networks that outsource certain aspects of trafficking, making them flatter, more nimble, and harder to disrupt.[17] With the command-and-control system being dispersed and alliances being mainly of a temporary nature, the intelligence community identifies these networks as "flat" and "adaptive." They are flat because the hierarchy is shielded from view by disparate cells that interact as equals. They are adaptive because alliances can shift quickly in response to enforcement threats or simply for a better return on investment.

Los Zetas, who have earned a reputation for brutality by gunning down thousands of Mexicans in the ongoing battle for drug smuggling routes to the United States, now control much of the illicit trade of moving migrant workers toward the US border, experts say. They have brought a cold know-how, using tractor-trailer trucks to carry ever-larger loads of people and charging high prices, as much as $30,000 per head for migrants from Asia and Africa who seek to get to the United States. They have also brought an unprecedented level of intimidation and violence to the human smuggling trade. Los Zetas or their allies often kidnap and hold for ransom migrants who try to operate outside the system. If relatives do not send payment, the migrants are sometimes executed and dumped in mass graves, or might be pressed into jobs with the criminal group.

The ascendancy of Los Zetas in migrant smuggling, formerly the preserve of relatively small independent operators known as "coyotes," who'd smuggle groups of twenty or fewer migrants north, has transformed the business. Mexican officials report regularly finding tractor-trailer trucks loaded with as many as 250 migrants in their holds. The heavily armed drivers, who travel with escort vehicles, make payoffs to police and immigration officers at the various checkpoints along their route. Aside from the classic *plata o plomo* paradigm, there is another form of bribery: every month at least one of the smuggled illegal immigrants is given as a slave to the cartel or to the gang capo, for her to be used as a prostitute by the recipient or his friends, or to be sold to others. Unlike a kilo of cocaine, a woman can be resold many times.

GROWING TIES BETWEEN CRIMINALS
AND TERRORISTS AT THE SOUTHWEST BORDER

Retail-level distribution of drugs from Mexican drug trafficking organizations is handled by smaller drug trafficking groups and gangs under the direct or indirect control of the Mexican cartels. The drugs cross the Mexican border through underground tunnels, in concealed compartments in passenger vehicles, or commingled with legitimate goods in tractor-trailers. Increasingly, drugs such as cocaine and methamphetamine are dissolved in liquids until they reach distribution points near the border (a big one is in Phoenix, Arizona). Lookouts are placed on elevated locations across the border desert to supervise the shipments and to communicate through advanced radio communications that evade law enforcement surveillance. Unmanned aerial vehicles—drones—are also used. Then the shipments are broken down into smaller units and sent to more distant distribution points such as New York City, Chicago, or Millville, Indiana.[18]

Associations between the Mexican cartels and the gangs who do their distribution inside the US are heavily based on geography and familial ties. The purpose is wealth generation: everyone makes money from the association. Arizona's gangs have wholesale-level drug contacts with the Mexicans. In California, the Mexican Mafia prison gang acts as an intermediary: it controls Southern California's Hispanic criminal street gangs, but has a long history with the Mexican cartels operating the Tijuana-California corridor. In Texas, you have the Texas Syndicate, the Texas Mexican Mafia, and a gang called the Tango Blast, which further breaks down into cliques, including the Houstones, Orejones, Vallucos, La Capirucha, D-Town, and West Texas Tangos, all of whom have strong working relationships with the Mexican drug cartels Los Zetas, the Gulf Cartel, and the Knights Templar.[19]

There are several case studies of documented instances of drug trade networks working with terrorist networks on America's Southwest border.[20] These connections and cooperations can be viewed as driven by a particular need or skill set to benefit either the terrorist or the criminal organization in question. Although there have been no confirmed cases of Hezbollah moving terrorists across the Mexico border to carry out attacks in the United States, many experts think Hezbollah members and supporters have entered the country this way.

This seems plausible: as far back as 2003 nearly sixty thousand illegal aliens designated as other-than-Mexican, or OTMs, were detained[21] along the US-Mexico border. In May 2012, the *Los Angeles Times* reported that intelligence gleaned from the 2011 raid on Osama bin Laden's compound indicated that he sought to use operatives with valid Mexican passports who could illegally cross into the United States to conduct terrorist operations. Authorities think that Al Qaeda terrorists hope to take advantage of a lack of detention space within the Department of Homeland Security, which has forced immigration officials to release non-Mexican illegal aliens back into the United States rather than return them to their home countries. Fewer than 15 percent of those released appear for immigration hearings.

TERRORISTS, DRUGS, AND DIASPORAS

Despite assertions by the Mexican government that no Middle Eastern terrorist has been found attempting to cross the US-Mexico border, there have been several cases verified by US authorities of just that. For example, in 2001 Mahmoud Youssef Kourani crossed the border from Mexico in a car and traveled to Dearborn, Michigan. Kourani was later charged with and convicted of providing "material support and resources . . . to Hezbollah," according to a 2003 indictment.[22]

Kourani was able to travel to Mexico from Lebanon through what is known as the "Lebanon-Tijuana Pipeline." He paid a $3,000 bribe to a Mexican consulate official in Beirut in order to get a Mexican entry visa. This allowed him to travel from Lebanon to Mexico, where he was able to connect with the human smuggling operation. He was then smuggled across the Southwest border on February 4, 2001, in the trunk of a car. While in the US, Kourani was reportedly involved in fund-raising for Hezbollah, and sent the group around $40,000. According to US Attorney Jeffrey Collins, Kourani is accused of conspiring with his brother, Haidar Kourani, chief of military security for Hezbollah in southern Lebanon, to provide support for the group.[23]

Then there is the case of Adnan el-Shukrijumah. El-Shukrijumah was born in Guyana on August 4, 1975, the firstborn son of Gulshair el-Shukrijumah, a forty-four-year-old radical Muslim cleric, and his sixteen-year-old wife. In 1985 Gulshair migrated north to the US, where he assumed duties as the imam of the Farouk mosque in Brooklyn, which raised millions for the jihad and served as a recruiting station for Al Qaeda.

In 1995 the Shukrijumah family moved to Miramar, Florida. It was there that Gulshair became the spiritual leader of the radical Majid al-Hijah mosque and where Adnan became friends with José Padilla,[24] who planned to detonate a radiological bomb in midtown Manhattan along with Mandhai Jokan, who was convicted of attempting to blow up nuclear power plants in southern Florida, and a group of other homegrown terrorists. In April 2001 Adnan spent ten days in Panama, where he reportedly met with

Al Qaeda officials to assist in the planning of 9/11. He also traveled to Trinidad and Tobago.

The following month, he obtained an associate's degree in computer engineering from Broward Community College. During this time, he managed to amass passports from Trinidad, Saudi Arabia, the United States, and Canada. On May 27, 2004, Adnan was spotted at an Internet café in Tegucigalpa (the capital of Honduras), from where he made calls to friends in Canada and the United States. At his table were Mara Salvatrucha leaders from Panama, El Salvador, Mexico, and Honduras. Officials from the Department of Homeland Security have asserted that el-Shukrijumah is known to have crossed the US-Mexico border at least twelve times, proving the synergistic effectiveness of the crime-terror pipeline.

The pattern in Central America repeats in several places around the globe. Migrants flee desperation and violence in Syria, Sudan, and Venezuela and are vulnerable to indenture into slavery. The flow of people away from violence and toward a better life often tracks the flow of goods to a richer market: in the world of illicit trade, humans are just one more commodity to be sold to the wealthy American or European. I have come to understand how trafficking in one good piggybacks on the trafficking of other goods (might as well fill that empty space on the truck) and how networks connect through the flow of money.

There are also "push" and "pull" factors. Migrants are pushed by violence and wars and poverty (often resulting from violence and wars and corruption) to find a better life elsewhere. If they are traveling to destinations that are pulling, with a demand for narcotics or counterfeits or prostitution or cheap labor, the conditions are ripe for people to be smuggled as just one more object from which to make money. Awaiting them at their destinations are not only vast human misery but serious threats of violence.

The answer, however, does not lie in opposing immigration,

but in rooting out its cause: end the demand for illicit goods and support good governance and the rule of law in people's home countries. After all, the migrants would rather stay at home with their families and prosper, if only we would stop funding and profiting from their misery.

Khans, Bags, and Triads

LAND OF THE GREAT KHANS

From Guatemala City I hopscotched the globe to the other side: the US Department of Defense was sending me to be a speaker at a seminar on countering transnational threats (the smuggling of goods and people) in Central Asia. Geographically, Mongolia is East Asia, but ethnically it is considered Central Asia. Like all aspects of group identity or black market cross-border trade, it's complicated. The trip would steepen my learning curve.

From Mongolia I would go to China, to give me a different perspective on illicit financial flows and development, and how they are impacted by Western consumers. China is the world's second-largest economy, run by a Communist Party that oversees a hegemonic capitalism, as it backs its companies to compete aggressively around the world. Its military, the People's Liberation Army (PLA), oversees an aggressive cyber-attack and hacking operation for the strategic advantage of China's industries. China is also the world's largest source of counterfeits. It all combines to create what pundits call "China, Inc."

Mongolia, on the other hand, is only really known to most as the home of the Mongols and their conqueror kings, Genghis and Kublai Khan, who conquered the known world with sheer kill-them-all brutality from the backs of sturdy little horses. Mongolia is large, landlocked, and mostly empty, except for lots of horses, yaks, and gold. It is completely surrounded by Russia and China. Everything about Mongolians reflects the combination: they physically look similar to the Chinese, but their architecture looks Soviet. In the main square, their idols stand on pedestals inscribed in Mongolian, which is written phonetically using the Russian Cyrillic alphabet.

Despite being rich in minerals and having only three million people, Mongolia exhibits all the signs of the resource curse and corruption. The resource curse (sometimes called "the paradox of plenty") is the statistical tendency of countries rich in natural resources (like oil or gold or diamonds) to be less economically developed (have many more poor people) and less democratic than countries with fewer natural resources. The explanation is simple: it doesn't take management competence to dig a hole in the ground and put what comes out onto a boat and sell it. The international market is more than happy to buy it; there is little transparency from either the government or the foreign companies in joint ventures, both of which pay and take bribes as they like. The money rarely gets reinvested into the country's infrastructure, beyond that needed to get the commodity in question, or spread around to the broader economy. Innovation is hampered because the government puts all its efforts into selling the commodity, not stimulating any other economic activity it does not control. Once you have traveled to a few of these countries, the signs are familiar. But I had to get there first.

To get to Ulaanbaatar, Mongolia, I had to take four flights and travel more than thirty hours from Guatemala City. My last flight connection to Ulaanbaatar was in the Beijing airport. It was August 2012, and I had never seen anything like it. I gazed up and around like some country cousin arriving among Manhattan's skyscrapers for the first time. Beijing's massive airport had the latest in technology, from screens to trains, and it all ran impeccably.

The Beijing airport flaunted the might of the Chinese security apparatus. Once I made it through the biometrics scanning my face or my eyes (I couldn't tell which), the customs agents had me take out every single item from my carry-on. They were bemused by all my charging cables for phones and laptops and camera. They were suspicious of my intent: I had to explain why I had each item with me. I was naïvely amused.

I hadn't yet learned that none of my colleagues would dream of traveling to China with their laptops and cell phones. China's People's Liberation Army famously infiltrates the machines and systems of anyone who appears even remotely interesting. When you turn on your cell phone or laptop and join a Wi-Fi, you're cooked.

I waited for hours at the gate for the flight to Ulaanbaatar, which was delayed. My brain was shrouded in fog and my eyes were failing from exhaustion. I slept as we flew for hours over empty steppes before landing at the rather more ramshackle Chinggis Khaan International Airport.[1]

Yep, I thought as we pulled into the center of town from the airport, *this is a country set up for extractive industries, all right.* In Ulaanbaatar's central square, sculptures were interspersed with Soviet-style buildings framed by Louis Vuitton, Chanel, Bulgari, Cartier, and Ferrari showrooms. On the roads beyond the square, some of those Ferraris struggled to navigate potholes big enough to swallow them and yaks carrying loads or pulling carts. The inference was clear: a few people were making a lot of money, but it wasn't being spread around broadly to the locals or even being invested in the infrastructure. The people buying the Ferraris were whisking their money elsewhere.

But I wasn't there to discuss corruption or asset repatriation; I was there to speak about illicit trafficking at the Central Asia Counter Transnational Threats Symposium, cohosted by the US

Defense Department and Mongolia's Institute for Strategic Studies. Situated between Russia and China, Mongolia is in what pundits call "a tough neighborhood." Though geographically far to the east, in some respects Mongolia is considered part of another tough neighborhood, Central Asia: Azerbaijan, Uzbekistan, Turkmenistan, Kyrgyzstan, Tajikistan, and (lest we forget) Pakistan and Afghanistan. Central Asia and Mongolia are tied by ethnicity and history. The Mongolian empire, the largest contiguous land empire in history, was founded in 1206 by Chinggis Khan. His grandson, Kublai Khan, conquered China and established the Yuan dynasty. The Mongol's stocky physique and straight black hair, framing a flat, broad face with narrow eyes, have left a strong genetic imprint from China to Uzbekistan.

I joined the rest of the congregants checking into a massive Soviet-era hotel, whose bizarre blocks in triangulated interlocking shapes made it look like a game of Tetris played by giants. Inevitably, it, too, was named Chinggis Khan. It would be our home, as well as conference site, giving us (in typical US Defense Department fashion) little reason to leave its walls. I, of course, had other plans: there was no way I would fly all the way to Ulaanbaatar and not slip away at an opportune moment to do a little sightseeing.

The overall mood of the place was of neglected grandeur. Right in the middle of the lobby, an enormous portrait of the great Chinggis Khan himself peeked from behind streams of crystals that gave it simultaneously a demure and a grandiose appearance. It struck me as a flashier version of those curtains behind which noble European families of the Middle Ages hid their religious paintings, lest the painted subject bear witness to the unholy activities of the house's residents. The rooms were terrible: the Formica bathroom countertop and the monastically plain wooden night tables all had cigarette burns; the carpets were stained.

Our Mongolian hosts were kind enough to break us into the time zone gently. Before we got down to business, they took us on a half-day field trip so we could see a sliver of landscape beyond the capital and get to know each other before we were locked into a room together for three days of work. The big bus bounced its way along, shedding the buildings and heading straight onto a narrow highway, at some section of which we stopped for a display of falconing. You could photograph the tribally attired men and their birds, but donations were requested, of course.

Then back on the bus for more bouncing along until we arrived at the pièce de résistance: the massive edifice in honor of Chinggis Khan, out in the middle of nowhere. Legend has it that it was at this spot that the great Khan found the whip that he used on his horse through his conquests over what is now Russia, China, and Eastern Europe. A man and his horse. He faces east to symbolize the sun rising on the Mongol empire.

Inside the huge rotunda under the horse's feet, we were treated like dignitaries and given a sumptuous feast to enjoy while exotic boys and girls danced and sang in full tribal regalia. After lunch, we exited at the top of the horse's mane to check out the view: other than the parking lot, there was nothing but hills and fields as far as the eye could see. It would be quite something to be part of a Mongol horde out here: nothing but horses, men, whips, and weapons— a military reductio ad absurdum.

Upon returning to the hotel, my head was swirling from the jet lag. I worried I wouldn't be able to string a coherent sentence together at the conference. My standard remedy is to seek out the gym. The elevator told me it was in the basement. When I got there, it was locked and dark and looked like no one had visited in years.

Indeed, they were downright confused when I asked at the front desk if someone had the key or knew how to get in. One person at reception was surprised to hear they had a gym; the other struggled to find where such a key might be kept. Finally, the helpful man found it and emerged victorious from some nether region of the reception desk. But our joy was short-lived: the musty, dark room had machines from the 1980s—yes, the Soviet era.

The conference hall, however, was enormous and designed to impress. The outsized ballroom had been arranged with large tables in a U shape to frame the alternating presenters under the fluorescent lights. I was one of the presenters, and discussed what had become my security terrain: how criminal groups and terrorists were increasingly benefiting from collaborating in the gray areas of illicit trade.

In one of the breakout sessions (held in glass enclosures), we worked directly with the military and political representatives of the Central Asian nations, mapping out on whiteboards different ways to approach solutions to their smuggling problems. These illicit economies were big, and some of the people in the room were probably benefiting from them. But no one could say that; we were there to advise on "capacity building," helping them identify security gaps that allowed illicit goods to flow through their countries.

For Central Asia, the goods are heroin (coming mainly from Afghanistan), terrorists, and weapons (particularly into and out of Afghanistan and Pakistan). Azerbaijan and Kazakhstan have a lot of oil and gas and a great deal of corruption; few people know where that dark money ends up. Mongolia's legal system and financial structures to fight money laundering are weak, despite its being a signatory to the UN Convention Against Corruption and its commitment to the Financial Action Task Force standards, leaving it wide open not only to its own corruption but to exploitation by Russian and Chinese organized crime groups.

The 2004 reopening of North Korea's embassy in Ulaanbaatar raised international concerns that would be used to finance North Korea's illicit financial activities through narcotics trafficking and counterfeiting. Office 39 is a North Korean government bureau dedicated to raising hard currency for the sanctioned country through illicit activities, including the manufacture of counterfeit US$50 and US$100 bills (of which North Korea is the main source) and counterfeit cigarettes, narcotics manufacture and trafficking, and the sale of missile technology.[2] Mongolia is in a tough neighborhood indeed.

"Tell me about your border controls," I inquired of one Central Asian military commander, as I stood by the whiteboard in one of the glass-enclosed rooms.

"What border controls?"

Great. I think my work is done here. Where do I send my invoice?

They were charming, though, in their own Central Asian way. During coffee breaks, when I emerged seeking sunlight to keep me awake, it was into a fog of cigarette smoke: to a man, they puffed away on strong brands no one had ever heard of. It made accepting a cigarette from them a pleasure that was extra-guilty.

"Oh, I think it's a legal requirement throughout Central Asia that everyone over the age of fourteen smoke relentlessly," said Brianne Todd of the Defense Department's Near East South Asia Center for Strategic Studies (the NESA Center), as her boss, Roger Kangas, nodded his head.

I have yet to meet greater experts on Central Asia than those two. They taught me a lot about the region, including what to order off the Mongolian menu when we made a break for dinner outside the hotel one night. Brianne Todd in particular impressed me: she is unrelentingly smart and tough, her wit taking no prisoners, and though much younger than I, she had spent an inordinate amount of time traveling through Central Asian capitals and badlands, working with (and no doubt schooling) many of the region's strongmen, in a region that takes particular pride in them: presidents-for-life are the norm.

I persuaded Roger and Brianne to take a little excursion with me that was not on the official schedule: to Hustai National Park, to find the elusive Takhi horses, the wild horses of Mongolia. These are not the horses the Khans rode into battle; no one has ridden them. They are the only breed of horse never to have been tamed, and are therefore legendary. They run only at dawn and dusk, and you are not supposed to get within three hundred meters of them.

It was a long drive in the dim light of a rainy crepuscular penumbra. After paying our entry fee, we stood by a field a guide had recommended. We were quite sodden and tired, heading toward despondent. And then, they appeared: the horses, a little horde of their own. They galloped over the hill, wild and free, shaking their manes as if taunting us: *You will never touch me, much less bridle me.* We were lucky: they ran by closer than they apparently usually do, allowing us to admire them all the more. And then, just like that, they were over the hill and into the horizon. We chattered with delight all the way back to our hotel.

On our last night of the conference, our Mongolian hosts thanked us by giving us commemorative mugs filled with desiccated nuggets of curdled yak's milk—a local delicacy to which I didn't take a liking. Using the excuse that the foodstuff might not survive the journey home or be approved by US Customs and Border Protection, I dumped the nuggets, but kept the mug. I still have my morning coffee in it.

ENTERING BEIJING

On my way back to New York, I decided to take a few days on my own in the Chinese capital, since I didn't know when I might return to that side of the world. I was still climbing the learning curve of the gray markets of illicit trade.

Upon landing back in Beijing, I got into a tiny but tidy taxi and handed the driver the address of my Western chain luxury hotel, not too far from the Forbidden City. Vast highways channeled cars that ran without delay past towers, the most gleaming of which was the headquarters of the CCTV, the state-run channel, on which I have since been interviewed a few times. The enormous reflective square (not cube) building looks like some giant tried to pull it apart, gave up the effort, and plopped it on one of its crooked sides. From a different angle, it forms an upside-down U, like a magnet fallen from the heavens and stuck to the Earth.

My first stop was not the Imperial Palace or Tiananmen Square or the Great Wall, but a *hutong* that a friendly China expert had recommended I experience and given me a book (which I read) explaining why. *Hutongs* are old, crowded neighborhoods with crumbling housing and very narrow streets that were standard in the China of yesteryear. Not just geographic locations, they often center on an activity or a family, giving each its distinct character, with names like "Drum and Bells" and "9 Turns." One of the most popular is Wudaoying Hutong, now hip and popular with strolling tourists, hunting the boutiques and cafés lining the narrow alleys.

It is somewhat ironic that both the Chinese and tourists are enjoying the coolness of what have been Beijing's truly residential areas for centuries; sequential government programs sought to raze them in the interest of modernization, first during the Great Leap Forward when communism was fresh, and then in time for the 2008 Olympics. By the time the Olympics rolled around, though, China's understanding of soft power (the power of exporting one's culture and ideas) had grown. Some in the Chinese Communist Party had come to appreciate that the preservation of some of those *hutongs* would be good for the Chinese narrative that would be sold to the world. So they are maintained (some even slightly "improved," cleaned up to the point of sterility) as jewel-like curiosities in all their messy, crowded, noisiness, as slices of true Chinese life for consumption by the tourists.

THE SILK ROAD MARKET: COUNTERFEITS AND TRIADS

While the tourists wonder at Chinese history—from the boisterous to the cleansed, from the imperial to the Communist—they also consume another Chinese claim to fame: counterfeiting of Western products. China's consumption of Western intellectual property has been ravenous, as any manufacturer (not just of luxury goods) can tell you. From Louis Vuitton handbags to Apple chargers to Viagra, it is all counterfeited in China. According to the Organisation for Economic Co-operation and Development (and anyone else who hasn't been living under a rock), China is the number one source of counterfeited goods.[3] Behemoth Chinese online retailer Alibaba may have undertaken measures to clean up its act since it floated its shares on the New York Stock Exchange, but in Beijing there remains the Silk Road market: a whole shopping mall full of counterfeits, from the luxurious to the mundane.

The Silk Road market is a five-story, all-counterfeit shopping center featured in "Best of Beijing" lists on Web sites, including TripAdvisor. It has learned some things the hard way, though: you can tell which companies are the most aggressive in pursuing copyright infringement, because those are the products for which you have to ask. I walked through every floor. Tory Burch and Chanel shoes were mixed in with frankly fake Rolexes. But I felt like I hadn't hit pay dirt yet, like I was missing something. I went in search of expensive luggage and handbags. Louis Vuitton and Hermès were the real prizes.

I knew women on New York's Park Avenue and London's Mayfair who bought fake Hermès from other genteel women who sold them out of their apartments. They even ranked them by quality of copy. A good fake Birkin went in New York for about $1,000—much cheaper than the $15,000 often paid for the real thing, if you were lucky enough to get off the waiting list. If Londoners and New Yorkers were getting them from here, and I was in the epicenter of counterfeiting, I was sure I could find the source if I pressed hard enough. I browsed nonchalantly through one more upscale luggage vendor and opened with a slightly easier target.

"Have anything more interesting?"

"What you want?"

"Louis Vuitton."

The woman looked me over suspiciously. She glanced around the tiny shop to make sure no one else had entered. She stepped outside the door to scan for anyone who might be within earshot. Then she came back to me.

"Follow me."

She opened a door in the back of the shop and shut it behind me promptly. There were lots of LV-emblazoned suitcases, hand-bags, wallets, and cosmetic cases, some of them wrapped in clear plastic.

"We careful. Louis Vuitton. They send spies and they sue. So we hide."

I nodded and looked around.

"Tell no one. What you want?"

I felt like an undercover DEA agent doing a drug buy. "A carry-on. Small suitcase."

She showed me several. She explained that the better ones came with the logo-stamped locks and keys, and she showed me the certificate of authenticity inside.

"Better. No difference. More money."

Judging by the relative fluency of her English, she likely did this negotiation a lot, covert or not. She wanted around $600. I haggled with her, then thanked her for her time, saying I would think about it, and walked away. I was intrigued that this was so easy.

The next day, I hired a guide and driver to take me out to the Great Wall of China. In fit shape, I trekked high and far, but what I was seeing for myself was only a minuscule fraction of the huge snaking structure that can be seen from space. The counterfeits remained on my mind, though. Descending from the Wall, I asked my guide (who had waited in the car) if she knew where one could buy counterfeit Hermès Birkin bags.

"Yes. I know the best." Lily's English was perfectly fluent. Her other job was as an interpreter.

We drove back into central Beijing, just a few blocks from my counterfeit shopping mall of the day before, to a business known as "Jinyie Xi Li." The car wound its way through low buildings toward the back of a warehouse. It stopped at the top of the alleyway, and we got out to walk the rest of the way.

"You're from New York?" Lily asked.

"Yes. How can you tell?"

"You walk fast. People from New York always walk faster than any other American."

"That's true. We are always in a hurry," I agreed.

Ascending some small metal steps, Lily pressed a buzzer next to a small metal door. A voice on an intercom under a camera answered. They spoke in Mandarin, and the door was buzzed open. Inside there was a glass-enclosed window, with a man behind it. Lily approached the man, provided some sort of identification, and spoke more Mandarin, gesturing to me, presumably explaining I was a client. He emerged and unlocked another metal door.

Behind that door, there were rows and rows of Hermès Birkin bags, the *non plus ultra* status symbol of New York society mavens. They were stacked on shelves, floor to ceiling; they covered the walls. I gasped. I was in the presence of many millions of dollars' worth of counterfeit handbags: a supermarket of counterfeits, in effect. I had Hermès bags at home; these were indistinguishable, right down to the locks, logos, keys, and certificates of authenticity. Their biggest size Birkins sold for $500. So many women back home would have wet themselves with excitement and willingly scooped up several of them.

Counterfeiting luxury goods is big business. Based on World Customs Organization data, the OECD estimates that in 2013, counterfeit goods accounted for up to 5 percent of imports into the EU, making that trade alone worth 85 billion euros. This is a rising threat in a global economy whose value generation is increasingly driven by intellectual property. And the marketers are savvy: like any well-run business, the counterfeiters target consumers across market segments. The primary market segment is buyers who think they are buying a real car part, a real iPhone charger, a real medicine, and are surprised when they don't work or (in the case of car parts or medicines) cause serious harm or death.

The second market segment is represented by my fake Birkin- and Louis Vuitton–buying buddies: the consumers are aware, but think there is no harm being done. The only harm, in their view, is to some major corporation that is overcharging anyway, to pay for all that marketing in glossy magazines and the rent on all those beautiful boutiques sitting on prime real estate. Buying the fake Louis Vuitton or Hermès is, in that construct, a victory for the little guy, against corporate greed.

In our March 2016 newsletter, my company Asymmetrica featured an analysis of this pattern of consumption. A study conducted by Paris-Sorbonne University Abu Dhabi analyzed why people who can afford genuine luxury goods persist in buying counterfeits. The results reveal the psychological drivers that effective strategic messaging must address if luxury goods producers wish to protect the integrity of their brands, and if law enforcement hopes to stymie illicit financial flows to transnational criminal organizations. In short, the wealthy Emiratis (like those on Mayfair and Park Avenue) buy genuine goods for high-profile events with wealthy peers who will spot the difference; they buy counterfeits for everyday wear-and-tear.

A third market segment is the aspirational middle class, who can afford the occasional $500-$1,000 bag but not the $15,000 bag.

Interestingly, when top brands come out with limited editions, they are subject to another phenomenon involving the knowing counterfeit consumer: the fashionista. She wants to be on trend, but knows another trend will replace it next season, so is not willing to (or cannot afford to) invest the money on staying on trend season after season. Furthermore, counterfeits of high-profile but limited-edition goods are the easiest to get away with: not enough people will know the details to spot the difference. In short, the only effective deterrent to buying counterfeit goods is shame: embarrassment among one's social peers.

There is plenty of reason for shame. This massive illicit trade transits through the same main hubs as legitimate trade: Hong Kong, China, Singapore, Panama. The large shipments are then broken down in safe havens such as free trade zones, which have lax enforcement, and get sent out from there in small-parcel shipments, through the mail or UPS, creating a huge enforcement headache for private shippers and law enforcement. Other transit points, which we know all too well at Asymmetrica, are chosen— places where there is weak governance or weak enforcement capacity.

More darkly, counterfeiters also use routes and transit points where there is a strong presence of criminal or terrorist networks, funding serious violence as these handbags move along their routes to the consumer. The production and distribution are heavily controlled by ultraviolent Chinese triads, which, in their diversified criminal portfolios, also traffic in narcotics and women bound for prostitution. The problem is, the society women don't know they are carrying "blood handbags"; if they did, they might think twice before buying them, either on the sidewalks of Lexington Avenue or in the genteel drawing rooms of Park Avenue.

The answer lies in making this illicit business bad business. In December 2015, the US Trade Representative (USTR) gave a very stern warning to Chinese online retail behemoth Alibaba (which is much bigger than Amazon) about the sale of pirated and counterfeit products on its online platforms. The USTR very nearly put Alibaba's Taobao marketplace (a Chinese online shopping Web site similar to eBay and Amazon) and Alibaba.com back on the Notorious Markets List, from which Alibaba.com was removed in 2011 and Taobao in 2012. The USTR has been pressured to relist them as Notorious Markets after complaints from various intellectual property rights holders' associations.

The USTR report[4] stated: "The Internet traders who use these online markets to offer counterfeit goods are difficult to investigate and contribute to the growth of global counterfeiting." A relisting as a Notorious Market would adversely affect the Alibaba group, which is now listed on the New York Stock Exchange and is in the midst of complex negotiations with more rights holders, including Disney. Both the stock price and the negotiations would be severely damaged by blacklisting.

Within days of the USTR's threat to list Alibaba as a Notorious Market, Alibaba Group Holding Ltd. announced it had hired Matthew Bassiur as vice president, head of global intellectual property enforcement, to reduce the prevalence of counterfeits on its Alibaba and Taobao platforms, which is costing the firm heavily in lost licenses, lawsuits, and fines. Bassiur previously oversaw anticounterfeiting for Pfizer Inc. and Apple Inc., and prior to those private sector positions was a federal prosecutor for the US Department of Justice.

Whether Bassiur sticks to his enforcement roots and cleans up Alibaba or simply becomes a front man only time will tell, but other online sites are worried about the trouble counterfeits bring. Google had similar concerns about impact to its revenue stream, and on January 22, 2016, it was announced that the company had hired more than a thousand people dedicated to removing advertising of counterfeits[5] (particularly pharmaceuticals) and other scams, such as phishing and malware. Google claimed its staff removed over 780 million "bad ads" and suspended more than 30,000 Web sites in 2015.

TO THE BENEFIT OF STATE AND CRIMINAL

Fighting illicit trade stemming from China (as an Apple executive and many others have told me) is particularly challenging, because it not only benefits triads, which have an interestingly intertwined relationship with the government, but parts of the Chinese government apparatus as well. Many of China's largest companies are state-owned enterprises. While all countries have such companies (especially in critically important industries like energy), in China they are particularly concentrated in the hands of the Communist Party elite, or their sons, referred to by policy analysts as "the princelings."

One high-ranking member of the British government told me in a private meeting in London in 2015 that he had just returned from senior-level meetings in China and that members of the People's Liberation Army had boasted that they owned the tobacco industry in China, both for domestic consumption and the illicit brands for export. The Chinese tobacco industry is run as a state monopoly, from production to wholesale distribution.[6] In the 1980s and 1990s, Chinese production and distribution could not meet demand and an illegal market emerged[7] as Chinese distributors illegally imported all the major brands from Western companies, including Philip Morris and British-American Tobacco. The latter's Hong Kong executives were caught supplying a smuggling organization (Giant Islands, Ltd.), receiving US$6.5 per box; it amounted to US$257,000 a month. In the 1990s, British-American Tobacco had 50 percent of China's cigarette black market, which accounted for 20 to 30 percent of the company's worldwide profits.[8]

China has the world's largest population of smokers: 300 to 400 million. One in three smokers in the world is Chinese, and the entire market is under the exclusive control of the Chinese government, which derives as much as 60 to 70 percent of local government revenue in cigarette-manufacturing regions from tobacco. The profitability is clearly obvious to corrupt government officials: in 1987, state-run cigarette-marketing agencies illegally sold 11 million cartons (that's 2.2 billion cigarettes) to 125 traders in the Chinese coastal province of Zhejiang.[9] The business is so profitable that military trucks and aircraft have been used in cigarette-smuggling schemes.

Worryingly for the West, both China and Russia—as well as many other countries—use their intelligence services for commercial espionage. They pass the information to their businesses, stealing innovation from the West to compete more effectively. Security and profit are intertwined objectives in China. A cyber-expert and former spy wrote me in July 2016 that in cyber-attacks, the real question is attribution: who is doing it. The second question is motivation: why they are doing it. China is the world's greatest cyber-hacker for the theft of intellectual property, but parsing out attribution and motivation (who exactly did it and why) is particularly complicated, even if you know the hack was Chinese: military interests, private corporate interests, nationalistic interests, and general hacking interests are often thickly intertwined in the intrigue of hacking.

Broadly, though, Beijing's primary focus in intellectual property theft is military or military-industrial items. The theft is part of its quest to develop twenty-first-century armed forces as quickly and cheaply as possible. China is in a race against time to establish the world's premier force to replace America in the Pacific by 2030. So it wants to steal all the military information it can in order to retrofit or reverse-engineer it. Cyber-espionage is China's key to winning the arms race for global domination.

That use of state power to steal intellectual property (like the counterfeiters do) for power and money puts the West at a disadvantage: we do not operate that way. Intelligence services in the US and almost all European nations are barred from passing information to industry, by laws and codes pertaining to the disclosure of classified information,[10] as well as treason, sedition, and subversive activities[11]—violations of which can carry the death penalty. The un-level playing field in global commerce and the dark money of illicit trade connect to the shadow wars of espionage.

Up in Smoke

By the autumn of 2012, I was getting pulled into the circle of subject matter experts (SMEs) who influence policymaking. I had to apply what I had learned from my observations in Venezuela, Colombia, Guatemala, China, and Mongolia and identify the patterns and strategic nodes that policymaking could target to promote peace and prosperity. By then I was focused on the nexuses between transnational crime groups and terrorists—namely, the willful collusion of corrupt government officials. I had started to formulate my position: pro-industry and anticorruption. The industry in which I would become immersed is that of illicit tobacco: how the high taxes on cigarettes become profit margins for criminals and terrorists directly involved in some of the biggest attacks around the world. As long as people continue to smoke and seek discounts for their habit, that dark money will continue to flow from the consumer to the hostile enemy.

On my return to the US from Guatemala, Mongolia, and China, I was invited to participate in a two-day conference at the National Defense University in Washington, D.C., where I presented my theory and observations of crime-terror pipelines. The conference was cosponsored by the US and UK governments, so at the end of it we were treated to a reception at the UK ambassador's residence in Washington: a more sprawling and grandiose place than even the special relationship between the two nations would lead you to imagine. I was on my magic carpet ride, my career ascending fast. On my magic carpet, I kept flying to London and Paris.

The second part of the binational conference series was in London in October 2012. From London I would move on to Paris for my first time at the Organisation for Economic Cooperation and Development, to discuss illicit trade. I always liked Paris (I used to borrow my brother's apartment on the rue de l'Université when I lived in London), and the follow-on was logical enough. I was invited to both by the US State Department's Bureau of International Narcotics and Law Enforcement (INL) director of anticrime programs, David Luna.

LONDON AND PARIS

At the two-day counterterrorism meeting in London, I gained a bit of notoriety when, with Home Secretary (now Prime Minister) Theresa May in the room, I contradicted a senior British official.

"Crime-terror pipelines may be a problem for the Americans," he said, "but we don't have that problem here in the UK."

I stood up.

"You'll forgive me, sir, but you have a problem with a huge marginalized and angry Muslim population. You have the highest per capita consumption of cocaine in the world at the highest price per gram in the world. I would say you have a problem. Shouldn't we look into the connections?"

The Americans bought me a drink at a local bar that evening.

The next day, I was thrilled to arrive in Paris, and I was not too disappointed when, at the end of the week, I had to extend my stay because all flights back to the US Northeast were canceled due to Hurricane Sandy. The OECD in Paris is a very different environment from from that of the close-knit meetings and planning sessions in US government buildings or military bases. The Paris headquarters does have more stringent security protocols than some US government buildings, though: airport-style baggage screeners and metal detectors, followed by sliding glass partitions that box you in completely if your magnetic ID card fails. The OECD's motto is "better policies for better lives," but it is often disparagingly called the "rich boys' club": it encompasses thirty-five of the world's most advanced economies, as well as global corporations and international organizations. The power of its analytic publications to move markets and government policy is well established.

Its headquarters in Paris's 16th arrondissement has two buildings: the Château de la Muette, a *gentilhommière* mansion, like a lord's *petit château,* where its social events are held, and the postmodern minimalist building next door, where the work gets done. The large double-story walls of its lobby are adorned with photos of heads of state beaming as they shake hands and sign accords. Down the escalators and in one of the giant conference rooms—which features booths for the simultaneous interpreters, a giant screen, and very long tables forming a rectangle with a placard at every seat (Interpol, United Kingdom, France, World Customs Organization, Novartis, Diageo, Spain, Philip Morris)—is where I met my first major long-term client.

"I understand you might be able to help us," he informed me. David Luna had told him to come talk to me. He was from one of the major tobacco companies. "We have a big problem with the illicit trade in tobacco."

No kidding.

"MR. MARLBORO"

Quite literally, the explosive consequences of the illicit trade in tobacco hit the world stage three months later, in January 2013, when I was in Dubai. Ambling through the sumptuous and expansive halls of the Palace Hotel on my way to the buffet breakfast, I picked up my usual clutch of newspapers: *The New York Times*, the *Financial Times*, and then at least one local one, in this case Abu Dhabi's *The National*, which a close friend of mine had been instrumental in setting up. Usually I get a variety of coverage. On that day, they all had the same headline: a terrorist group had besieged a gas facility at In Amenas, Algeria. Eight hundred thirty hostages (both Algerians and foreigners) were trapped inside. The leader of the terrorist group's nom de guerre: Mokhtar Belmokhtar.

The remote site, run by BP, Norway's Statoil, and the Algerian state oil company, accounted for 10 percent of Algeria's considerable natural gas production. It lay deep in the southern desert: eight hundred miles from the Algerian capital of Algiers, but only thirty-five miles from the Libyan border. Islamist leader Belmokhtar (aka "Mr. Marlboro") issued a video statement claiming responsibility for the kidnapping. (The moniker Mr. Marlboro refers to the money he made smuggling cigarettes across the Sahel, the semi-arid belt that separates the Sahara from greener Africa to its south. "Sahel" in Arabic means "coast," while "Sahara" means "desert": the Sahel's sparse vegetation is the coastline of the Sahara's ocean of sand.) The authenticity of the video (and therefore the claim) was confirmed by SITE Intelligence Group, the premier monitor of jihadist media. The militants, who numbered around forty, had inside intelligence and detailed plans of the important fifteen-hectare site, according to the Algerian prime minister, Abdelmalek Sellal, but the opening shots of the attack were likely opportunistic.

On their way to the plant, the terrorists intercepted two buses taking plant workers to In Amenas Airport. Three foreigners who tried to escape the bus attack were shot as they ran through the sand. The terrorists kept driving to their target. At around 5:40 a.m., Toyota Land Cruisers crashed through the entrance of the gas plant and heavily armed militant gunmen headed to the living quarters. As workers were preparing for the start of their shift, some still eating their breakfast, the alarm sounded. An Algerian security officer was shot, but managed to activate the gas facility alarm system before he died.

Foreigners were rounded up; many had their hands tied behind their backs with rubber cable ties, some had their mouths taped. The hostage-takers, whom Algerian officials said included at least three explosives experts, set about strapping Semtex bombs around the necks and waists of some of the hostages. (Colombia's FARC have also used this tactic; Colombians call it a "bomb necklace.") Some survivors said foreigners were shot as they tried to escape. One of the casualties was Liverpool-born Paul Morgan, a former soldier in the French Foreign Legion who fought in the first Gulf War and was working as a liaison between gas field workers and local security staff. The Algerian prime minister later spoke of "numerous foreigners killed with a bullet to the head" in the course of the siege. They were lucky: many terrorist hostages face a fate much worse than a swift death.

When the Algerian Special Forces ended the four-day siege, the blazing noonday sun shone down on the corpses of thirty-eight hostages and twenty-nine militants. The US, UK, France, and Japan were shocked and confused: they had received no advance word of the assault, had no idea how many of their citizens had been killed. Even the rescue itself had been brutal, in keeping with the Algerian government's history of violent responses to Islamist militancy.

Algeria's interior minister, Daho Ould Kablia, confirmed that the 830 hostages had been held by forty members (not thirty, as first reported) of an Al Qaeda in the Islamic Maghreb (AQIM) offshoot, Al-Mourabitoun ("The Signed-in-Blood Brigade"), commanded by Mr. Marlboro.

Belmokhtar had learned to fight as a mujahideen in 1980s Afghanistan, against the Soviets. Because of the successful expulsion of the Soviets, jihadists consider Afghanistan hallowed ground:

the site of their first successful jihad against an outside and apostate oppressor, the Soviets. It was in Afghanistan that Belmokhtar met Osama bin Laden, joined Al Qaeda, and named his son Osama in homage. When he returned to North Africa, he led AQIM, and it was then he became known as "Mr. Marlboro." After a falling-out with Al Qaeda (some say because they felt he was more focused on making money from the illicit cigarette trade than on waging jihad), he founded his own terrorist militia, al-Mulathamun ("The Masked Men").

In 2013 Mr. Marlboro's al-Mulathamun Battalion merged with the Movement for Unity and Jihad in West Africa (MUJAO), both of which were offshoots of Al Qaeda in the Islamic Maghreb. In May, they carried out joint suicide bombings in Niger that killed at least twenty people. The merger was complete, and the Signed-in-Blood Brigade was born.

The newly formed brigade announced its intentions to "rout" France and its allies in the region and to violently implement sharia (Islamic law) in West Africa. The group carried out attacks against French interests in the region, including African military units coordinating against Islamist forces, and African civilians. According to the US State Department, the Signed-in-Blood Brigade poses "the greatest near-term threat to US and Western interests in the Sahel."[1]

Commanded by Mr. Marlboro, the Signed-in-Blood Brigade was also responsible for the November 2015 attack on the Radisson Blu hotel in Bamako, Mali, that left nineteen hostages and two attackers dead, and the January 2016 siege of the Splendid Hotel in Ouagadougou, Burkina Faso, where twenty-two (out of 148) hostages were killed. Mr. Marlboro has been declared dead three times, but all indications are that he is still alive.

According to the UN Office on Drugs and Crime (UNODC), about 15 percent of the cigarettes smoked in the West African region are bought on the black market and trafficked through West Africa. AQIM and the splinter group MUJAO have been taxing traffickers in return for safeguarding their passage for decades. The smuggling of cigarettes to North African markets began to thrive in the early 1980s, and it developed into a large-scale business controlled by a few major players. Cigarette smuggling in particular has greatly contributed to the emergence of the practices and networks that have allowed drug trafficking to grow, eroding state institutions and thereby further destabilizing countries throughout the region, including Libya and Algeria.

Mr. Marlboro's cigarettes often enter West Africa through Ghana, Benin, and Togo. A second route is via Guinea, where the supply, according to the UNODC, vastly exceeds the country's demand. The cigarettes are then moved to Mali by road or by boat on the Niger River, where there is little risk of detection. Mauritania is a third distribution hub, for smuggled goods bound for Senegal, Morocco, and Algeria. In each case, Mr. Marlboro makes enormous profits, either by charging a "tax" for the safe passage of the cigarettes along the route or by facilitating their transport, using 4×4s, trucks, motorcycles, and even bicycles.[2]

Cigarettes imported through Mauritania supply a large portion of the Algerian and Moroccan markets, while those imported through Cotonou in Benin and Lomé in Togo are routed through Niger and Burkina Faso to Libya and Algeria. In 2009, UNODC estimated cigarettes smuggled along these routes accounted for around 60 percent of the Libyan tobacco market (or $240 million in proceeds at the retail level) and 18 percent of the Algerian market (or $228 million).[3]

The collusion between smugglers and state officials has compromised the customs services through corruption. For part of its journey, the merchandise is transported in large trucks on main roads, with the collusion of corrupt Malian and Nigerian security officials. In Libya, cigarette smuggling is controlled by networks in the security apparatus dominated by members of the Qadhadfa tribe. In the triangle connecting Mauritania, Mali, and Algeria,

Sahrawi networks—often with the direct involvement of officials in the Polisario Front, which seeks independence for Western Sahara—trade subsidizes Algerian goods and humanitarian aid southward in exchange for cigarettes bound northward to Algeria and Morocco.[4]

THE BIRTH OF ASYMMETRICA

It was in 2013 while smoking *shisha* (the molasses-based tobacco concoction smoked in a hookah, the ornate water pipe used throughout the Middle East)—under the shadow of the world's tallest building, the Burj Khalifa in Dubai—that I conceived of my company, which would become Asymmetrica. The sun had set and I was chatting poolside at the Palace Hotel with Michael Waltz, a friend and colleague who was also in Dubai on business. Waltz is a former Green Beret who spent an exceptional amount of time in Afghanistan, then served in the White House and the Pentagon before returning to the field. He has the unusual perspective of being part of the Washington, D.C., policymaking machine, then living the consequences of implementing those policies on the ground, and then returning to Washington. He is also a successful entrepreneur.

On this particular trip to the United Arab Emirates, he was introducing Afghan Pashtuns (the tribe from which the fierce Taliban are drawn) to people who would help them set up businesses to rebuild Afghanistan, to make them productive citizens rather than insurgents: the Afghan version of the DDR (disarmament, demobilization, and reintegration) Colombia implements. I was there for different reasons, but I had a business idea of my own.

"There are two segments of people who care about illicit trade," I said, "businesses and security agencies. Businesses see it as a market problem—illegal competition eating at market share and damaging their brands by counterfeiting. Security agencies see it as a 'threat finance' problem, a generator of funds to bad guys. But they can't speak each other's languages. I understand business more than security, but if I can be the bridge between the two, I think I have a business."

Waltz liked my idea. Since 2010, I had been in business as Vanessa Neumann, Inc., consulting on Venezuela, Colombia, and the flows of dark money between and from them, but in that moment I saw clearly my targeted growth niche and began to develop a strategy to conquer it.

Waltz invited me to join him on his trip with the Pashtuns to Abu Dhabi the next day. The bus ride from Dubai to Abu Dhabi was civilized enough. I knew enough to put a hijab (the Muslim head scarf) in my bag, but I did not wear it on the bus. Neither did the woman who sat next to me: Shahla Nawabi, who owned a business in Kabul but lived half of the time in London. Shahla was quite forceful and opinionated: a fellow woman born in a country that celebrates male domination but who then got accustomed to the ways of Western liberalism. I recognized the phenomenon; we got on well.

Our first stop was the Sheikh Zayed Mosque, the United Arab Emirates' religious heart. Enormous and gleaming in perfect white marble, it made you feel as if you were entering Heaven—which is the point. My hijab wouldn't cut it. I had to cover my clothes with an abaya, the long flowing robes devout Muslim women wear over their clothes. I put on one of the all-black, sweaty, and rather smelly ones they had to lend visitors, but I made a mental note to visit the shopping mall right next to the Palace Hotel when I got back to Dubai and purchase a couple of my own for the future.

Great Muslim mosques are spectacular to behold. Figurative depictions of the human form and of Allah are not allowed in Islam. The elaborate decoration centers on Arabic calligraphy of unimaginable delicacy and ornateness. The walls and ceilings and floors are inlaid with lapis lazuli, onyx, opals. The feeling these mosques impart is one of transcendent peace.

From the mosque, we went to the Afghan Embassy. Here my hijab would suffice, but I committed a cultural faux pas. Entering the drawing room where we would be received by the ambassador, I found a free spot on a sofa. No sooner had my rear end touched the fabric than the two seated men sprang up as if it were on fire and promptly scooted to the other side of the room. I sat there alone, until the Afghan-British businesswoman Shahla joined me.

"Geez, that's no joke, is it?"

"No," she answered. "Just wait until the lunch. Not only will we women be seated alone at our table, we'll probably have empty tables around us."

Before lunch, however, we sat through a presentation on the changes in Afghanistan since the American invasion in late 2001. At the question-and-answer session, Shahla raised her hand. The presenting Muslims ignored her as they took questions from the men. She kept her hand raised. The Muslim presenters continued to ignore her and started to move on as if she did not exist. I protested. So did a few men in the audience. In the end—because other men protested—the presenters relented and acknowledged Shahla, but they only answered her vaguely, and rather dismissively.

On our way to the lunchroom, I noticed a Pashtun I had not seen on the bus. He took my breath away. He was in full tribal dress, and an intricately wrapped turban of the most exquisite colorful weave sat atop a face that seemed to have popped right out of one of those Romantic portraits in the Frick Collection, with pale blue eyes thickly rimmed in kohl, a long narrow hooked nose, and a long beard died red with henna. He was glorious, and unrepentantly proud of his tribe. He must have noticed my stunned reaction, because he smiled at me, which is unusual for such a traditional Muslim man.

Shahla was only partly right about lunch. When we sat down to eat, it was indeed only the two of us at the table. But then the ambassador joined us, clearly making a point. Other men followed. The ambassador smiled at us.

"I believe in progress," he said.

I smiled back. It was a reminder of how women's equality is by no means the norm in the world. It hardened my resolve as an entrepreneur.

EVOLUTION

My professional profile ramped up another notch on March 5, 2013, when my phone started ringing nonstop. The news confirmed what I suspected was the cause: the Venezuelan president, Hugo Chávez, had died. I was flooded with requests for comment by the world's media, both international and local. I called my assistant, Danielle Schwab, to come over to my house and help me manage the chaos, and I stayed up all through the night and the following day giving interviews, often just fifteen minutes apart. As producers altered their schedules, I was sometimes in the crazy situation of giving two interviews simultaneously, one on Skype, the other on the phone. Poor Danielle also traipsed with me to television studios; she set up a Google Hangout for me to do an interview with HuffPo Live as soon as I stepped off the stage at Fox.

Every media outlet had its own agenda: the right-wingers were gleeful he was dead; the left-wingers thought it was the tragic death of a hero and crafted complex conspiracy theories that ultimately blamed the CIA. I tried to stick to the facts of Chávez's rise, his consolidation of power, the country's economic troubles, the causes of the inefficacy of the opposition, and what might come next for Venezuela's economy and foreign policy. Regardless of where the interviewers stood on the political spectrum, they all predicted a warming of US-Venezuela relations, with Venezuela returning to being an American ally, as it was when I was a child growing up in Caracas. *No*, I contradicted. *Why would it change? What would drive that change? Chávez may be dead, but the*

Chavistas *remain deeply entrenched, and hating America has been* *good for them, bringing them power and money. Until they have* *more to gain with the US than they do with Russia, Iran, and China,* *this pattern won't change.* I could hear the deflation in their voices, but I was right.

The night of March 4, I had to fly to Geneva to sign what would become my long-term corporate client for the next several years. I had not slept in two days. I picked up my suitcase, without any idea what my housekeeper had put in it, and headed to JFK. Upon arriving at my hotel in Lausanne the next day, I had three hours to rest, shower, and change before going to my would-be client's massive headquarters to lay out my strategic plan to combat illicit trade in their industry.

A month later, in April 2013, I returned to the OECD for the start of its Task Force on Charting Illicit Trade (which in 2016 was renamed Countering Illicit Trade, to everyone's relief), chaired by David Luna. In 2013, we had our work cut out for us: it was a bit like herding cats. Government and industry do not tend to work well together and, because of their differing objectives, in many cases are barred from doing so. Getting industry and government to share information and their experiences was not simple, though that is exactly what this task force was supposed to accomplish. I was appointed to head the tobacco group, which I did for two years, until 2015. The work entailed gathering data on cigarette smuggling from the major tobacco producers, law enforcement agencies, and multilateral groups like the World Customs Organization, then collating it all into a text that was balanced and gave an accurate portrayal.

To call it complicated and politicized would be an understatement: each group had divergent agendas, and everyone knew it. At first, the only ones who provided detailed information were the tobacco companies, who had reams of data on what brands were illegal and how much of each was being sold in which country. The government agencies disputed their numbers, but refused to provide their own. There were even heated arguments about how the measurements were taken and who was behind the smuggling. It was interesting, if often frustrating, and it seemed that the only countries that cared much about it were the US and—to a much lesser extent—the UK. Both countries criticized plenty, saying they had different information, but refused to share that information or add any comments to the documents. I suspected something else was going on.

By that time in 2013, I had a strategic business plan, a steady client, and my pro bono role at the OECD, but I still kept my finger on the pulse of what was happening under the Bolivarian Revolution in Venezuela as Nicolás Maduro, a former bus driver who'd become foreign minister and then vice president, assumed the presidential mantle after Chávez's death.

The encrypted exchanges with what I termed "my kids"—a network of young tech-savvy university students who wanted change in Venezuela—continued until I landed in Caracas on May 12, 2013, and arranged to finally meet a couple of them in person a few days later. We alternated our meeting sites between random public lunch spots and one trusted friend's home. To meet the first of the kids, I went with what had become my standard security contingent: an armored SUV with a driver and a shooter in the front seat beside him, with a second car following us as backup. In 1970s Caracas, when I was a child, there were a lot of organized kidnappings of the wealthy, so it was not uncommon for me and my friends to have bodyguards, or at least a driver with a weapon and training in "close personal protection." When I worked in Caracas in the early 1990s, it was normal that our cars, which looked like the average Toyota or Nissan, would be armored with reinforced doors and thick bulletproof glass.

Since the *Chavista* rise to power, however, criminality, popular anger, and political repression had all skyrocketed and law enforcement had fallen into chaos: Caracas became one of most violent cities on earth. By the time I landed in May 2013, I had three

In January 2010, I was touring Colombia with an international delegation observing Colombia's reintegration of paramilitary fighters under the Justice and Peace Law. The FARC, though, were still very active, so we relied on snipers, Black Hawks, and Counter-Terrorist Special Forces like these guys to keep us safe, even in the capital city of Bogotá.

In July 2016, "Chris Howard" was on duty again in Somalia, where he has spent an inordinate amount of time. During that tour, the Al Shabaab terrorist group set off two bombs simultaneously, just outside the Mogadishu International Airport compound where he was living. A quarter century of hunger and war have made Mogadishu's beautiful coastline into an outdoor museum of misery.

In April 2016, I was one of the panelists at a plenary session of the OECD's Integrity Week. Our topic: corruption and illicit trade. My conclusion was simple: I have never seen a major case of smuggling or trade-based money laundering without corruption, and corrupt government institutions recruit corrupt people, so they can all enrich themselves without threat. On the far left is the then-chairman of the OECD Task Force on Countering Illicit Trade, David Luna, a State Department contractor.

On May 20, 2017, there were simultaneous protests all over the world commemorating fifty days of ongoing demonstrations for food and elections in Venezuela. In this protest in New York's Washington Square Park, organized by the NGO SOS Venezuela NY, chalk outlines with name cards represented protesters killed by government forces.

A view from a neighboring building into the backyard of a "rancho" in Medellín, Colombia, in 2009. The makeshift (likely pilfered) building materials are typical, as are the mountains of uncollected trash. Both point to the marginalization of Latin America's poor and the lack of public services.

Hills of slums in Medellín, Colombia, in 2009, as the city boasted advances in infrastructure, the rule of law, and economic inclusion. In neighborhoods like these in the 1980s, Pablo Escobar, the *capo* of the local cartel and the "King of Cocaine," would have been revered as a Robin Hood hero and protected by the locals.

عيد مُبارك

Jama Masjid
Islamic Foundation of Panama

Postcard given to me at the Jama Masjid Islamic Foundation on Mexico
Avenue in Panama City. The mosque is identified by US security services
as being involved in Islamist recruitment and radicalization in Panama.

The monument to Genghis (Chinggis) Khan outside Ulaanbaatar, Mongolia, in August 2012. Its remote location in the middle of the steppes is allegedly the site where he found his horsewhip (which he holds), enabling his conquest of Asia all the way to modern-day Europe from the back of his horse. He faces east to symbolize the rise of the Mongol Empire.

This Fernando Botero sculpture of a bird, exploded by a bomb, stands as a memento of more violent times in Medellín, Colombia, when drug cartels, Marxist insurgents, and paramilitaries all fought for territorial control over narcotics distribution routes.

Authentic contraband Marlboros ("illicit whites") sold in the market of Mogadishu, Somalia, in July 2016. This photograph was taken by a source of ours, just days before two bombs were set off at Mogadishu International Airport by al Shabaab while "Chris Howard" was there. The sale of illicit whites benefits the Islamist terrorist group (37.5 of these cartons will buy one rocket-propelled grenade launcher).

The aquarium in Medellín, Colombia, in 2009, as the city's mayor was showcasing infrastructure and economic development after the dismantling of the Medellín drug cartel (whose late leader was Pablo Escobar) and during the reintegration of right-wing paramilitaries.

A counterfeit Hermès Birkin bag from Beijing, sitting on a sofa in an apartment on New York's Park Avenue, where the bag is considered one of the key status symbols of that social set. Most people cannot tell this $500 fake from the real one, which often retails for $15,000 or more. If these socialite women understood the human suffering along the counterfeit bags' supply chain, they would be ashamed.

things to fear: general criminals who would shoot you just for your cell phone or, if you looked like your family might be able to afford a $30,000 ransom, take you in an opportunistic "kidnap express," release you, and do the same thing to someone else the next day; the half of the population (*Chavista*) that hated my half (opposition), leading to class violence with racial underpinnings; and an oppressive regime that used Soviet-style surveillance and detained and tortured critics like me. I had to be careful to keep me, my family, and anyone I spoke to out of trouble.

Three days after my arrival, on May 15, 2013, I met the kid with whom I had established the greatest rapport. He hopped into my SUV and we drove around fairly randomly while we chatted in person for the first time. He asked whether I in any way worked for the US government.

"No. I wouldn't touch it with a ten-foot pole. I have a brother in Caracas to protect." The *Chavista* regime is rabidly anti-American; if I were mistakenly perceived as working for the US government, he could be imprisoned, tortured, or killed by the regime. "I'm just an academic trying to understand what has happened here," I explained.

He was disappointed; I guess he thought I would be more helpful to their cause if I were working with the US government.

After about twenty minutes of driving around, we made it to a downtown street and went to an *arepera*. Arepas are corn patties shaped like hamburgers that you cut open and stuff with whatever you like: eggs for breakfast, or chicken or pork with avocado for lunch.

Later, in 2017, it was nearly impossible to have an arepa: Empresas Polar, the country's largest food and beverage company, which makes the Harina P.A.N. (the corn flour used to make arepas) and Polar beer, halted production because they couldn't obtain the foreign currency needed to purchase raw materials. Currency controls had been imposed by the government: you had to ask permission to convert your sales in the local currency of the

Bolívar Fuerte into US dollars to pay your suppliers. The government regulated both the price at which you could sell your goods in Venezuela and your access to dollars to pay the suppliers.

It did not help the company that its owner and CEO, Lorenzo Mendoza—a billionaire who was beloved by all because his products were consumed by everyone, but particularly the poor—was loudly critical of the *Chavista* regime. The government sent in troops to take over some of his plants, and that, on top of the economic pressures, led to the unthinkable: the collapse of Empresas Polar and the supply of the basic food basket for the Venezuelan poor. Venezuela without arepas is like Asia without rice—and with this change, Venezuela could not feed itself and the poor were starving.

When we arrived at the upscale *arepera,* my "shooter" got out first, scanned our surroundings, and covered me as I exited the car and he escorted us to the front door. There was a sign prohibiting weapons and an airport-style metal detector.

"I can't go in with my weapon, but I will wait right here. Try and stay in my line of sight," he said.

I nodded.

As we munched our arepas and yucca fries, the boy asked me a bit about my upbringing in the US, my feelings toward Venezuela, whether I had enjoyed living in London. I was happy to discuss all that: he seemed genuinely curious (almost like a fan), and due to my public press, it was all stuff that was already in the public domain. He was about to share information that could get him killed by the regime, so he wanted to bond with me first. We chatted as we ate until he felt comfortable enough for me to ask him some pressing questions.

"Is it true," I asked in between bites of my *reina pepiada,* an arepa stuffed with chicken and avocado, "that there is heavy Iranian infiltration here? Rumor is they're mining for uranium for their nuclear program."

"Yes. They are."

"How do you know?" I sipped my Coca-Cola Light.

"I've seen the bills of lading. One of us has access, works for the head of the mining company."

Loud rumors had circulated that Iran was extracting uranium and shipping it out of Venezuela to Iran, with the assistance of the highest levels of the Venezuelan government through the state-owned Venezuelan conglomerate, CVG Ferrominera; CVG is located in the Guayana region in the southeast of the country, which is rich in aluminum, gold, and uranium. The "head of the mining company" about whom the boy was talking was Radwan Sabbagh, who was to be arrested on June 12, 2013, on charges of pilfering over Bs. 295 million (about US$45 million at the time).[5]

"How interesting," I answered as flatly as possible. "You guys be careful."

A few days later, I met with a retired military officer to whom a friend had referred me. He came to my friend's home at the base of the Ávila, the green mountain range that separates the city from the Caribbean Sea and gives the city its perfect weather: hot but not humid. He was personally acquainted with some of my family, and although he was retired from the military, some who were still in it and who were unhappy with what they were seeing had talked to him; and now he was talking to me.

"I know this neighborhood well." His voice had more than a tinge of nostalgia. "We used to have secret meetings in that building there, and that one there," he said, pointing at two buildings across the street. "It reminds me of old times."

"It's amazing how things have changed, though," I responded. "What's going on? What's going to happen?"

Scenario-building was not his expertise, but he did go on at length about the extent of Hezbollah and Iranian infiltration in Venezuela. I kept taking notes, kept observing, kept trying to find patterns that might be replicated in other parts of world, to see what lessons we could learn, what we as humans could do better. It felt like an application of my political philosophy roots. I kept writing, too: my paper "The Global Convergence of the Crime-Terror

Threat" was published in the academic journal *Orbis* in the spring of 2013. I was closing in on my specialty, establishing my turf.

On July 11, 2013, I changed my company's name to Asymmetrica, at the suggestion of a friend: "Like Oxford Analytica, you should name it Asymmetrica, because you're the asymmetric warfare chick." My being an entrepreneur working at the intersection of big corporations and security, it resonated.

By the time the OECD task force met again in March 2014, Asymmetrica had hired about half a dozen staff with special operations and intelligence experience, and I'd divided a 30 percent share of the company between the two most senior people, to secure their long-term commitment and to encourage them to develop business. I took my new chief operating officer and my business partner with me to the meeting in Paris. They would betray me later. It turns out military guys do not take kindly to a female boss and undervalue not just women, but also civilians with a business perspective.

It was at that March 2014 OECD meeting in Paris that I first came across an NGO called the International Center for Sport Security (ICSS). It was backed, incongruously, by the Qatari royal family, which afforded the NGO quite a lot of independence by locating its key staff in France. Its mission: to investigate money laundering and other illicit financial flows through sport. When Fred Lord, a gregarious Aussie, started his presentation on the ICSS's work, some of us had had a long day and were answering emails on our computers. Then came the whammy: he said once you added in online sport betting, the amount of criminal money flowing through sport was in the trillions. Now he had our attention. The ICSS had made quite the splash. It would make a bigger splash when the FIFA scandal broke.

CIGARETTE SMUGGLERS, SYRIA, ISIS, AND OTHER BAD GUYS

Later that year, in August 2014, the US Department of Defense identified[6] a cigarette-smuggling network extending from Bulgaria into Turkey and offering material support to the Assad regime, in contravention of international sanctions, as well as to the Islamic State of Iraq and the Levant (ISIL, or Daesh) terrorist organization. Prestige and Victory cigarettes (brands owned by the Bulgarian company Bulgartabac) are shipped across the Black Sea, through the Strait of Bosphorus, and then either directly to Syria or down to the Red Sea and around to the Persian Gulf. Western Syria "is controlled by and benefits the Assad family,"[7] the Department of Defense's maritime security publication states. As cigarettes move through various transshipment points near the Turkish border (in areas controlled by Daesh), Daesh taxes their transportation—despite the group's public burning of cigarettes as a violation of Sharia law. The cigarettes are then sold at a premium price in Syria or smuggled onward into Turkey.

According to Chris Rawley, the author of an article on the smuggling network: "The product and profit not only support ISIL and their organized crime network, but other Al-Qaeda affiliates and foreign fighters drawn to the region. The illicit tobacco trade is an instrumental part of their funding portfolio, which also includes weapons trafficking and sale of stolen oil."[8]

The shipments are processed through the port of Latakia by Fadi Adam Allosh, an Alawite (like the Assad family) from Jablih, Syria. The customs processing company is a front for his real business, connected with the Assad family and the Syrian regime, which during the ongoing Syrian civil war has been focused on smuggling narcotics and human organs between Syria and Iran. Latakia is an Assad family stronghold, controlled by the wealthy Makhlouf family, headed by Bashar al-Assad's cousin, Rami Makhlouf, and his twin sons, Hafez and Ihab. Rami Makhlouf was designated by the US Treasury Department in 2008 under Executive Order 13460, which "targets individuals and entities determined to be responsible for or who have benefitted from the public corruption of senior officials of the Syrian regime."[9] He was also sanctioned by the European Union for financial support to the Assad regime.

In the dirty business of illicit trade, in which money doesn't care who owns it, the shipments are transferred to revolutionary-controlled areas near Qalaat Al Madiq, where they are guarded by people who work for the well-known revolutionary leader Jamal Ma'arouf and his deputy, Miskal Al Abdulla of the Syrian Revolutionaries Front (SRF), a moderate faction of the Free Syrian Army rebel group. Miskal Al Abdulla was a cigarette smuggler before the war began in Syria. Ma'arouf and Abdulla are getting a share from the profits of the smuggled cigarettes. The Assad regime's affiliated gangs can deliver any requested amount of cigarettes over the minimum order of $50,000, which amounts to ten to fifteen large cargo trucks. In other words, cigarette smuggling is partially funding both sides of the Syrian conflict, helping to escalate the conflict, while civilians in the middle continue to be slaughtered in the crossfire or to flee to a Europe that does not want them.

As in all illicit trade, a lot of the funding that ends up in terrorist coffers comes from developed economies, including the US. The links between the illicit traffic in tobacco and terrorism are well known in New York, covered even by the local *Daily News* in May 2013.[10] Over the previous seventeen months, a cigarette-smuggling ring had bought $55 million worth of cigarettes in Virginia, trucked it to New York, and sold packs tax-free to small stores across Brooklyn, the Bronx, Queens, and Staten Island. Investigators in the case, dubbed Operation Tobacco Road, had found evidence the group pocketed $22 million in profits, of which authorities have found only $7.8 million in cash and bank accounts.

Former New York police commissioner Ray Kelly said the group included several "individuals on our radar with links to known terrorists," starting with Mohannad Seif, a cigarette reseller from Brooklyn, who had lived in the same three-story walkup in New York as the personal secretary of Hamas's main fund-raiser in the US, Mousa Abu Marzouk, who was deported from the US in 1997 but continues to raise money for Hamas in

Egypt. Furthermore, Youssef Odeh, of Staten Island, a suspect in the case, had financial ties to the imprisoned blind sheik, Omar Abdel-Rahman, who was convicted in a 1993 plot to blow up New York landmarks. Before he got into the cigarette business, Odeh sold baby formula. In the early 1990s, the sheikh invested $10,000 in Odeh's business, Kelly said.

In Operation Smokescreen, a federal jury in Charlotte convicted Mohamad Hammoud of violating a ban on providing material support to terrorist groups by funneling profits from a multimillion-dollar cigarette-smuggling operation to Hezbollah. The jury also found Hammoud, whom prosecutors described as the leader of a terrorist cell, and his brother guilty of cigarette smuggling, racketeering, and money laundering. The two men, natives of Lebanon, were accused of smuggling at least $7.9 mil-lion worth of cigarettes out of North Carolina and selling them in Michigan. Hammoud was sentenced to 155 years in prison,[11] though the sentence was later reduced to 30 years.

AN ALL-TOO-OBVIOUS SOLUTION

Working illicit trade in tobacco is the kind of challenge I love: a legal consumer good that is highly controversial (all the more fun) is being counterfeited or smuggled into countries where it does not pay duties and is literally used as currency by criminals at an exchange rate of so many AK-47s or RPGs (rocket-propelled gre-nade launchers) for so many crates of cigarettes. The high taxes create a profit margin for criminals, who are not known for their tax compliance. This makes the profit margin as high as that for cocaine, with much lower penalties. As a security consultant, I would have to get the security issues taken seriously without wad-ing into the quagmire of tobacco politics—no easy task.

Worldwide, over 1.1 billion people smoke some 5.7 trillion cigarettes each year. Illicit trade in tobacco products (ITTP) is es-timated to approach 11 percent of that market. Every single producer making filtered cigarettes uses cellulose acetate tow (from which cigarette filters are made) provided by one of the six manufacturers in the world. While there are substitute materials for cigarette filters, they are not adequate, in their function or their flavor.

The industry of cellulose acetate tow is very capital-intensive, with an estimated investment of approximately $500 million for a medium-sized unit of forty kilotons of acetate flake and acetate tow production. Such capital intensity and concentration implies that all acetate flake and tow must be processed at one of the major known plants around the world. Although cellulose acetate flake can be used to make LCD screens, among other products, 90 percent of flake is used to produce cellulose acetate tow, 80 percent of which, in turn, goes to produce cigarette filters—at least 11 percent of which are for illegal cigarettes made and/or smuggled by serious criminal organizations.

There is likely no way a commodity company could operate year to year with no idea where 10 percent of its total sales were going or why the companies making those purchases were not known and reputable. So a producer of cellulose acetate tow, with equal access to public data, is (or should be) aware that its products are used to produce illegal cigarettes and to finance transnational organized crime. Since the relationships between illicit producers and the criminal networks engaged in the illicit trade in tobacco products are now widely known and understood, any key input supplier that sells its products to illicit producers should know that by supplying these key inputs (including cigarette paper and cellulose acetate tow) to illicit tobacco producers (even by oversupplying the legitimate market), they are ultimately aiding and abetting organized crime, corruption, terrorism, and other forms of conflict and political unrest.

A known Interpol case study verifying oversupply of acetate tow to illicit manufacturers was based on a visit to a factory in the Hong Xi Industrial Area in Ma Xiang Town, Xiamen City, China. Interpol found a storage site of raw materials for manufacturing fake cigarettes and seized 719 filter pieces, 1,470 rolls of wrapping paper, and another 33.3 tons of acetate tow. This amount of raw materials was capable of producing millions of illicit tobacco products, which would generate millions of US dollars in profit for the criminals involved, as well as deprive governments of potential revenue[12] from cigarette taxes or import duties.

Interpol's secretary-general at the time, Ronald K. Noble, stated in a press release of March 5, 2014—while I was at the OECD task force meeting—that a vast oversupply of cellulose acetate tow is a major enabler of illicit trade and an enormous source of funding for criminal networks.[13] Key input oversupply provides billions of dollars to illicit manufacturers and the criminal networks that move the cigarettes.

"It is in the interest of all governments to establish due diligence frameworks and 'know your customer' programmes such as those required for banks, and to demand track and trace systems for key component manufacturers to help combat the illicit trade in tobacco products and avoid millions being siphoned out of the public purse," said the Interpol chief. "Regulating identifiable, consolidated components industries, such as of acetate tow, is one step towards achieving our goals."[14]

That should not be too hard: there are only six manufacturers in the world. The two biggest (Eastman and Celanese) are in the US—the same country that spends the most on the Global War on Terror, ironically. Five of the six are in OECD countries—and therefore subject to OECD policies. The three biggest (Eastman, Celanese, and Solvay) are all members of GAMA, the Global Acetate Manufacturers Association. These companies are both natural chokepoints in the illicit supply chain and legitimate targets for OECD policy.

The Protocol to Eliminate Illicit Trade of the World Health Organization (WHO), adopted in 2012 by the parties to the Framework Convention on Tobacco Control (FCTC), "sets out international guidance for national action on supply chain security, offenses and enforcement and international cooperation."[15] However, while the Framework Convention has issued specific track-and-trace technology requirements to ensure that legitimate production is not diverted into illicit channels, it has taken no measure to combat counterfeiters or producers of illicit whites (cigarettes that are not counterfeit, but are smuggled into a country where they are not licensed and not taxed or subject to duties). Neither has it targeted the suppliers of key inputs (such as acetate tow cigarette filters) to illicit manufacturers.

The UK's National Crime Agency (previously known as the Serious Organized Crime Agency) has led the way in upstream criminal investigations to more effectively disrupt illicit trade. As part of its Programme 9, whose aim "is to reduce the harm caused to the UK by the cocaine trade focusing on the 'upstream' elements,"[16] it investigated and helped prosecute employees of pharmaceutical companies who knowingly sold precursor chemicals to criminals engaged in illicit manufacturing. The sale of cellulose acetate tow or cigarette paper to counterfeiters or manufacturers of illicit whites would seem a direct parallel, one that should be explored under the US government's numerous counter–threat finance initiatives of the Departments of Defense, Treasury, and Justice.

In the years I have been working on the topic of illicit trade in tobacco, the Global Acetate Manufacturers Association (GAMA) has changed its message (and its Web site) from defiance to some acknowledgment of the problem industry and law enforcement have been trying to get it to address for years. The GAMA Web site[17] now acknowledges that 11 percent of the tobacco market is illegal and funds organized crime and terrorism. The association says it is addressing the problem with a know-your-customer (KYC) due diligence program it instituted in 2006—voluntary for its three members—and that it "supports cigarette companies and public authorities in their fight against illicit trade."[18] Though it says that an "independent auditor audits every GAMA member participating in the KYC" every two years, it does not identify who participates in the program, it does not give the standards for the program, and it does not cite any penalties for noncompliance or any enforcement mechanisms. It is, after all, voluntary.

Though the association claims to be "committed to complying with all applicable legal obligations and cooperates with public and private actors who share GAMA's goal,"[19] its "goal" is to promote cellulose acetate as a product, not to regulate it. Since the chemical companies that make cellulose acetate tow for filters are not themselves in the tobacco industry, they suffer no regulatory downside from the illicit 11 percent of sales. As long as the government refuses to regulate them (especially the largest two, which are American), these companies will keep funding criminals and terrorists, causing our soldiers to lose their limbs and lives fighting them, while the chemical companies continue banking the money. The addition of industry complicity in illicit trade furthered my understanding of the complex global puzzle of how our habits as consumers fund terrorists.

9

Bad Sport

The twelve-month period from the summer of 2014 to the summer of 2015 tested my mettle as a businesswoman. I fell in love, came face-to-face with real bad guys in a whole new crime-terror pipeline involving Islamists in the free trade zone in Panama, learned all about yet another form of corruption and money laundering (in sports and online gambling), and had to part ways with my partners in Asymmetrica.

This next level of adventure started in June 2014. Some members of the OECD's Task Force on Charting Illicit Trade were beckoned to task force chairman David Luna's office in a satellite building of the State Department for a briefing with a senior member of the Office of the Director of National Intelligence. I was one of them. So was Chris Howard.[1]

He sat across the table from me, next to his International Centre for Sport Security colleague Fred Lord—his friend, Australian compatriot, and polar opposite. While Fred is slim, swarthy, chatty, and long-haired, with tie askew and the permanent demeanor of one who has only just barely escaped some harrowing situation, Chris is broad, pale, taciturn, impeccably attired, and chillingly self-possessed. He watches.

I didn't realize then that he was watching *me,* in my favorite slim-cut emerald-green trouser suit, about which he would later tease me endlessly. He seemed nice enough (the little that he spoke) when, at the end of the meeting, we exchanged a few pleasantries about his plans that evening. He gave some vague answer about hitting the town and getting some drinks. Vague, brief answers, I was later to learn, are his default. I was going to Virginia to visit my retired horse, and then one of my new business partners and I were going to shoot targets with a Glock, an AR-15, and an M-4. I had no inkling of the role the quiet Australian would play.

PANAMA: "YOU ARE NOT WHO YOU SAY YOU ARE"

On July 13, 2014, I received an email from a Washington, D.C., friend introducing me to "Bill," saying Bill had a project for me for which he thought I would be well suited. I routinely get requests to find out who is really behind a business transaction or where a network is getting its support: how the money and goods flow, who is connected to whom and how—particularly if the networks connect Latin America to the Middle East or Africa. We turn down clients we think are dirty or "on the wrong side." In a follow-on email later that day, with a link to some of his work, Bill explained what he wanted: for three to four days of in-country work researching Islamism in Panama, he needed a fluent Spanish speaker; the work would be time sensitive and there would be limited funding for about ten days' worth of work.

I said that given my past (and well-publicized) work on Hezbollah in Latin America, I might be interested in the expansion of my regional knowledge.

In a follow-on email, Bill explained the terms. The money was minimal, for a four-thousand-word report that would be published in Arabic in a forthcoming edition of the "monthly book" of a Persian Gulf think tank that would focus on Islamist movements in South and Central America. The think tank had a growing following in the region and a liberal, pro-Western leadership, and would host a forthcoming conference in Dubai, "for which there will also be compensation, as well as an opportunity to connect with some remarkable people."

Three days later, I flew into Panama. Numerous flight delays made me thirty minutes late for my first meeting, with a liaison who knew the organized crime and terrorist landscape quite well. We met in the lobby of the Waldorf-Astoria Hotel, where other members of what she referred to as her "team" sat in the background as we chatted. She was very warm and friendly, and I gave her a brief backgrounder on how I came to do this work, on Asymmetrica, and on what I was seeking in Panama. She hoped we could establish a long-standing relationship that would be mutually beneficial.

My liaison asked whether I had noticed upon arriving how at the Panama airport the arriving passengers mix with the transit passengers, making Panama an ideal transit point for anyone who wishes to hide. Overall she stressed that Panama is a place that is growing economically, so the government has little will to offer greater transparency because it is economically beneficial not to look too deeply into illicit trade or money laundering.

This was two years before the Panama Papers scandal, but money laundering had gained political importance in the two weeks since the new administration had been sworn in: Panama had just been placed on the gray list of the Financial Action Task Force (FATF, a financial policymaking and monitoring organization that sits inside the Paris headquarters of the OECD), based on an International Monetary Fund report chronicling the country's lack of financial transparency.

The consequence of being gray-listed was that now everyone doing business through Panama would have their books more closely examined, and, more important, the price of borrowing money for the country's sovereign debt was higher—being gray-listed flags a country as risky. As anyone who has ever applied for a loan knows, the riskier a client you are, the higher the interest rate on the loan. So this lack of transparency carried a heavy financial cost for the country.

Two of the main problems with illicit trade and corruption are the disconnection and the asymmetry between those who profit and those who pay the costs. While facilitators (like the law firm Mossack Fonseca, which gained notoriety in the Panama Papers) make fees for hiding money, the cost of stolen money (whether in higher interest rates or crumbling infrastructure) are borne by residents, who have no share in the profit. The profits are funneled into the hands of a few, while the costs are spread out among the populace. It takes a lot of stealing to get the populace to feel enough pain that they are motivated to rebel, so corruption can exist in a country for a long time.

Panama, my liaison said, is a remarkably small place where everybody knows everybody else and everybody is a consultant. I told her that my next meeting was with a lawyer who was a former narcotics prosecutor; she asked whether it was "Roberto," and I confirmed that it was. She said the talk around town was that Roberto had offered his consulting services to the American Embassy, but was turned down because it was unclear what his area of specialty was and he had done nothing official in some time, so his information was not current. (Nearly everyone in Panama is a *"licensiado,"* the title used to designate a lawyer, because the law degree requires only four years of undergraduate study, but most function as consultants or managers of shell companies.) By the end of the meeting, I had two starting points for my research into Islamism in Panama: the mosque in El Chorrillo and the free trade zone in Colón.

Unusually for a Latin American, Roberto arrived bang on time and suggested we find another place to have dinner that would be more fun and jovial. Assessing the risk, I got into his car and he drove me to another part of town with a view of the water, and we had dinner at a very casual place with live music, the El Ranchito restaurant. Dinner consisted of fish and a couple of beers, which we consumed as the band played, silhouetted against a moonlit sea.

Roberto offered no insight of value but was offering instead his professional services for any clients that we might have with local business, saying his particular area of expertise was investigations into shell companies and money laundering. I said that that sounded like a great idea, that I had no doubt we would be doing business together, and that I would let him know as soon as we could use his services—which I knew we would not. Exhausted from many hours of travel after only three hours of sleep, I asked him to take me to my hotel.

The following day I met with "Eduardo," who had been until two weeks earlier a very high-ranking intelligence officer for the Panamanian government. Unlike Roberto, Eduardo was a fountain of information. He talked about Palestinians in Chiriquí, on the border with Costa Rica, as well as about the many Lebanese in the Colón free trade zone, who were of all stripes, including Sunni Muslims and Maronite Christians, some of them angry that the US Embassy had been canceling their visas.

He also spoke of Nidal Waked, a Spanish, Lebanese, and Colombian national who owned two newspapers (*La Estrella* and *El Siglo*), an import-export business called La Riviera, the duty-free zone at the Panama airport, and his own bank, Balboa Bank & Trust. His business was the second largest in the Colón free trade zone, and he was investigated in the 1980s by the Americans for money laundering. In May 2016, almost two years after this conversation, Nidal Waked was arrested by the DEA at the airport in Bogotá, Colombia, as one of the world's biggest drug lords. The US

Treasury Department said Waked's family-run operation "uses trade-based money laundering schemes, such as false commercial invoicing; bulk cash smuggling; and other money laundering methods, to launder drug proceeds on behalf of multiple international drug traffickers and their organizations."[2]

Eduardo said the Arabs are viewed very positively by the local population in the Colón free trade zone, because they help the poor with food and jobs. He spoke also of his long friendship with Fernando Núñez Fabrega, the former foreign minister of Panama. He said China is the biggest provider of goods entering the free trade zone, followed by Taiwan.

Eduardo talked about two operatives of the Iranian Revolutionary Guard Corps who had set up an office in Managua, Nicaragua, then came to Colón and met with the Arab community there, requesting more money from their charities. When I pressed as to names and dates, Eduardo was vague: he said it had happened over the last couple of years and he could not recall the names. He mentioned that Lebanese Hezbollah, Hamas, and Islamic Jihad all traffic from Colón to Maicao, Colombia, on the Guajira Peninsula, which I know well as a transnational trafficking hot spot, as well as a hot spot for a significant Arab diaspora—one that is also Marxist and that has extensive relations with the Colombian narcoterrorist group FARC. Many of the most radical *Chavistas* of the Venezuelan government were either raised on the Venezuelan side of the border in this region or went to school there, particularly at the Universidad de los Andes.

Eduardo said there were approximately five thousand Palestinians and Lebanese in Maicao, and that they were suspected of shipping Venezuelan uranium to Iran. Iranian merchant marines operated out of Venezuela, and the Americans were increasingly concerned about dual-use technology transiting through the Panama Canal on its way to Iran. Iranian influence, he said, was a huge problem in the region: an Iranian university (in Iran) was giving scholarships to fifteen hundred Mexicans a year to come study in

Iran and learn about Islam, but the kids were effectively becoming radicalized. It was his view that Iran had a much more aggressive radicalization program in Mexico than anywhere else in Central America.

He also spoke of a Muslim Indian community in Agua Dulce in Panama, and said they were mostly peaceful and mostly involved in the business of used cars in Panama City. I answered that used cars was a very well-known money-laundering scheme, seen also in West Africa. He spoke of the flight of Jews from Venezuela to Panama, as a result of the anti-Semitism under Chávez and since. He said that since the Israeli Embassy in Venezuela was closed, most of Mossad's intelligence operatives had been moved to Colombia. He claimed that Russian Jews who are Israeli Mafia traffic drugs and weapons through the Panama Canal, in collaboration with Mossad, and that he knew this because he had excellent relations with the Israeli Embassy in Panama.

He also said that Dino Bouterse, the son of Suriname's president, had been trying to set up an Islamist training camp in Suriname, but was captured in Panama and is now in prison in New York. As a result, he said, he had strained relations with the elder Bouterse, but was very good friends with another presidential candidate: Chan Santokhi. Eduardo also mentioned that San Pedro Sula, in Honduras, had lots of active Arabs; it had been known as the most violent city on earth, with the world's highest homicide rate, until it was overtaken in that dubious distinction by Caracas, Venezuela. He said that the Islamic Foundation of Panama had been funded by Moammar Qaddafi, but he did not know who was funding it since Qaddafi's death.

After the meeting, I went up to my room and called my driver, Miguel, asking him to take me to two of the three mosques I had identified as being of interest: the Islamic Foundation on Mexico Avenue in Panama City and the Islamic Cultural Center in Colón. The Colón mosque was funded by the Saudis, according to Eduardo, just as was the Islamic Center in Santiago, Panama. A US-based colleague who focuses on the Muslim Brotherhood identified the Santiago center as a probable hub for the Brotherhood, so I wanted to visit that the following day, as it would be a four-hour drive each way.

I arrived at the Islamic Foundation wearing the traditional Muslim clothing of a hijab (the head scarf that covers the hair and encircles the face) and an abaya (the voluminous robe worn over a woman's clothing), one of the two I had bought in Dubai. I arrived at the Islamic Foundation mosque and was received very politely by an imam, a religious teacher. I told him I was seeking to learn more about the great success of the Muslim community in Panama and how they had come to be so loved and such an economic force in the country. I waited while he made a phone call. He told me to return at 6 p.m., when Professor Yunus Magda would be there to speak to me. The imam handed me his own card. The name matched one of the two muftis identified by a colleague as cause for concern: responsible for increased jihadist activity in Panama. I told him I would be back at 6 p.m. and had Miguel drive me out to the Colón free trade zone to find the Islamic Cultural Center in the meantime.

TROUBLE IN COLÓN

In Colón, I arrived first at the Ramadan Karim mosque, but found it empty. I walked around the corner and found the Islamic Cultural Center. Young Muslim men were unloading trucks of food in a quantity that far exceeded what any party might require, but might instead feed an entire town. One of the Muslim men escorted me into the entrance of the center, where they were stockpiling the food. All of the Arabs spoke Arabic but very little Spanish.

"*¿Qué país?*" asked one man. What country?

I said I was Venezuelan, and held up my Venezuelan passport.

One of them fetched me a chair and used his phone to call some-one to come and speak to me. While I waited, I was approached by the only man who could communicate with me even minimally: a Moroccan who told me his name was Rafiq. I initiated a conversa-tion with Rafiq in French about Ramadan. I told him I had a very dear friend in New York who was Saudi, indeed part of the Saudi government delegation to the UN, and that he told me that he was struggling with Ramadan. I told him that I had always wanted to go to Saudi Arabia, as it seems a great country, and then I asked him whether all this was funded by Saudi Arabia.

"Yes. Saudi. All Saudi."

"Is this the most important mosque in the country?"

"Yes," he answered. "Colón most important. All other mosques in Panama controlled by Colón."

"That's wonderful," I said.

My ride arrived: a young boy named Osama, who pulled up in a white SUV and received instruction from one of the Arabs who had let me into building. I introduced myself in typical demure Muslim fashion, with my hand on my chest and a nod of the head, so I was surprised when he shook my hand. He told me to get into his car and he would take me to see his father inside the free trade zone. I told him I wanted to go with my driver and his wife. He suggested I should get into his car and they could follow in their car, but they'd have to wait outside the gates of the free trade zone, as their car did not have permission to enter. I counteroffered that the two of them should come with me in his car. He agreed, so that is what we did.

On the drive to the free trade zone, Osama was very friendly and chatty. I told him that I was surprised by the poverty in Colón, as I thought there would be much more prosperity spilling out from the free trade zone. I asked him what all the food was for. He said that every Saturday during Ramadan, they give out food to two thousand local non-Muslim families, who come to the Is-lamic Center with tickets that are given to them to claim their food—one ration per family, which is estimated at five people. Two people from the same family cannot claim food. He said they kept order by going to the houses to distribute the tickets before Ramadan. I said that for this to be possible, there must be a local census with a listing of every family member living in each household. He said yes, they do keep a list of all the locals and in which houses they live. I suggested that this was very kind and considerate of them and explained why they were so loved by the community. This made him smile.

Upon arriving at the free trade zone I was taken to a shop with a sign on the door, ARCO IRIS (Spanish for "rainbow"), and was told to enter. It was a wholesale shop of small electronics. A woman in an abaya at the back of the shop asked my name. I told her I was there to meet with Osama's father, to whom I had been referred by the Islamic Cultural Center. She called him on the telephone and then said I could go in. I rounded a wall behind the counter and entered an office. At a desk facing the door was a gray-haired, bearded man who was very obviously the man in charge and the one I was going to meet. At a table positioned perpendicular to that one, at some distance to the right, sat another woman in an abaya, this one middle-aged. A man in his thirties stood between me and the door as I sat down in the chair in front of the man I was there to see, who never introduced himself. But he had a lot of questions.

"They told me you were here to convert to Islam."

"Well, I'm Catholic, but I'm very mixed. Many members of my family moved great distances to escape oppression," I tried to explain, and at the same time bond.

The woman asked: "Are you Jewish?"

"I am not, but my ancestors had been considered Jewish, although nobody practiced."

"You're a Jew," she repeated.

"I am Catholic, but greatly interested in Islam, because I have many great friends from the Middle East and travel there often and am very impressed by the culture and tradition."

The man looked me over.

"Where are you from? To what countries in the Middle East have you traveled? What do you do that you travel to the Middle East?"

"I am a consultant on trade relations, particularly between the Middle East and Latin America, because I am Venezuelan."

"Who are you working for?"

"I am working for a client in the Gulf, who is extremely impressed with the wonderful relations the Arabs of the Colón free trade zone have with the Panamanians. My client thinks you are a model to be replicated across the region."

"I don't believe you. If you are working for someone in the Persian Gulf, why would they send someone from New York who does not speak Arabic? We do not speak Spanish here—we speak Arabic."

"I don't know why. I just do what the client asks." I tried to disarm him with a smile; it didn't work.

"You are not who you say you are."

Shit. He thinks I'm CIA. The only thing worse than being CIA is people thinking you are when you're not. I'm going to get killed here. I'm going to end up inside one of those shipping containers bound for Asia. My body will never be found. But surely he realizes that if I were a covert agent, I would be better at this. He must realize that. He has to realize I have no training, that I'm just making this up as I go along.

He looked me over again.

"If you want to understand community relations, I am not the person to speak with. I am in charge of religious conversions and religious education. I will send you to speak with Jamal Saker, the head of the board of directors for the organization that manages community relations."

"That is incredibly thoughtful and kind of you, sir," I said. "I am very grateful for your time and kindness in receiving me."

I took one of his cards off the desk and put it in my handbag.

This flustered him. "Do you have a card for me?"

"No."

He ripped a Post-it note out of its holder and handed it to me and told me to write down my name and telephone number.

"Of course," I answered, smiling. I weighed the consequences of putting down a fake telephone number. Would he have my handbag emptied and find my phone? Would he then dial the number to make sure it rang? If it didn't, how would I explain the lie? "Perhaps we can stay in touch."

I was then escorted out of his office and taken around the corner (I had Miguel in tow) to meet with Jamal Saker. However, when we arrived at the lobby of the building that houses his office, I was informed by a woman in a suit that he had just left. I asked whether she might be so kind as to give me his card so that I could perhaps call him the next day. She did. The company specialized in sporting goods: shirts with insignias from teams from around the world. I could not tell whether they were real or counterfeit, or whether they were bound for consumers in the US or elsewhere, but I wondered whether the team owners knew about their brands being here. Probably: it was a free trade zone, after all.

When we returned to the Arco Iris office, a young man came out and told me that I had to come back inside and give back the card I had taken and that I would be given the card of the person I needed to speak to. I said that was incredibly kind and thoughtful of him, but he need not bother, as I had gotten the card of the person I needed to speak to and I would be calling him the next day. He urged me to come inside again. Again I thanked him and said that I was really enjoying the beautiful weather outside, which reminded me of home, Venezuela, which I missed terribly as where I now lived did not have weather such as this.

I then rummaged around in my handbag and used my iPhone to take photographs of the two cards I had just taken and texted them to one of my business partners in the US. That way, if I were about to be kidnapped, someone would know who had been the last person I had seen. I stood my ground and waited outside until

Osama came to pick us up and drive us back to the Islamic center outside the free trade zone. At the mosque, Miguel, his wife, and I got into the car and drove back to Panama City for my 6 p.m. appointment with the professor at the Islamic Foundation.

BACK WITH THE IMAM

We arrived just a few minutes ahead of my appointment, and I was very well received. The professor was there and ready for me. I was escorted into a small room, completely carpeted and with a small window set high up on the wall, at the back of the mosque.

I was told to wait.

A young man then brought in two folding metal chairs, which he placed facing each other at a forty-five-degree angle. Then in came the professor with a little boy, his son. The professor had a rather improbable-looking long black beard with a nearly perfect white streak right down the middle. I said I wanted to learn about the history of the Muslim community in Panama, so I could understand its great success in maintaining its identity while integrating into the socioeconomic fabric of the country and becoming such a force for good. Pleased by this, the professor proceeded to tell me all about the history of Islam in Panama. His son brought me a glass of pink *chicha,* a popular Latin American rice-based drink that I'd loved during my childhood in Venezuela.

He said that the history of Muslims in Panama falls into two big stages: pre-Canal and post-Canal. He said that around the sixteenth or seventeenth century, the first Muslims arrived as slaves from Africa. They had a leader known as "Bayano," who led the resistance in the area of Darién; this is the first known Muslim community in Panama. Panamanian lore reveres Bayano as a symbol of resistance to repression of all Panamanians, not just Muslims. The professor suggested that this is one reason why Muslims are so accepted in Panama, as evidenced by the naming of the river Rio Bayano.

The second phase occurred when Muslim workers were brought in from the Antilles to build the canal. These Muslims had a great affinity for the African culture found in Isla Colón and Bocas del Toro; there are mosques in both these sites today. Then waves of immigration from other countries started in the 1940s, when Bangladeshi Muslims first arrived.

Their first congregation was established around the Rio Abajo prayer site. Muslim Indians started arriving the 1950s, and their numbers really spiked in the 1980s, when Panama's military government imposed few restrictions on entering Panama. In the 1960s and 1970s, Panama had an influx of Lebanese from the peninsula of La Guajira, on the border between Venezuela and Colombia.

The professor said that more than 150 businesses in the Colón free trade zone were owned by Lebanese, mostly Sunni. More recently, there had been an influx of Palestinians. The professor estimated that there were approximately ten thousand Muslims in Panama. He enumerated on his fingers the number of mosques, which came to twelve; that was three more than Bill had told me. Sensing resistance to my going off-topic or asking more pressing questions, I thanked the professor and left. He gave me a postcard of the mosque. When I got into the car with Miguel, he showed me he had gotten the same postcard from the people at the mosque.

Back at my hotel, I Skyped with my partners, who were seasoned intelligence professionals. They were concerned that I might be targeted by the people I had met in the Colón free trade zone.

"Do they know where you're staying?" they asked.

"No. They didn't ask; I didn't tell them."

"It won't take them long to figure it out. Stay in your room and lock your door. Get on the next flight home."

I locked in and called Miguel to pick me up early in the morning.

"I thought you were staying longer," he said. I would not be going to Santiago.

At Tucumen International Airport, I kept looking over my

shoulder and scanning my surroundings. As the wheels went up, I leaned back in my seat, relieved, and smiled.

BONDING

It wasn't until the following plenary meeting of our OECD task force in Paris, in March 2015, that I realized there was something mysterious about the quiet man from Down Under I had met in Washington, D.C., the previous June. I was, you might say, a bit slow on the uptake.

I nearly didn't go. I had emailed David Luna, the chair of the task force, and informed him of my intention to spend the Easter holiday in the Caribbean with childhood friends. The Paris meeting had been scheduled at the last minute, and the tobacco paper I was overseeing had been "embargoed" (the exact term used in the email) by Luna and his acolyte, Dr. Susan Melzer, an intern in his office at the State Department. They insisted that the government take over the handling of the topic, and were refusing to release any draft until they rewrote it.

I'm not going, I wrote. *I'm on a holiday that was planned more than six months ago and I don't have a paper to discuss, so there's no point.* Luna viewed it as my betrayal of the task force; I viewed it as the task force's betrayal of me, and wrote him so in no uncertain terms. Besides, my work on the task force was uncompensated, while my holiday travel was expensive and logistically complicated.

"It really takes the full force of the US State Department to be so culturally obtuse as to schedule a meeting in Europe during Easter week. There's a reason why our diplomatic corps is based in a swamp," I quipped to my hosts, referring to Foggy Bottom, where the US State Department is located in Washington, D.C. To be fair, Luna's office is not in Foggy Bottom, but is an ancillary in a different part of D.C.

In the end, I relented: I cut my holiday short and, at a financial loss in the many thousands of dollars, went to Paris for the meeting, which was sparsely attended—many others who were also working on the illicit trade in tobacco expressed their displeasure at the withholding of the paper by boycotting the meeting. In 2016 I was informed why: it was a business power struggle disguised as political. The US State Department wanted control and credit, probably for funding purposes, either from government or the tobacco industry. Dr. Melzer, the intern for the State Department, insisted that her name had to appear as the author of that chapter, so she would get publication credit. Until that was agreed to, neither the US nor UK government agencies would share any information on tobacco smuggling and would condemn the paper as biased.

Our first night in Paris, before the meeting's opening, Chris Howard emailed me asking me to meet him and Fred Lord that evening for drinks, but Luna insisted I join him at a dinner hosted by a technology company that was seeking to sell its offerings to the corporate members of the task force. I wrote Chris that I felt compelled to join the dinner in the interest of smoothing over the task force dynamics, but the dinner made me uncomfortable: it was enormously flashy, held at one of Paris's top restaurants, with an endless stream of expensive wines. The bill, picked up by the technology company, had to be well into the thousands of euros. I had started my consultancy as a subcontractor in 2011 investigating violations of the Foreign Corrupt Practices Act, and I knew that a government official accepting this largesse from a vendor broke that act's rules.

After dinner, I emailed Chris from my iPhone, asking him and Fred to join us for after-dinner drinks. Chris entered like a breath of fresh air, wearing a somewhat dirty polo team shirt: he had just returned from a polo match near his country house outside Paris. *Who is this guy?* I thought. *Who is this quiet Aussie who plays polo, lives in Paris, and has an English cell phone? What's his story?* I didn't get to find out much that night; our conversation was overtaken by the others in the group.

At the plenary session the next day, Luna announced that he was appointing a government "working group" on tobacco, with his acolyte Melzer to be in charge. The message was clear: any work that would be done on tobacco would have to flow through him and her. Never mind that government had historically done very little to tackle the very serious threat from the illicit trade in tobacco products in any strategic manner, because of its adversarial relationship with the tobacco industry. As we left the OECD building after the announcement, Luna's intent became all too apparent to me.

"How much do you earn in a year?" he asked. "Are you on retainer? Is it an annual contract? Do you get paid monthly or quarterly? When I leave government, I'm going to set up a rival company to Asymmetrica."

Yeah. Good luck with that, I thought. *You'll never cut it in the private sector.* Nevertheless, I carried on professionally and responded vaguely, with a smile.

At the next day's session, Chris sat on the other side of the giant rectangle of tables and watched me. During one of the coffee breaks, he approached me.

"I want to talk to you about Africa," he said, in his charming Aussie accent. "Maybe we can work together."

"I'd like that," I answered.

Back at our seats, we started sending emails to each other across the room, each watching the other's reactions as we read them. He sent me the link to the company on whose board he sat: Chelsea Holdings, a conglomerate with electricity grids in Africa, security contracting in the Middle East, and aviation services in Latin America. I wanted to work with him, but we were much smaller. It wasn't clear to me what I'd bring to the table that he didn't already have. Fortunately, he persisted.

It wouldn't be until nearly a month later that we would get closer, when he and Fred came to New York on sport integrity business.

They were coming in from some location in New Jersey, where

they were doing a briefing on money laundering and corruption in sport, and he agreed to meet me at the red bar in the lobby of the Four Seasons hotel on 57th Street and Park Avenue. They arrived an hour late. I kept promising my waiter that my friends were not imaginary, as I tucked into my second bowl of mixed nuts and second martini.

Two days later, on his last day before returning to Europe, I took him to the Williamsburg headquarters of Vice Media, the edgy journalists who now have their own TV show on HBO and their own channel. They had become famous for their ride-along with ISIS. I knew those guys, and I knew they would be interested in Chris's work on sport integrity.

"Oh my God," said a senior producer. "This could be the biggest story in the world."

He was right. The story was FIFA.

"MR. 10 PERCENT"

It was a month later, at 6 a.m. on May 27, 2015, when president of FIFA (the International Federation of Association Football) Sepp Blatter's morning coffee was interrupted by a phone call with unwelcome news: seven senior FIFA officials had been arrested by Swiss police, acting at the behest of the US Department of Justice, in a predawn raid at the Baur au Lac hotel in Zurich, where FIFA officials were meeting. Marco Villiger, FIFA's legal director, called Thomas Werlen for help. Werlen had been general counsel to Novartis, the Swiss pharmaceutical group, when it battled Justice Department accusations that it had illegally marketed a number of drugs and paid doctors to prescribe them. The case was settled in 2010, with Novartis agreeing to pay $422.5 million in criminal and civil liabilities.

Two years later, in 2012, Werlen became a Zurich-based partner at Quinn Emanuel, the US law firm that began advising FIFA in 2014. Bill Bruck, a former special counsel to President George W.

Bush and a former US attorney in New York, also got involved, becoming a main conduit between FIFA and the Justice Department.[3]

When the Swiss investigators finished sweeping the hotel, they moved on to FIFA headquarters. FIFA senior officials were outraged at the timing: two days before a FIFA presidential election—which, despite the growing scandal at his organization, Sepp Blatter handily won, again.

The Justice Department investigated FIFA under RICO, the Racketeer Influenced and Corrupt Organizations Act, originally designed to target the Mafia. FIFA had $5.7 billion in revenues in the four years before the 2014 World Cup. Its books were approved by the behemoth accounting firm KPMG. Quinn Emanuel hired Teneo, a public relations crisis-management firm that advised BHP Billiton and Novartis in their battles with US prosecutors. Teneo was charged with making FIFA look transparent, cooperative, and less political than it was. It did not work.

At the center of the charges of racketeering, money laundering, and wire fraud brought by the US Department of Justice, the US Attorney's Office for the Eastern District of New York, and the Internal Revenue Service are allegations that US and South American sports-marketing executives paid more than $150 million in bribes and kickbacks in exchange for broadcasting rights of major soccer tournaments. The investigation is expected to take another four to five years: the Office of the Attorney General has nine terabytes of data to trawl through—equivalent to a Word document of 750 million pages.[4] Extradition proceedings have begun.

The story of FIFA's massive corruption really started in Donald Trump's eponymous icon Trump Tower, on New York's Fifth Avenue, just three blocks away from where Chris, Fred, and I had met a month before the story hit the front page of every newspaper in the world. Chuck Blazer had moved the paltry CONCACAF (Confederation of North, Central American and Caribbean Association Football) headquarters from Nicaragua to Trump Tower and masterminded the election of his buddy Jack Warner

(from Trinidad and Tobago) to the head of the organization. Warner repaid the favor by making Chuck Blazer FIFA's general secretary. As the sponsorship and broadcasting deals rolled in, Chuck
Blazer started collecting 10 percent, earning him the nickname
"Mr. 10 Percent," and bought two apartments in Trump Tower:
one for him and his partner, one for his cats.[5]

When Jack Warner was forced out of FIFA in 2011 under accusations of "systemic corruption," the US tax authorities came
knocking on Mr. 10 Percent's door. Needless to say, the friendship
came to an abrupt end: in exchange for leniency, Chuck Blazer
became the asset of US investigators. During the London Olympics of 2012, Warner ensnared his buddies in a Mayfair hotel
room: the key fob he was carrying was an FBI-provided listening
device. The Justice Department got a lot more than it had ever
bargained for. Three years later, FIFA came undone.

DIRTY MONEY IN THE BEAUTIFUL GAME

Very few people, even in law enforcement, understand how huge
money laundering and corruption are in the sports world—much
less have an effective way to tackle it. The mechanisms of money
laundering in sport gambling and online betting are more akin to
high finance and hedge funds than they are to other forms of illicit
trade. The opportunities for ill-gotten lucre are vast, and transnational criminal organizations manipulate both sports competitions
and sports betting.

It is huge: the sports market—including teams, stadia, merchandise, and broadcasting rights—accounts for almost 2 percent
of gross global product (GGP). That is without the larger parallel
market of illegal sports betting. The majority of the value lies in
services (television broadcasting deals and sports betting), rather
than the physical goods of the teams, stadia, and merchandise.

The media are the primary source of funding for sports teams,
more so than investments by their wealthy owners. The owners

can then turn a profit in one of two ways: by trading promising amateurs they have trained and developed or, on the capital markets, by forming joint stock companies with tradable shares. "Following the money" is difficult for law enforcement, precisely because of the sophisticated manner in which value is generated in sport: the globalized markets of finance, consumption, ownership, broadcast rights, and sponsorship. No large football club has any national affiliation among these anymore.

The simplest form of sport corruption is sport manipulation, the corruption of players: inducing them to participate in a fixed game—to take a loss, make a bad kick, lob, or dunk. The manipulation of sports competition is defined by our OECD task force as "an arrangement, act or intentional omission aiming to improperly change the result or the progress of a sports competition in order to totally or partially remove the unpredictability of that competition for the unwarranted personal material gain of oneself or others."[6] This encompasses four types of cases, two related to sports bets and two not[7]:

1. A player or players purposely underperform, either to save their energy for a future game or to avoid facing a fiercer competitor.
2. A player or players accept pay to alter an outcome, such as a boxer who "takes a dive." This is corruption and covered by both criminal and disciplinary sanctions, though enforcement is lax.
3. A player loses voluntarily because he has bet on his defeat, but is not externally manipulated. This is internal fraud: difficult to sanction criminally (because it is not usually codified in law) and usually dealt with through disciplinary sanction.
4. A player loses voluntarily to allow someone else to win, when that someone has promised him an advantage or a payoff.

The fourth is the most egregious form of match-fixing: it incorporates corruption and is the preferred form for organized crime syndicates. It runs afoul of both criminal law and the disciplinary code of any sport. Instigated and/or controlled by external criminals and groups in order to secure an illegal profit, it is also the most common and the most threatening of the manipulations.

Europe is where the most cases of match-fixing have been discovered and prosecuted, likely because that is where the greatest value is and (ironically) where surveillance and judicial systems are more reliable. The most manipulated sport is the "beautiful game" of soccer (football to everyone outside the US). It is played on every continent and at all levels, so its popularity provides ample opportunity for betting, and a concomitant strong financial incentive for manipulation. The realities that players are temperamental and renowned for exaggerating injuries and that referees have a great deal of latitude without any instant replay to second-guess their decisions also help conceal bad calls, poor kicks, and faked injuries that can be used in a "fix."

Cricket is the second most manipulated game (particularly in Asia), but hanky-panky has also been uncovered in snooker (a form of billiards), basketball (particularly in the US), volleyball, wrestling, motor racing, boxing, badminton, and handball. However, true numbers, comparative or absolute, are hard to ascertain, as some federations have few surveillance or fraud detection resources, and leagues are multitudinous.

The sports betting market is so vast, liquid, and transnational, its bets have algorithms more complex than hedge funds. Chinese triads and many other criminal organizations launder money through sports betting, whether or not the game is fixed. Sports betting operators can themselves be owned by criminal organizations, and often evade taxes and regulations by operating transnationally out of jurisdictions that provide permissive environments, such as the unregulated Internet. The big money at play in sport betting provides the financial incentive for sport manipulation.

The enormous liquidity of the financial market around sports makes these illicit transactions extraordinarily difficult to spot. Some of the wilder (and perhaps more questionable) bets that paid off[8] include:

- That Frankie Dettori would ride the winning horse in seven races in a row
- That the Saint Louis Cardinals would win the 2011 World Series (the odds were 999–1)
- That Germany would beat Brazil in the 2014 World Cup, 7–1, *and* that Sami Khedira would score a goal. When the 2,319–1 odds prevailed, the $20 bet turned into a $46,000 win.
- That the New Orleans Saints would beat the Indianapolis Colts in the Super Bowl. Billy Walters, a man called so "notoriously lucky" Las Vegas bookmakers prefer not to take his bets, wagered $3.5 million—and won.

The multiplying complexity of the types of odds on which one may place a bet has transformed the market from one for amateurs to one for professional investors—as well as a preferred platform for money laundering. The 200- to 500-billion-euro transnational sport betting market is highly attractive to organized crime.[9] "A bettor in one country can access an online betting platform located in another country to bet on the results of sporting events taking place in a third country in real time."[10]

The final form of corruption in sport is corruption in the leagues, such as in the FIFA case. The league executives can take kickbacks to grant broadcasting rights or to grant a major sporting event to a particular host country: such is the allegation in FIFA's granting of the 2022 World Cup to Qatar. Evidence is showing that Qatar colluded with the Spain-Portugal bid to trade votes in the contest for the 2018 and 2022 finals. Qatar then bought the votes of other countries in various ways: it paid handsomely for a "friendly" match between Brazil and Argentina in Doha; it offered to relocate the headquarters of the Asian Football Confederation to Doha. The crux, though, is FIFA presidential candidate Mohamed Bin Hammam, a Qatari, and Amadou Diallo, a Guinean national accused in the British Parliament of facilitating bribes on behalf of Qatar's World Cup bid. They were close colleagues and collaborators for more than six years. Bin Hammam and Jack Warner are facing stiff disciplinary action for allegedly offering bribes to members of the Caribbean Football Union in exchange for votes in an upcoming election.[11]

THE LURE OF LUCRE

The International Center for Sport Security estimates that the global sports betting market is worth around $1.5 to 2 trillion. This is nearly equal to the World Bank's estimate of the gross domestic product of Russia, which was $2.1 trillion in 2013. In 2013, it was claimed that $15.5 billion a year was made by organized crime from fixing matches. This seems entirely reasonable when one realizes that up to $2 billion was being wagered per match in the 2014 FIFA World Cup. In the US, where sports betting is legal only in Nevada, the illegal market is the invisible part of the iceberg. About $100 million is bet legally on the NFL's Super Bowl; $3.8 billion is bet illegally. The illegal pool is thirty-eight times the size of the legal pool.[12]

Worldwide, most gambling havens are also tax havens: places where weak regulation and anonymity are not only prized but monetized assets. Panama is an example; so are many Caribbean islands, like Aruba and Curaçao and the Bahamas. From these tax and gambling havens, sporting bets operators offer their services via the Internet, without the required licenses. According to a joint study of the Sorbonne and the ICSS in 2012, "80 percent of today's global bets are illegal."[13] The winnings are transferred into bank accounts in well-regulated countries, and in that way illicit money is not only transferred, but laundered.

Up to US$140 billion (a full 10 percent of global revenues of organized crime) are laundered through sporting bets,[14] yet illegal betting is not usually an offense, much less a crime. So there is no risk and few deterrents to laundering vast sums of money this way. This is a win-win for both the client and the service provider. Money launderers are great clients for gambling operators because they agree to regularly lose a lot of money without jeopardizing the financial interests of the fixed-odds operators.

Large established, legal, and regulated betting establishments such as Las Vegas casinos, however, would have a reason to help law enforcement. In 2014, a Malaysian with a net worth of US$300 to 400 million, who was also a renowned high-stakes gambler, was arrested with his son and six others in Las Vegas's Caesars Palace hotel. They had asked casino personnel to set up a large amount of electronic equipment and began running a billion-dollar illegal gambling operation right from their residence in Caesars Palace. When the personnel recognized the similarity with the casino's sports books and betting odds for Web sites that were illegal in Nevada, they saved themselves from complicity by contacting the Gaming Control Board, which then launched an investigation in conjunction with undercover law enforcement. The ringleader was a high-ranking member of the Hong Kong–based 14K triad and owned IBCbet (one of the two online betting platforms he was using—the other was SBOBET), one of Asia's largest online gambling Web sites.[15]

Chris Eaton, the director of sport integrity at the ICSS (he was previously at Interpol and FIFA), says that all sports are manipulated, and that such corruption is "huge" in badminton.[16] The money mainly flows into and out of Asian organized crime syndicates. It is a $2 billion-a-week turnover for triad-controlled Asian bookmakers.

"It's as big as Coca-Cola. And it does not produce anything. It's just paper," says Eaton.[17]

Other estimates peg the value of Asian gambling on sports at $1 trillion per year, with 90 percent of it (a full $900 billion) being illegal, "wagered in the dark."[18] The trio of illegal online lotteries, betting, and gambling has been called the "Wild West"[19] of illicit finance. Nigeria, with broad swaths overrun by Boko Haram, is a case in point.

The Lottery Regulatory Commission is only concerned with the regulation of the operation and business of the national lottery of Nigeria. Nigeria has strict gambling laws, yet due to a lack of enforcement, hundreds of illegal online lotteries, betting and gambling schemes, slot machines, underground casinos, and football betting all operate freely, with lax regulation and no strong consumer advocacy groups to protect the individuals and families who lose money to dangerous criminals or terrorists. Neither the Economic and Financial Crime Commission (EFCC) nor the Nigeria Communications Commission (NCC) has the mandate to regulate the nearly 9,100 retail lottery terminals currently available in Lagos, Abuja, Port Harcourt, Aba, Benin City, Enugu, Ibadan, Onitsha, and other major cities.

The easiest games to manipulate are those that do not matter for advancement in professional leagues—i.e., the "friendlies." Criminal syndicates themselves can set up these matches in order to manipulate them. This scheme is effective and lucrative because of the dual willingness of bettors (who bring the cash liquidity) and the players. The players themselves don't much care whether they win or lose a friendly, as it does not impact team ranking, so they are happy to take the money the fixers offer them. The bettors, on the other hand, feel tremendous national pride in these national games of their country playing against another, and so wager a lot of money.[20]

In betting on national games, even if the match is just a

friendly, the bettor has to root for his or her country. For the bettor, it is a matter of national pride in a country-versus-country contest. The national supporters for each team place their bets, putting a lot of liquidity into the system, from which the criminals may draw their winnings—sometimes with dire consequences for the patriotic bettor, who is not in on the fix. Once again, the criminal entities profit from the manipulation of the emotions of an uninformed consumer: the sports fan.

When a young student placed his bet in the African Cup of Nations that Angola[21] would defeat Mali, the bet seemed a safe one: Angola was winning 4–0, with eleven minutes left in the game. He wagered his entire student loan funding of £4,400 on the outcome, and—against the odds—lost, as Mali made an incredible comeback over Angola. The kid lost it all. Such stunning against-the-odds-and-the-clock comebacks are just the sorts of events that spark the interest of sports integrity investigators.

Not only do bookmakers take bets on actual matches, they also take bets on "ghost matches"—matches that have not actually been played. Yet major legal bookmakers post odds and results and pay out winnings, while their onsite data operative reports confirm the match and the stats.[22] These operatives are the key to the ghost matches. With so many matches being played in so many places around the world at so many different levels, the lower-level games have scouts dispatched to them. They may be paid as little as $50 a game, and are easily bribable by some crime syndicate representative who wants their help in reporting the details of a match that never took place so that the syndicate can take bettors' money and/or launder its own. It could hardly be simpler, really.

CAN MATCH-FIXING BE FIXED?

Ultimately, though, money talks—specifically: the money of corporate sponsors. In early October 2015, Coca-Cola, Visa, McDonald's, and Anheuser-Busch InBev (AB InBev) grew tired of the tarnishing of their brands by being seen as patrons of corruption, and called for Sepp Blatter to step down[23]—particularly when the investigation turned to his own personal corruption. By early December 2015, Coca-Cola had penned an open letter to FIFA, urging it to embrace reforms and create an independent oversight committee, and posted the letter on its Web site.[24] Adidas, AB InBev, McDonald's, and Visa also signed it. In the end, though, everyone's outrage faded and the corporate sponsors went back to business as usual.

People's appetite for gambling, though, is not going to go away. Making it illegal does not work: it only makes the gambling "dark." One proposed solution is to make it more legal and regulated, and thus more transparent. As for league corruption and match-fixing, the solution lies with consumers—sports fans: they have to demand that their sport and their sporting heroes be returned to them. They must pressure the leagues to eliminate corrupt players and boycott corporate sponsors who fund crooked leagues.

Chris Howard explained the multifarious interests, from the top down in sports and sports betting, thus:

> Well, the government sees it two ways. It sees it as a piece that unifies a country—sport is a process of bringing people together. So it always wants to make sure . . . If football is the number one game in your country, you as a Prime Minister or President, you want to make sure that there is [sic] games being played, and people like a good outcome. So there are some people who use it in that way. Taxation, and also, kickbacks. There are some governments that use it for the sports betting market and the market has a way of funding. So, to some degree, it works for the government. And also, it's a protection thing: if you really don't want the police to look at it, you should just own the government,

and the government will say to the police: "Turn a blind eye." And in some cases, the government doesn't want to recognize this, because, I'll tell you what, the government says, uh, sitting around the table, what problem is this? You go to the prime minister and you say: is it a sport problem? Or is it a police problem? Or is it a gambling problem? Or is it a cyber-crime? Where did this money come from? Or is it the sporting federation? It is such a complex piece that people pull back.

NEW TEAM

In the summer of 2015, I had to clean house in my business. It was Chris who first realized that three of my key personnel were betraying me, by stealing corporate property and trying to steal clients. I acted swiftly and decisively.

"Can you take over running my intelligence operations?" I asked Chris, showing him some of the work we did. He perused some briefs containing personal identifying information of smugglers, routes, political facilitators, and their associated crimes.

"That's so hot, babe. You're so badass. It's so sexy."

I asked again. "Can you take over running my operations?"

"Absolutely. I can do it with my eyes closed. It's what I've been doing for twenty-five years."

"Great. You're hired."

"Get on the next flight to D.C.," advised Chris, "and cut them off at the pass."

That's exactly what I did, and my clients stayed with me. I then signed a new contract to map and disrupt a crime-terror pipeline from Eastern Europe through Iraq and Syria and into Turkey, where Chris's expertise in corruption and money laundering and competing tribalism would be invaluable. Unsurprisingly, even though we were working the problems of a different industry, some of the money was laundered through sports teams and gambling operations with which Chris was familiar. Now every time I see a Knicks game, I wonder how much dark money is flowing, and to whom, and whether the fan merchandise is real or counterfeit, and if it's funding some Islamist in Panama.

Trading in Sickness and Violence

MALARIA AND ISLAMISM

I carved gently into my *aller retour* steak—"come and go," for a steak whose two sides have touched a searing pan but is otherwise raw. In early September 2015, I was having lunch at La Grande Armée, in Paris's posh 8th arrondissement, with Jean-Luc Moreau, a former French spy from the DGSE (*Direction Générale de Securité Exterieure*, the French CIA), whose private sector transition was to head corporate security at pharmaceutical behemoth Novartis. Pharmaceutical companies hire a lot of spooks. It was during that lunch that Jean-Luc, a genteel roué whose rumpled expression tells you he has seen more than he cares to discuss, first told me about the Coartem case, where pharmaceuticals given to NGOs were diverted to fund corruption, criminality, and religious radicals thousands of miles from their intended recipients.

Coartem is an antimalarial drug that was supposed to be distributed free to the population of the endemic area in East Africa by the United Nations Global Fund to Fight AIDS, Tuberculosis and Malaria (aka the Global Fund). The Global Fund takes donated medicines from all the major pharmaceutical companies and sends them to countries that have a need and request them. In each country, there are local NGOs, clinics, et cetera—the "local implementing partners"—that distribute them to the local populations in towns and villages.

While at Novartis, Jean-Luc had noticed that the amount of malaria pills Novartis was giving to Tanzania as part of the Global Fund program far exceeded the market size: the incidence of malaria is low in Tanzania. He also knew that other big pharmaceuticals were giving the country free malaria pills. In all, Tanzania was getting from the Global Fund much more than it needed. He wondered what Tanzania could be doing with all those excess medicines.

He called the Global Fund and asked about its market assessments. It had not done any; it had simply responded to demands from the Tanzanian government.

Then some British journalists doing a story on West Africa came across blister packets of Coartem openly for sale in the huge outdoor market in Cotonou, Benin, not too far across the border from Touba, Senegal. Local police officers openly collected their "tax" from the street vendors and let them carry on with their illegal sales.

When the journalists contacted Novartis, seeking comment, Novartis obtained samples and checked the lot numbers. The lot numbers matched those distributed to Tanzania. Five thousand violent kilometers separate Cotonou, Benin, from Dar es Salaam, Tanzania. The batch numbers of some four hundred samples were collected in a subsequent on-the-ground operation, during which Novartis inspectors confirmed more disturbing facts: 73 percent were from East Africa, mainly Tanzania (51 percent), but they were also from Ethiopia, Kenya, and Malawi—these four countries' governments received forty-five million free treatments in 2009 alone. Statistically, 25 percent of the freely distributed medications—more than ten million treatments—have been methodically collected and diverted for sale in informal markets of West Africa, generating a profit of about $60 million.[1]

The charitable distribution chain of Coartem and other antimalarials is infested with transcontinental trafficking on a large scale. It can be assumed that this is the result of a sophisticated criminal organization, with high-level complicity and huge logistics. Novartis's own investigation led it back to Tanzania's capital, Dar es Salaam—specifically the warehouses of the Medical Stores Department of Tanzania's Ministry of Health. This confirmed the Tanzanian government was complicit in the systematic predation or misuse of 20 to 30 percent of international antimalarial donations. In other words, corruption was the key facilitator, as it is to all illicit trade. Novartis even identified a regional industrial group suspected of providing logistical cover to the traffickers.

Unfortunately, this was hardly the first scandal involving the Tanzanian government's misappropriation of aid. But when Novartis brought the case to the local Interpol commissioner, he replied that he could do nothing.

Jean-Luc Moreau asked him: "Why? Do you fear for your career?"

"No," answered the Interpol officer. "I fear for my life."[2]

The key node for this pan-African traffic in medical aid is the corruption of the regime of Senegalese president Abdoulaye Wade. Wade also leads the *Confrérie des Mourides* (the Mouride Brotherhood), a powerful Sufi Muslim organization headquartered in Touba, the site of the Great Mosque. The Mourides control a caliphate, ensuring both impunity for the smugglers and the spread of Sufi Islam. Aid for poor and sick Africans is partly funding a West African caliphate.

Corruption is the decisive factor in successfully injecting fake drugs in the health chain of a country. Very often in the most exposed regions, the institutional interlocutors such as Interpol liaison officers are themselves linked to organized crime—like the Mauritanian Interpol officer imprisoned for heading a cocaine trafficking ring.[3] The syndrome has been known since the Prohibition era in the US: in the Great Moonshine Conspiracy of Franklin County, Virginia, in the 1920s, the police became the protectors of the mobsters.

In Jean-Luc's view, investigating after a crime is too reactive and, in the vast majority of cases, ineffectual, as the fake drugs are undetectable. Combating the illicit trade in pharmaceuticals requires a more strategic approach. To effectively disrupt or dismantle transnational networks that bridge at least two governments, one criminal organization, and one Islamic resistance group, a two-pronged approach is required. First, greater strategic and operational intelligence has to be collected. Second, pharmaceutical manufacturing firms and big NGOs and their implementing partners need to design a proactive risk-management system to better protect patients.[4]

As of the end of 2015, the UN's Global Fund had disbursed $33 billion in aid to governments and other local implementing partners[5]—all without any due diligence of the local distributor of the medical supplies. Sadly, it has been accepted that corruption is a part of the system of these governments.

"As long as at least some of the help gets to the people who need it" is what one of them said to me as I sat in the Global Fund's Geneva office, after the 2015 Easter week meeting of our OECD task force. I had taken the train from Paris to Geneva to see my friend Katie Silk, a former agent for MI-5 (the British equivalent of the FBI), who had done hard counterterrorism work in Iraq and Afghanistan before going to work for Jean-Luc at Novartis. When he left Novartis, so did she, and went to run investigations at the Global Fund. Katie's task: to institute an effective due diligence program for the group's inspector general.

"They don't get it," said Katie when I arrived at the Global Fund offices to catch up with her. "Humanitarians just want to disburse aid. They don't understand how it can fund bad guys. But they're starting to."

The issue is not new; it has been raised by a number of credible voices. Zambian economist Dambisa Moyo has been railing against the scourges of foreign aid in Africa since 2009; renowned anticorruption activist Sarah Chayes (who lived and worked in Afghanistan for years) argues that aid from well-meaning NGOs is simply another revenue stream for kleptocratic ruling networks.[6]

It is not surprising, then, that aid can end up fomenting the corruption and instability that caused the problems that afflict the populations that the aid workers are there to help. Not only does it fuel the corruption that justifies extremism in a citizenry who want to overthrow a corrupt and oppressive regime, but it also fuels the paternalism that keeps the criminally corrupt in power: it keeps the people suckling at the teat of that oppressive regime, by making them beg for handouts and promise fealty in order to get their food or medicine. In other words, the lack of due diligence in foreign aid engenders corruption that funds the violence that prompted the need for foreign aid in the first place: and, thus, a never-ending cycle of violence, bad governance, poverty, and dependency ensue.

PHARMA'S GRAY MARKETS

The Coartem case is a vivid example of supply chain diversion: real product (these were real medications) gets sent to the right person, but gets diverted. The Tanzanian government purposely got an oversupply and diverted what it got through criminal organizations, funding another regime with extremist religious views. That happens with many goods, and it is what we call the "gray market"—neither white (entirely legitimate) nor black (completely illegal). It starts out legal, and becomes illegal on its way to distribution. Those gray markets are in addition to the all-black markets of counterfeiting.

The illicit trade in each industry is slightly different, but knowingly making fake medications is a nearly perfect crime. If someone sick takes a falsified medication and recovers, there is no investigation. If a sick patient dies, the underlying illness gets blamed. And die they do: the World Trade Organization has estimated that counterfeit antimalarial drugs kill a hundred thousand Africans annually, while seven hundred thousand deaths a year have been attributed to counterfeit drugs across the board. The number of individuals whose health has been jeopardized because they took a counterfeit drug could well be in the millions. This huge problem is growing.

In the 2015 OECD publication *Illicit Trade*, the World Customs Organization estimates counterfeit medicines to be a $200 billion-a-year industry.[7] The World Health Organization (WHO) estimates that 10 percent of medications sold are falsified; the figure can be as high as 50 percent in certain developing countries and on the Internet. That 10 percent represents around $75 billion a year, which is roughly equivalent to the traffic in heroin.[8] China is the largest producer, and the United Arab Emirates (particularly Dubai) the biggest transshipment point. But the problem is everywhere, from sub-Saharan Africa to the United States, where the Food and Drug Administration, arguably the world's most draconian drug regulator, reported an 800 percent rise in counterfeit medicines in the years between 2000 and 2006.[9]

The definition of counterfeit medicines is just the first of many complications in the topology of the illicit pharmaceutical trade. Some countries do not have a definition; many have different definitions; some countries define it but do not criminalize pharmaceutical counterfeiting. The most standard definition since the 1990s is that of WHO: "A counterfeit medicine is one which is deliberately and fraudulently mislabeled with respect to identity and/or source. Counterfeiting can apply to both branded and generic products and counterfeit products may include products with the correct ingredients or with the wrong ingredients, without active ingredients, with insufficient active ingredients or with fake packaging."[10] The critical aspect of the definition is the intention to deceive, to commit a crime: "mens rea," in legal parlance. Unwitting sale or distribution of illicit medications is not criminalized.

Based on confidential counterfeiting reports received between January 1999 and October 2000, the World Health Organization grouped the counterfeits into six categories:[11]

- Products without active ingredients (32.1 percent)
- Products with incorrect quantities of active ingredients (20.2 percent)
- Products with wrong ingredients (21.4 percent)
- Products with correct quantities of active ingredients but with fake packaging (15.6 percent)
- Copies of an original product (1 percent)
- Products with high levels of impurities and contaminants (8.5 percent)

The term "falsified" medicines has come into common usage in discussing this trade to separate its discussion from anything to do with the intellectual property debate surrounding "branded"-versus-"generic" medications, as well as to separate the deliberately falsified from the "substandard." Falsified medications are deliberately fraudulently produced; substandard medicines are legitimately produced by the authorized manufacturer, but "do not meet national pharmacopeial standards because of errors in the quality or quantity of raw materials or in manufacturing."[12] The former is a deliberate criminal attempt to deceive; the latter results from poor quality control. Since their origins are different, so are their solutions.

According to the Pharmaceutical Security Institute, in 2012 counterfeiting incidents rose 2.2 percent over the prior year to 1,664 new counterfeiting incidents reported, involving 207 different pharmaceutical products, which impacted the legitimate supply chain in forty-seven separate countries. With or without mens rea, the results of counterfeit medicines infiltrating the legitimate supply chain and being administered by health authorities can be disastrous:[13]

- 1990, Haiti: a cough suppressant mixed with a toxic solvent killed eighty-nine people
- 1995, Niger: counterfeit meningitis vaccines administered to fifty thousand people by health authorities during an epidemic killed twenty-five hundred of them
- 2009, Nigeria: fake pediatric paracetamol syrup killed eighty-four children
- 2016, China: a scandal involving corrupted measles, mumps, and rubella (MMR) and meningococcal disease vaccines sold to three hundred distributors is labeled a "genocide" by the Chinese people

As per capita GDP rises, so does the use of higher-quality medications, but then, that also opens the branding path for counterfeits. In wealthier countries, the Internet makes their consumption much easier: thirty-six million Americans are estimated to have bought medications online without a valid prescription.[14] In the US—as everywhere—the problem is spread in both the very-expensive-but-particular markets (like when counterfeits of Roche's Avastin cancer drug were found in the US health care system in February 2012) and in the more popular markets (like counterfeits of the diet drug Alli or Botox,[15] which were made in concentrations far too high, putting people at risk of paralysis and death). "Somewhere around $10,000 GDP per capita, substandard drugs become less significant than counterfeits."[16] A broad cross-section of Novartis medicines, for instance, has been counterfeited, including: Glivec (cancer), Exelon (Alzheimer's), Diovan (high blood pressure), Neoral (immunosuppressant for organ transplants), Zometa (bone cancer), Femara (breast cancer), Optalidon (pain), and Coartem (malaria).[17]

Like other cases of illicit trade, the transnational trade in illicit falsified medications is a global business that encompasses multiple players, that is facilitated by corruption, and that has a business model that mimics that of the legitimate manufacturers.[18] The illegitimate manufacturer will use machines similar to his legitimate counterpart's to produce similar pills and similar packaging, with ingredients that may be completely false, or authentic but inadequate, contaminated, or degraded. The illegitimate marketing division often infiltrates the supply chain by managing the covert distribution to trick inspectors, wholesalers, and downstream retailers. Sophisticated bookkeepers will launder the illicit financial gains.

HOW TO EXPLOIT SUPPLY CHAIN GAPS: THE CASE OF RXNORTH

The RxNorth.com case is a prime example of how illicit pharmaceutical traders purposely make the supply and distribution chains much longer and more complicated than normal business interests would require they be, in order to conceal actors and complicate enforcement. Jean-Luc described the process of illicit distribution (and the challenges it poses for law enforcement) vividly in his congressional testimony.[19]

In May 2006, Customs officers at London Heathrow Airport in the United Kingdom seized a shipment from Dubai, en-route to the Bahamas which contained several thousand packs of eight confirmed counterfeit pharmaceutical products from seven companies, including more than 3000 packets of a counterfeit Novartis medicine for hypertension.

The counterfeit products had been manufactured in China, transported by road to Hong Kong, flown to Dubai where they were stored in a duty free warehouse before being shipped to the Bahamas via the UK. Based on information provided by the pharmaceutical industry, local authorities in the Bahamas executed a search warrant at the destination address where additional counterfeit drugs were seized, including more of the counterfeit Novartis hypertension drug as well as a fake Novartis treatment for Alzheimer's.

The counterfeiting facility in the Bahamas was a fulfillment center established by RxNorth, an Internet drug Web site. The facility processed orders placed on the Internet by American and Canadian patients and shipped pre-addressed orders for RxNorth to mail forwarders based in the UK and the Netherlands Antilles. The products were then shipped from the UK or Netherlands Antilles direct to individual customers in the United States and Canada. These routes were used in order to reduce suspicion and avoid Customs inspections.

In August 2006, the Food and Drug Administration issued a warning to consumers not to buy or use prescription drugs from certain Web sites, including Rx North. In September 2006, RxNorth.com informed prospective customers that responsibility for order fulfillment would be transferred to Canadadrugs .com. Canadadrugs.com had previously been implicated in incidents of counterfeit pharmaceutical products and later became the center of another international counterfeit drug scandal, mainly affecting U.S. patients.

Following investigations in all of the countries impacted by Rx North, a Dubai-based trading company general manager and three co-defendants were convicted in the United Arab Emirates and imprisoned for terms ranging from one to eight years. Two men in the UK were also prosecuted and convicted for their roles in the RxNorth operation. Andrew Strempler, a Canadian citizen, pleaded guilty in the Southern District of Florida for his role in a scheme to defraud consumers purchasing pharmaceuticals online through his ownership of RxNorth. In January 2013, he was sentenced to 4 years in prison and also ordered to pay a forfeiture of $300,000 and a fine of $25,000. He was also ordered to pay restitution to the companies whose products he counterfeited.

As in almost all forms of illicit trade, pharmaceutical counterfeiting and supply diversion is also facilitated by diaspora networks, which provide access to shipping and distribution. An established African Bakongo diaspora in Guangzhou, China, arranges the manufacture of the drugs with local facilities as well as the shipping for the fake medicines under covering loads to Africa through a complex structure of export and import companies with associated sister companies in recipient countries in Africa. The associated tribal networks in Africa ensure the passage of counterfeit product upon arrival and distribution to illicit street retailers.[20]

"A CRIME AGAINST HUMANITY"

The main policy objective of pharmaceutical companies has now become the implementation of effective transnational legislation. Roger Bate (a scholar on the illicit trade in pharmaceuticals) illustrates why such international legislation is needed. For simplicity's sake, let's turn it into an illustrative fictional example.

If a counterfeiter from country A (call it "Albania") produces and exports fake drugs to country B (call it "Burma"), normally only Albania has the authority to prosecute the criminal, because that criminal act occurred in its territory. Even if lots of people die in Burma as a result of taking the fake medicines, Burma, the recipient country and home of the victims, likely has little criminal jurisdiction over acts ancillary to the counterfeiting, such as fraud or smuggling. Not only are fraud and smuggling not the same crime as counterfeiting, it is nearly certain that the smuggling and the fraudulent sales were not committed by the same person or group of persons as the counterfeited manufacturing, and these crimes likely do not carry an appropriate penalty. Without an international agreement to treat medicine counterfeiting as a serious crime, the courts and police of the two countries will likely not cooperate. As a result, medicine counterfeiters have practical immunity.[21]

Extradition treaties are not good enough either: they often have a double (or dual) criminality stipulation.[22] This requires that if someone is to be extradited from country B (Burma, in our fictional example) back to country A (Albania), Burma must agree to the extradition. National laws in Burma are required to criminalize the act in question in a similar manner; that is how such mutual extradition obligations are established between states. It is premised on the legal maxim *nulla poena sine lege,* or "no punishment without law." In short, for a person to be extradited, the deed for which he or she is wanted must be a crime in both the country that is harboring him or her and the country that is petitioning for extradition—in our example, it must be a crime in the legal code of both Albania and Burma.

Many countries do not even recognize pharmaceutical counterfeiting as a crime; different jurisdictions probably have different motivations (including lack of investigative or prosecutorial capacity), but one factor is that pharmaceutical counterfeiting is viewed—like all counterfeiting—as a crime of intellectual property, where the people most being hurt (except in some exceptional cases) are major pharmaceutical companies that want to profit at the expense of the poor. As the demand for cheap medications prevails over the enforcement of intellectual property rights, there is not much of a will to draft the requisite legal framework. Criminals can therefore effectively hide in different jurisdictions.

Just as the fight against the illicit trade in tobacco products gets hijacked by arguments about tobacco control, the fight against the illicit trade in pharmaceuticals gets hijacked by arguments about access to cheap medications. The only universally adopted rules applicable to illicit trade are those of the World Trade Organization, but when pharmaceutical companies invoke international trade rules to dismantle the cross-border operations of drug counterfeiters, their efforts are met with suspicion, especially by Brazil and India, which accuse the companies of using intellectual property statutes to limit sales of Indian generic drugs.[23]

As is often the case, the truth lies somewhere in the middle: yes, the intellectual property rights holders ("Big Pharma") use international trade rules to eliminate competition from cheaper brands; yes, criminals also exploit the gaps in these rules to make money, too. After all, illicit trade is trade; the business might be criminal, but it is still business, and the money doesn't care who owns it.

"Falsified medicine producers" are astute enough at business to take advantage of the gaps and arbitrage opportunities that the regulatory, trade, and enforcement structures present. There are many gaps through which criminals, counterfeiters, or falsified medicine producers and their cohorts can profit. Many countries have lax regulation of their drug manufacturing and distribution networks. Where there are laws, they are poorly enforced by investigators and/or the punishments are weak. Exporting countries have weak regulation, and it is downright minimal in free trade zones. Pharmaceutical companies (like every other industry) have long complained that free trade zones repackage and transship illicit goods with impunity.[24] Complex transactions involving many intermediaries complicate investigations, as does inefficient cooperation among stakeholders. This entire illicit trade in medicines is driven by the high demand and prices for (genuine) curative and preventive drugs and vaccines: if there weren't money in the legitimate market, there would be no money in the criminal market either.

Pharmaceutical expert Roger Bate uses the terms "widespread" and "systematic" in describing the trade in falsified medicines in his push to get it criminalized in international law as a "crime against humanity." Because falsified medications can kill either directly by virtue of their toxic contents or indirectly by not treating sick patients properly, their trade can approximate the "extermination" crime against humanity, which is defined as: "the intentional infliction of conditions of life, *inter alia* the deprivation of access to food and medicine, calculated to bring about the destruction of part of a population."[25]

While the mens rea may not rise to the intentional extermination of a portion of the population, there is an interpretation where commercializing a product with willful disregard to the fact that it will cause significant harm or kill on a large scale can fall into the legal definition of *hostis humani generis*—"enemy of humankind." The term was first used with regard to pirates at sea. In the modern era, it has been applied to terrorists, slave traders, and torturers.[26] However, the underpinning reason it was applied to pirates at sea (and now to terrorists) is because at sea the victim was not on terra firma and so was at a significant disadvantage, with limited resources and no escape route. This would certainly seem to apply to the sick—whether or not they are poor—taking a medication they need to cure or manage their illness: they have little choice, and therefore no reasonable escape from the counterfeited products.

One good option for such an international legislative framework, because of its global reach, is the World Health Organization's IMPACT (International Medical Products Anti-Counterfeiting Task Force), which encompasses NGOs, pharmaceutical manufacturers, enforcement agencies, and regulatory authorities. IMPACT has designed model legislation for countries that have not yet enacted effective laws. Barring such international legislation, the World Health Organization could formulate a treaty like its Framework Convention on Tobacco Control. Another option would be a process led by the UN Office on Drugs and Crime. For any option to work, though, effective rule of law needs to be implemented, and corruption eradicated. As we have seen, that is not so easy.

There is one international framework convention that criminalizes the counterfeiting of medical products as a human rights violation: the Medicrime Convention. According to the Council of Europe, medical counterfeiting and its related crimes violate the right to life enshrined in the European Convention on Human Rights and Fundamental Freedoms, partly by significantly undermining public trust in health systems and their supervisors. The

Medicrime Convention provides a framework for international cooperation and introduces criminal sanctions and measures of prevention and protection of victims. Unfortunately, as of July 2016, only twelve states (less than half the EU) had signed the convention. Critically, the UK, with its huge National Health Service, is not a signatory, while Israel, Russia, and Ukraine are.

ILLICIT EXCHANGES

The problem of smuggled consumer goods funding Islamist causes in Africa is not limited to pharmaceuticals. In late July 2016, Chris Howard was in Mogadishu, Somalia, best known to the public for its pirates. Locals informed him that cigarettes of all brands were coming in and being sold in a market five hundred meters from the port. In another area of the market: AK-47s—Kalashnikov Russian assault rifles that because of their near-indestructibility and ubiquity remain a favorite of insurgents, terrorists, and guerrilla fighters the world over. The Somali Islamist group Al Shabaab sells smuggled cigarettes and uses the money to buy AK-47s. A carton of cigarettes sells for $4.

There are warehouses full of them, and they appear to be legitimate product, made by Philip Morris International and British American Tobacco. They seem to be major-brand "illicit whites," smuggled into the country using criminal networks. The manufacturers claim their cigarettes are diverted from wholesalers, to whom the manufacturers legally sell after applying proper know-your-customer due diligence, as they are required to do by various laws and regulations. Their argument (which some people believe and others do not) is that they know their customers (the wholesalers), but they do not know the wholesalers' customers.

In the open-air markets of Mogadishu, rocket-propelled grenade (RPG) launchers and assault rifles like AK-47s or the American military–preferred M-16 or M-4 can be bought as easily as fruit.[27]

WEAPON	MOGADISHU MARKET PRICE	CIGARETTE EQUIVALENT
AK-47	$400	100 cartons
M-16 / M-4	$200	50 cartons
Rocket-propelled grenade (RPG) launchers	$150	37.5 cartons

These are the Mogadishu exchange rates between illicit cigarettes and weapons: how many illicit white cigarettes it takes to buy each weapon.

In one of his tours in Iraq, Chris had seen how cartons of cigarettes are transported alongside—and swapped for—suicide vests. He was in Mogadishu, Somalia, on July 26 and 27, 2016, when a suicide bomber detonated his vest and a car bomb in near-synchronicity around the Mogadishu airport. We wondered how many smuggled Marlboros those bombs had cost. More important, we wondered how many people were killed per smuggled carton of cigarettes. Smoking kills in more ways than it says on the package.

After the bombings, a few people traced the shipments of the cigarettes to their source: Dubai, United Arab Emirates. The United Arab Emirates is home to dozens of very large and important free trade zones; of these, the Jebel Ali Free Zone Area (JAFZA) stands out as a key transshipment and manufacturing point for many illicit products, including tobacco. Over ninety companies (including nine manufacturers) are licensed to trade in tobacco products in JAFZA, and many of these produce illicit whites,[28] unknown cigarette brands (not counterfeits) that are produced in order to be smuggled without paying taxes or duties, using criminal networks. Fifty-seven percent of the shipments of illicit tobacco that transited through Egypt's Port Said Free Zone to Libya during the height of Libya's unrest originated in Dubai's JAFZA.[29]

The lack of transparency in free trade zones is both a consequence and a cause of corruption. In most countries, counterfeit goods cannot be stopped if they are "in transit," so that designation is often applied to bills of lading, even when it is not true. A January 2012 case from Jebel Ali highlights this: when brand owners advised the Intellectual Property Department of Dubai Customs that sixteen containers of illicit goods were on their way to Jebel Ali Free Zone from China and asked the authorities to intervene, the Dubai director general's legal adviser said that he had released the eight containers they had detained, because the goods were designated for reexport to Iraq and had thus been released as "ship to ship," outbound to Iraq. (Ship-to-ship transfers occur between ships positioned alongside each other, so the cargo never touches land at a port.)

Public container tracking Web sites, however, "indicated that the containers did not go 'ship to ship' at all but were emptied at JAFZA."[30] After that the paperwork disappeared, and so no one knows what really went into those containers or whether they really went to Iraq or who their final recipients were.

The illicit trade in Chris Howard's Mogadishu case is entering through the port of Berbera in Somaliland (the northernmost of Somalia's three regions), which Dubai bought into for a $442 million investment in June 2016, turning it into the main entry point for shipments from the United Arab Emirates into the Horn of Africa. (The semiautonomous region of Somaliland signed a deal with the Dubai Customs World operator to boost trade through its Berbera port amid congestion at a facility in neighboring Djibouti,[31] which the Chinese had won the bid to run.)

The press release of Berbera's deal with the Dubai Customs World operator was nothing short of exuberant: "'The mayor of Berbera welcomes this agreement with Dubai World with joy and hope that this investment will have an effect and bring about many changes in terms of infrastructure and economic (growth) for the port of Berbera . . . Dubai Ports World is expected to pay

$5 million a year plus 10 percent on port revenue to Somaliland."[32] Presumably, a good portion of that money is going into the pockets of corrupt Somali officials. Somalia was seen as the most corrupt country on earth in 2016.[33]

Illicit trade isn't deadly just for the patients who take falsified medicines and for the victims of the suicide bombers who buy their vests with smuggled goods; it can also be deadly for us, working in the field. In the summer of 2016, Chris had to go into hiding for nearly a month at a safe house when one of our sources told him there was a price on his head: his name had been given to a serious organized crime group he was looking into and it had given orders to have him killed.

Not only was I worried, I was furious. Fortunately, our sources had not been blown; no one had been caught. The fact that this group had only Chris's name meant that the traitor only had Chris's name to give. It meant the traitor was someone we dealt with in the corporate structure of one of our clients. (Some clients insist on knowing everything about our sources, but we withhold detailed information specifically because of this type of scenario.)

We had a prime suspect, whose behavior we found telling during our briefings about our work. He was uncooperative and aggressive at the wrong time and for the wrong reason, as if he were not on the same side as us. Everyone at Asymmetrica, even the bookkeeper, had the same name on their lips. It was also on the lips of two of his coworkers when I mentioned my concerns to them in London.

"You take that personally?" said his boss at a meeting a few weeks later, in Washington, D.C., playing it a little too cool for my taste. The employee had been transferred to a rather less savory point on the map, away from headquarters, rather abruptly. So the company must have had its own suspicions that he was in cahoots with the enemy.

"Yes, I do. Such risk is part of our job, but would it be okay with you if we ordered a hit on your wife? Would you renew our contract?"

Silence. That's what I thought. As a businesswoman, I waited to see if the company would offer to pay us a bonus, to compensate for the trouble it had cost us. When it did not, I severed all ties and moved on; with every industry afflicted by illicit trade, nearly every major company is a potential client.

Meanwhile, Jean-Luc Moreau left Novartis and took his super-spy skills to Chanel, where he is helping the company fix its counterfeiting problems. Whether you buy medicines from the Internet, handbags off the street, or cheap cigarettes at your local bodega, there is always a gang of bad guys at the end to catch—and that is now a business all its own.

It's All About the Benjamins

Money doesn't care who owns it, and everybody wants money. Making money illegally is usually easier than making it legally: no regulations, no taxes, no labor unions. But criminal enterprises do face a lot of risk and (like any business) respond to market pressures. In order to disrupt and lessen illicit trade, we have to understand it as it is: criminal enterprises are profit-driven businesses. Understanding the business model will help us design strategies to stem the funding of criminal and terrorist networks.

What keeps illicit trade large, transnational, and profitable is corruption. Quite simply, fighting illicit trade will not be effective unless we fight corruption, too. Corruption not only enables illicit trade, it traps citizens by subverting the rule of law and corroding state institutions: government officials become more beholden to criminals than to their citizens. The state becomes criminalized, and the criminals take over the state infrastructure to serve themselves, particularly to move goods and money without hindrance.

State criminalization, then, benefits terrorists in two ways. First, terrorists make more money and operate more easily. Second, corruption gives terrorists an excellent recruitment pool: when citizens feel oppressed by a corrupt system that is aligned against them, they are more likely to become extremists and take up arms to overthrow the government and its perceived allies. Furthermore, the illicit money from corruption and criminal profit is usually moved to jurisdictions with banking secrecy, where it can easily be transferred to terrorist operatives or weapons traffickers, threatening our security. The Panama Papers revealed the enormity of the shadow world of corruption, secret finance, and other illicit financial flows. Hidden in the 11.5 million documents pertaining to the Panamanian law firm Mossack Fonseca were 140 politicians (heads of state, ministers, and other elected officials and their associates) with offshore companies in twenty-one tax havens.[1]

Some policy experts consider capital flight (money leaving a country to find a safer haven) a more dangerous aspect of corruption than the corrupt act itself. When money leaves the country, transportation, communications, and even food distribution systems collapse and national poverty accelerates into high gear, disproportionately impacting those at the bottom of the economic scale, the most desperate. However, the jurisdictions where the money gets laundered see multiple effects, not all of them bad. Businesses whose primary purpose is to launder money regularly outcompete clean businesses, driving them from the market and thereby distorting the economy.

On the other hand, money laundering is excellent for banks and real estate values, but that puts pressure on housing for working families. Miami is an example of a city built on the laundering of drug money. In the 1970s and 1980s, Miami was the main entry point for South American cocaine into the US. Cocaine was so plentiful that local residents joked that the white lines on the Miami Dolphins football field were painted with cocaine.

With the narcotics also flowed a brutal crime wave that lasted into the early 1990s and a whole lot of money that was laundered through front organizations and put into upscale nightclubs, commercial and residential real estate development, luxury car dealerships, and hotels. The Southeast Financial Center is the tallest skyscraper built during the 1980s construction boom, during which time most of the heart of the city's financial center was constructed. The classic drug money laundering paradigm is to bring a suitcase full of cash in small denominations, like $20 bills. The US Treasury at the time calculated that a suitcase stuffed with $20 bills could hold half a million dollars, yet many millions were being deposited every day. There were obviously a lot of suitcases. The money quickly muddied the US economy: in 1978 and 1979, the *entire* currency surplus of the United States could be ascribed to Miami-area banks.[2] The show *Miami Vice*, with its Ferrari Testarossa–driving undercover counternarcotics agents, glamorized the Miami drug wars for the world.

"Following the money" leads you to the convergence between criminal groups and terrorist organizations. The convergence touches our everyday lives.

PROFITABLE BUSINESS

Although the Mexican cartels have gotten a lot of media play these past few years (because of their brutality), Mexico's supply of drugs into the US is nothing new. The country was a source of marijuana and heroin in the early twentieth century, particularly from the Sinaloa region. By the 1940s Mexican drug smugglers had become notorious in the US.[3] Now, three-quarters of a century later, the Sinaloa cartel controls 40 to 60 percent of Mexico's drug trade, earns about $3 billion a year, controls crime in at least five Mexican states (Baja California, Sonora, and the "Golden Triangle" of Sinaloa, Durango, and Chihuahua), and distributes to fifty countries.[4] Cellular telephone SIM cards from Michoacán have been found in Singapore,[5] highlighting the cartels' criminal reach. Drug trafficking is a resilient business.

In order to effectively counter drug trafficking and all other forms of illicit trade—and understand where criminal networks might move next—we must understand the business drivers and develop strategies that address them. The corruption and payoffs and transportation expenses in a high-risk illicit trade like drug trafficking add significant costs at every border crossing between point of production and point of sale. A study done by the London School of Economics Expert Group on the Economics of Drug Policy compared the economics of narcotics with those of other commodities from the same region. Per unit of measurement (troy ounce for silver, pound for coffee, and gram for narcotics), from source country to single-serving retail to the end consumer (not wholesale or bulk retail), silver has a 9 percent markup; coffee, 635 percent; cannabis resin, 1,047 percent; heroin, 3,745 percent; and cocaine, 6,427 percent.[6]

In 1996, drug trafficking organizations employed 730,000 people—more than the Mexican state-owned oil company, Pemex. In 2000, despite the fact that business was booming, that number dropped to 364,000, due to better plant genetics that required less manpower per square meter of production.[7] Plus, after 9/11 border security tightened, causing domestic consumption to increase: the cartels had to create a new market for their product on their side of the border, and pushed to increase domestic consumption and distribution.

Diversification can be viewed as a sign of organizational strength and growth: once you have the pipelines, the connections, and the territorial control, you expand (as many large businesses do) into additional revenue streams. On the other hand, diversification can be viewed as a sign of desperation, because drug profits are being hampered by interdiction or changes in drug consumption patterns, including the growing legalization of marijuana.[8] Famed Mexican journalist Carlos Loret de Mola said at a talk at the Americas Society in New York on November 23, 2015, that his guide through the Sinaloa cartel had told him that the worst thing that could happen to the cartels is the legalization of drugs.

Under the administration of President Felipe Calderón (2006–12), the Mexican cartels' finances changed. First, the cartel monopolies extended down through local groups that had previously been independent, in what might be considered a brilliant success in branding. Second, they expanded into other illicit trades, including kidnapping, extortion, and human smuggling. Third, they expanded beyond marijuana and cocaine into other drugs that were gaining popularity in the US, such as heroin and methamphetamine. Mexico's Gulf cartel, under Mario Cárdenas Guillén—*"El Gordo"*—was the biggest importer of heroin into the United States. The major changes since 2012 (the expansion of designer drugs and human smuggling) have been in reaction to the threat of marijuana legalization in the US.

According to the journalist Don Winslow, who has been covering the US War on Drugs from the front lines for over twenty years (he even knew the Sinaloa cartel boss, *El Chapo* Guzmán, when he was just a cartel errand boy), the partial legalization of marijuana eroded cartel profits, so they had to diversify into heroin. Seeing that America was getting hooked on prescription opioids like OxyContin and Percocet, they saw a market opportunity to expand into heroin.

The Sinaloa cartel went into direct competition with the pharmaceutical companies: Mexican heroin production increased by almost 70 percent and the cartel imported Colombian cooks to create "cinnamon" heroin (also known as "Dark Horse") to compete with the product coming into markets dominated by the Asians. According to a former agent, the Drug Enforcement Administration knows cinnamon heroin as an "intermediate" product that enabled the transition from black and brown to Colombian white heroin, and there are only a couple of markets with really high purity levels (greater than 75 percent); in most markets purity runs 40 to 60 percent.

The Mexicans have adopted Colombian processing techniques to create their own white heroin from homegrown resources. Asian or Afghan heroin is not really a player in the overall US market; it is a more significant player in Europe. Addicts are steadfast about their heroin: they like what they like. Much like Diet Coke versus Diet Pepsi, there are not many converts to the other brand. In heroin's case, the loyalty is to color, not source. So even if consumption patterns stay the same, supply chains may not.

Then the Mexican cartels made another classic move of market economics: they dropped the price. A kilo of heroin cost $200,000 in New York City around the start of the decade; in 2013 it cost $80,000, and by 2016 it had dropped to around $50,000. More of a better product for less money translated into greater market share.[9] No wonder America is in the grip of an opioid and heroin epidemic: the transition makes perfect sense from the point of view of the consumer, in this case the addict. Pharmaceutical companies aggressively seek market share by pushing their opioid painkillers on patients via their doctors. Patients like them and get hooked. Then they realize that for a bit more money, they can get a much better high, so they move to heroin. In short, as cartels lose US market in marijuana (due to increasing legalization) and cocaine (because of its falling out of favor), the pharmaceutical companies are acting as entry points for the cartels' share in the heroin market.

According to Loret, there are two basic business models for Mexican drug trafficking organizations, each with a different risk profile. The model of the Sinaloa cartel under *El Chapo* Guzmán is limited to drugs, so the local population not only did not mind *El Chapo*'s drug trafficking activities, but actually viewed him as a Robin Hood hero, as Pablo Escobar was in his heyday. The Sinaloa cartel, for instance, is renowned for its brutal violence and its corruption of government officials, but it has largely stayed away from the "extractive" crimes of kidnapping and extortion, focusing instead on maintaining its majority control of the drug business and keeping a low profile otherwise. This helps the Sinaloa cartel garner the support of local populations,[10] who are content to allow the drug business to flourish as long as they are not subject to violence or victimization by kidnappings and extortions.

The other model is that of the Knights Templar under Servando Gómez, known as *"La Tuta,"* which took over all economic activity in its territory, controlling peasant farmers, governors, and the port of Lázaro Cárdenas. Mexico provides 50 percent of the global supply of avocados.[11] The Knights Templar cartel also extorts avocado and lime growers in Michoacán, reaping 13 percent of the farmers' profits. *La Tuta*'s predilection for giving press interviews raised the cartel's visibility, making it more of a target for government intervention, while its move into the illicit trade in avocados and lemons, and illegal mining, means that the locals it "taxes" find them oppressive. This made them less protective of *La Tuta* (who was captured in February 2015 and has none of the Robin Hood aura of Pablo Escobar or *El Chapo*) and less supportive of the cartel's activities.

The Mexican cartels rose by adapting from the disruption of the Colombian cartels: an unintended second-order effect of well-meaning interdiction efforts. The White Triangle of cocaine is comprised of Colombia, Bolivia, and Peru, the world's primary producers of the drug. In the 1990s, US military and law enforcement (US Southern Command and DEA, primarily) began shutting down the direct land and sea routes from the White Triangle to the US, particularly those that traversed the Caribbean. In response, smuggling networks shifted to overland routes through Central America into Mexico and onward into the US. Estimates are that now 60 and 90 percent of the illegal cocaine entering the United States travels through Central America and Mexico.[12]

As the powerful Colombian cartels were forcibly broken up by the violent and multipronged actions of the US-backed Plan Colombia, the Mexicans gradually took over the profitable cocaine traffic into the United States. Greater interdiction of the trans-Caribbean routes used by the Colombians and other Andean producers forced them to shift their routes into Central America through to Mexico. Initially subcontractors who were paid in cocaine rather than cash, the Central Americans and Mexicans evolved from couriers to traffickers for themselves. To convert the narcotics to cash, they had to find new buyers and distribution channels and to encourage local consumption. That meant creating new points of sale and fighting each other for points of sale that had been dominated by others. Both of these factors translated into a spike in violence.

As their dominance increased and they started controlling distribution into the US, the cartels became more vertically integrated. As will any business that makes its cost structure more efficient, it became more profitable. This raised the stakes for control over the routes, erupting in violent competition and turning Mexico—and particularly the border-crossing towns into the US—into war zones.[13] At its height, between 2008 and 2011, Ciudad Juárez had ten murders a day.[14] Former journalist and expert on Latin American gangs Doug Farah holds the view that President Felipe Calderón's decision in 2006 to attack the Mexican cartels led to the ascendance of the transnational organized crime groups in Central America and the expansion of their territory and power.[15] The Mexican cartels were under siege by the government and simultaneously brutally fighting each other in intracartel warfare. Those cartels that had the capacity wanted to protect the critically important Central America drug routes. So the biggest cartels, Sinaloa and Los Zetas, spread south into Central American gang territory, putting the gangs and the Mexican cartels into more direct cooperation by integrating the gangs into the cartel supply networks.

There is an inherent risk to adopting measures to winnow the size of the major cartels, as we saw in the case of Colombia—namely, the unintended consequence of splintering: the creation of a greater number of groups, which then further compete with one another and work to marginalize the state on even more fronts.

Also as in Colombia, mass killings have led to the emergence of paramilitary vengeance squads in Mexico.

Chief among these is the Zeta Killers group, which announced in July 2011 via a YouTube video that it would rid the Mexican state of Veracruz of Zeta criminals. Mexican authorities, however, are skeptical—and probably rightly so: they think that the Zeta Killers group is simply another organized crime gang battling the Zetas for supremacy and territory.[16] Ultimately, though, the sad truth is that as long as there are high margins and big markets and borders and enforcement disparities that offer the opportunity to arbitrage them (make a profit by buying an asset in a market where it is cheap and selling it in a market that will pay more for it), there will be violent clashes for territory.

COMBAT OR ACCOMMODATE?: THE KINGPIN STRATEGY VERSUS *PAX MAFIOSA*

The brutality of "Calderón's War" was the result of the militarization of what is known as the "Kingpin Strategy." In fighting transnational criminal networks, politicians have two options: the Kingpin Strategy or a *Pax Mafiosa*. In the Kingpin Strategy, enforcement takes out the leaders of the various groups. A *Pax Mafiosa*, on the other hand, is exactly what it sounds like: the government makes its peace with one mafia group so that there is no criminal power vacuum that prompts violent competition.

Former Mexican president Felipe Calderón's Kingpin Strategy was similar to the one the DEA implemented in 1992 in pursuit of Pablo Escobar and the other Colombian cartel capos. Rather than pick up the distributors or street dealers, the strategy was designed for upstream disruption, by attacking the organizations at their most vulnerable nodes: at the chemical labs needed to process the drugs, plus their finance, transportation, communications, and leadership infrastructure, particularly in the United States. "The

Kingpin program essentially controlled investigations from DEA headquarters and selected a finite number of targets for intensive investigative activity."[17]

Mexico, however, has a very decentralized political system, which is one of the factors Calderón proffered as an explanation for why Mexico has been more resistant to the strategy, and why its implementation triggered a fragmentation of the cartels. This escalated the violence, with vicious battles of succession and turf wars, due to the multiplication of new and more violent gangs and their rapidly shifting alliances.[18] Cartels are organized for stability. When they fracture and become small, they become fiercely competitive, fighting constantly with the others and then joining forces with some to try to regain some market power. Then they shift and try to join another group, triggering fighting with their previous allies, and so on.

The other argument against a Kingpin Strategy is that the convergent networks analyzed in the Combating Terrorism Center study[19] show that taking out the kingpins does not dismantle the network. That was the observation with the second capture (of three) of *El Chapo* Guzmán: the Sinaloa cartel continued its narcotics exports almost unabated. The explanation comes from analyzing the network interconnections (domestic and transnational, high-level and mid-level) and studying their number and redundancies. Even though the network may have global reach, its social connections are built from the bottom up. Kingpins are the people clearly atop the global illicit market: they have operational control and the most money and connections to other networks. Via money launderers, weapons traffickers, and lawyers, they connect South American cartels with Middle Eastern terrorist groups.

However, the greatest network connectivity redundancies (overlaps) in the network structure are mostly among mid-level individuals. While these individuals have less power than the kingpins, removing the kingpins will not crash the network. The redundancies in middle to upper-middle management of the network help the dark network reconstitute its activities quickly when its leader (the kingpin) gets taken out by arrest or assassination. So, while taking out the kingpin leads to a period of uncertainty, fracturing, and consolidation as underlings compete for leadership, historical evidence shows this plays out relatively quickly and that the network resumes business as usual in short order.[20]

Taking out the kingpin, as the security agencies like to do, is not as effective in the long term as having a more comprehensive approach of targeting the mid-level operators. This is, in fact, what the CIA has done against drug trafficking organizations and Al Qaeda: focused on disrupting both the money flows and the middle to upper-middle management of the organization. This strategy is effective, because organizations need to pay bills and vet their workers. The dual prongs of disrupting financial flows and taking out middle management cause substantial chaos in the organization for a long enough period of time for enforcement agencies to gain the advantage. According to a former spy who spoke to me confidentially: "Knock out the middle and upper-middle management. Big guys are replaceable; money and management guys are very disruptive."

The other side of the coin of a Kingpin Strategy is a *Pax Mafiosa*. Cartels are about market domination and stability. There is always an argument in the background as to whether it is better to allow one crime group, one warlord—one hegemon—to remain in power than to fight them all. That one group can then be managed or boxed in—or maybe not, but it certainly reduces the body count.

The price of a *Pax Mafiosa*, however, is a loss of state legitimacy: the hegemon becomes the ruler, supplanting the government. Various Mexican cities under cartel control provide vivid examples. Peace has reportedly been restored to Ciudad Juárez; the government has claimed victory (particularly since it instituted violence reduction programs there). But some observers have claimed this "peace" is illusory, and that the government has given up the fight and the Sinaloa cartel reigns supreme. Tamaulipas and Michoacán are both calm: there is no fighting; organized crime won, and the state lost. Michoacán has a crime rate lower than that of Canton Vaud in Switzerland. Now, Loret claims, Jalisco Nueva Generación is the wealthiest cartel, and the people in its territory get on with their lives. As a child, my mother lived on a street in Brooklyn where mob bosses lived. No one ever burgled a house or robbed a car on the street. Residents left their doors open. *Pax Mafiosa* indeed.

Mexico's biggest mistake, Calderón says, lay in not having combated the drug traffickers and criminals early enough. People did not realize what was happening. NAFTA (the North American Free Trade Agreement) made Mexico a middle-income country, which made it a consuming country—a consumer of drugs, cell phones, and banking, all of which are integral to the drug business. Calderón also takes a dim view of the Venezuelan government under Chávez and his successor, Maduro. "We need to convince Obama that part of his legacy needs to be change in Venezuela." But Obama left office with little impact on the hemisphere's biggest drug and terrorist facilitator or on the lives of Venezuela's thirty million citizens.

CORRUPTION, ILLICIT TRADE, AND VIOLENT EXTREMISM

Sitting on a panel at the OECD in Paris during its Integrity Week 2016, I was asked: "What is the connection between corruption and illicit trade?"

"It's simple really: at Asymmetrica we have never seen any illicit traffic that did not entail corruption. There is always at least one corrupt official. Usually there are several, all along the supply and distribution chains."

Corruption is what makes transnational criminal organizations enduring. The effective disruption of transnational crime is largely dependent on the success of anticorruption efforts.[21]

Corruption, activist Sarah Chayes argues, poisons the well, erodes governance, and engenders extremism. Profound corruption in post–Soviet Eastern Europe has left many young people there longing for the return of dictatorship, which would at least deliver some social justice and rule of law.[22] Chayes points out that the World Bank is coming to the conclusion that if your goal is to help the people,[23] it is sometimes better to work around the government and engage the target populations directly—or, in some cases, not to do anything, particularly if the government is oppressive and/or corrupt (the two frequently go together) and working with them would only harm the people one is trying to help.

In any form, corruption generates tremendous distortions on both the business environment and governance, causing citizens to lose access to basic goods and services and faith in their government. Roads and schools go unbuilt; laws are not adhered to; cops act like criminals; honest businesses cannot compete, and they go out of business; public trust in government erodes; and instability—or even violent extremism—ensues. People also die as a result: ". . . child mortality rates in countries with high levels of corruption are about one third higher than in countries with low corruption, infant mortality rates are almost twice as high and student dropout rates are five times as high."[24]

Numbers on the monetary loss due to corruption vary, but are alarming. A 2002 African Union study estimated that 25 percent of the GDP of African states, amounting to US$148 billion, is lost to corruption every year.[25] If even 10 percent of that were recovered through anticorruption programs, it would free up US$14.8 billion for poverty reduction. Other studies paint a bleaker picture of accelerating illicit financial flows (corruption plus tax evasion) pouring out of Africa. One estimates that US$814 billion was lost between 1970 and 2010, with one-quarter of that (US$202 billion) lost from 2005 to 2010. Whereas US$17 billion illicitly flowed out of Africa annually in the 1990s, this has risen to US$50 billion per year since 2000, with the continent's greater economic growth.[26]

The impact on the lives of millions of citizens is palpable.

Angola, for instance, is one of Africa's biggest oil producers, but about one-third of its annual revenue mysteriously disappears from state coffers, while three-quarters of the population live in abject poverty, and it remains one of the most undeveloped countries on earth.[27] The reason for this is that the impact of corruption compounds over time. Insofar as, without corruption, money would have flowed into good development investments, these investments would have paid dividends (education does this, and so do infrastructure, health care, child nutrition, and various other things). So corruption slows growth, and this slowing compounds over time. If, for example, a country has 20 years with average growth of 1 percent and, without corruption, would have had average growth of 5 percent, then it is true that, over those 20 years, without corruption the country would have had 56 percent (and in the last year 117 percent) more gross national income. The really staggering question is: Where would Africa and its states be today if they had been allowed to develop without the headwind of corruption since 1960? Chances are that they would have gross national incomes five or six times larger, on average.[28] The United States is not immune either. "The US health care programs Medicare and Medicaid estimate that 5 to 10 percent of their annual budget is wasted as a result of corruption."[29]

Foreign aid, particularly for security in the age of the Global War on Terror, creates an incentive for corruption and oppression. The regime receiving aid (from, say, the United States) has an incentive to close the democratic options for representative leaders to its people: the regime will portray itself (to both its people and the countries giving it financial aid) as the only viable option against fearsome extremists and terrorists. I concur with Chayes that the existence of the extremists is also good for the government: it justifies oppressive controls and the need for foreign aid, trapping people between the predations of a corrupt and oppressive government and the violence of extremists claiming to combat it.[30] In her years in Afghanistan and elsewhere, Chayes cited evidence that "several of these governments had deliberately targeted their repression against the most thoughtful, reasoned and moderate leadership over the years, while covertly facilitating militant groups to serve as ogres to scare people."[31]

Traditional Western thinking, she argues, is that security needs to be established before the project of good governance can be tackled. But since poor governance causes insecurity, violence cannot be addressed without reducing corruption.[32] I agree that there are three main ways "acutely corrupt governance"[33] is a threat to security. First, it supports and assists terrorist groups—it drives angry citizens into the terrorist fold, and corrupt politicians turn a blind eye to their presence or even provide logistical support. Second, corrupt officials who allow human smuggling and trafficking across their borders increase the likelihood of someone transporting a weapon of mass destruction into the country. Third, corrupt governments such as Algeria, Pakistan, and Yemen might purposely cultivate violent extremist groups to keep foreign aid dollars streaming into their coffers.

Corrupt governments are not "failed" or "failing." Indeed, they are tremendously successful at what they do: functioning as criminal syndicates, enriching the ruling elite at the expense of their people.[34] Corruption breeds corruption—it is nearly impossible to find honest people to serve in a corrupt government. One reason is self-selection: the honest will not participate in a corrupt system. A corrupt government is an effective criminal syndicate, like the Mafia: loyalty to its ways is rewarded, while anticorruption activists are punished as troublemakers.[35]

Corruption flourishes in spaces where regulations are complex, where there is little oversight of decision makers and public officials, and where the rule of law is weak (it is then made weaker by corruption). The remedies are long term, difficult to implement, and require periodic review to assess effectiveness: compliance must not cause greater harm than corruption or create new opportunities for corruption by generating more paperwork and opportunities for decision-making by petty officials, who can then wield their increased power to elicit more bribes.

"CALDERÓN'S WAR" AND THE RULE OF LAW

At our first meeting, on November 9, 2015, at New York's Instituto Cervantes, former president of Mexico Felipe Calderón mused on the challenges faced by his administration, which ran from 2006 through 2012.

The average Mexican family consumes a kilogram of tortillas per day. In 2006, when the price of cornmeal rose 20 percent due to demand for corn crops as a biofuel, it was disastrous for poor Mexicans, who were already spending a fifth of their daily wages on tortillas; unrest ensued, in what became known as "the Tortilla Riots."

"The [high] price of wheat and corn will not be tolerated, but thirty years of dictatorship will be," he cautioned any aspiring heads of state in the room.

Earlier, in 2000, when Vicente Fox won the presidency, it was the first time in seventy-one years that a candidate who was not from the Institutional Revolutionary Party (PRI) had won. It meant that the deals between the PRI political party and the cartels were no longer valid. Fox earned his new-sheriff-in-town credentials by violently pursuing those cartels that had become too comfortable, and the cartels themselves launched into violent competition with one another. The spiraling violence required an ever more concerted response from the government, which eventually brought in the military to fight the cartels. Though Calderón's legacy is marred by the widespread slaughter of the drug war, which brought his approval ratings down to 8 percent by the time he left office, he pointed to Mexico's economic development: when he took office, Mexico was the ninth-biggest exporter of vehicles in the world; by the time of his speech, in 2015, it was fourth, and it was slated to be third by March 2016.

Though nicknamed (perhaps a bit unfairly) "Calderón's War,"

according to Mexican journalist Carlos Loret de Mola, the violence started in 2004, under President Fox, in Tamaulipas. The same strategy of aggressively pursuing the cartel capos has held from the last two years of the Fox administration through Calderón and now with Peña Nieto.[36] The reason it is referred to as "Calderón's War" is that President Calderón "militarized" the war on drugs, enlisting the military to combat the cartels.

Under the Calderón government, the Mexican federal police were trained through the Mérida Initiative[37] and grew from a force of 6,500 to almost 37,000.[38] Though the military was considered more effective than the often-corrupt Mexican police forces, militaries are terrible at domestic policing, and human rights abuse complaints rose. So did the body count: "Drawing on data from Mexican government agencies, the Justice in Mexico Project maintained that between 120,000 to 125,000 people were killed (all homicides) during the Calderón Administration, with a gradual decline beginning after 2011."[39]

Since May 2014, the Mexican government has adopted a controversial approach to DDR (disarmament, demobilization, and reintegration, as we saw in Colombia in 2010): it has started incorporating the self-defense groups (i.e., paramilitaries) into legal law enforcement, inviting them either to disarm or to register their members and their weapons as part of a legitimate "Rural Police Force."[40]

Yet Calderón (contrary to his predecessor, Vicente Fox, and many other Central American leaders) does not advocate drug legalization; making drugs legal will not defeat the drug cartels, Calderón insists, and he thinks there is no point in legalizing drugs if you do not combat organized crime.

"Organized crime's objective is to capture the state," he says.

In other words, he believes that organized criminals want to co-opt the state infrastructure—financial, physical, and administrative—and make it work for them. They want to turn judges and cops to their favor, use the banking infrastructure to store and move money, and use the ports, roads, and warehouses for the goods they are selling and buying. Furthermore, Calderón believes that legalization will increase children's access to narcotics.

Over lunch in his New York office on February 24, 2016, former Central Command general and CIA director Gen. David Petraeus concurred with Calderón's view. Petraeus, often called "the most effective military commander since Eisenhower," literally wrote the manual on counterinsurgency ("COIN") for the US military. He then implemented his own theory in bringing Iraq back from the brink. When he was appointed head of Central Command in 2007, Iraqis were dying at a rate of ninety a day,[41] mostly by being blown up by suicide bombers; his strategy reduced casualties by more than 90 percent. Petraeus has said that Mexico's cartel-induced violence is akin to an insurgency and requires a counterinsurgency strategy like the one he employed in Iraq.

"The problem is that it's comprehensive and expensive," he said over our egg drop soup. "The key is instituting the rule of law."

I said that that's what Calderón told me, and he nodded.

"Effective rule of law," Petraeus continued, "has three legs: police, courts, and prisons. In Baghdad we instituted a judicial Green Zone, where the police, the judges, and the prisoners were kept secure; the transportation between the prisons and the courts was within the Green Zone, away from insurgent attacks."

He said the city elders in Monterrey, Mexico, a major industrial center, have done the same thing.

"They doubled the pay of police, provided the police, the judges, and their families secure homes and supervised transportation, and secured the prisons, with private money. It has worked," praised Petraeus.

"Good. But it means they have privatized some important functions of the state," I retorted.

"They have secured their homes and businesses," Petraeus replied.

In Calderón's view, there can be no real development without rule of law, the lack of which he considers Latin America's biggest problem, along with its transnational organized crime groups.

"Without rule of law, we will not be a developed country," Calderón believes. "When I took office, I found a capturable state."

President Calderón has very definite views on the drug cartels in his country. He believes that the motive behind drug cartel violence is to strike fear in order to gain control of people and territory. Violence is a valuable tool in the drug business: it secures the supply chain, by keeping suppliers, creditors, distributors, and competitors in line. He says that "the real business of organized crime is extortion," adding that people can't call the police to help them if they are at "the margins of the law," citing prostitutes and gamblers as examples. Corruption, he feels, is both a facilitator and an objective.

"Organized crime, in order to survive, needs the protection of the authorities . . . The lubricant of the old traditional system in Mexico is corruption."

But corruption, of course, is not limited to the Mexicans. In order to ply their trade, he says, the cartels need to bribe Mexican police, sure, but, more important, the American patrols at the border as well. Wherever vast quantities of illicit goods are crossing a border (like drugs in the Southwest), customs agents are in on it. In order to fight this scourge, Calderón identifies two priorities: first, fight the criminals; second, strengthen institutions. To the latter point, he advocates examinations to vet police and professionalize them, as well as raising their salaries. He says that Plan Colombia was successful because it helped strengthen Colombia's law enforcement.

"I didn't have enough support from Congress or the Americans," he stated.

The political operating environments are very different in Mexico and Colombia. Colombia has a centralized political system, while Mexico has a federalized political system—"which is a mess," Calderón says. Mexican feds cannot remove complicit corrupt cops or governors. It was police officers, he says, who kid-napped the forty-three students in Iguala, Guerrero, on September 26, 2014, a case that shocked not just the nation, but the international community.

In an age where money is being laundered through apps on phones, Mexicans also need better financial intelligence. Mexico's challenge is that it needs more human talent. It needs smart, hon-est, and brave patriots to track finances. Money and weapons coming from the US are what are generating the violence in Mexico. Calderón is not only quick to blame the US for insufficient support, he is also skeptical of its will to reduce drug consumption.

Calderón did not cite motives for this laxity, but there have long been whispers in policy circles that there is too much of a profitable industry around drug consumption. The banks receive cash; more police officers and DEA agents get hired for drug busts; and the prisons and the rehab centers receive the criminals and addicts, in-flating their revenues, either from the public purse or private ones.

But mainly, it's about the banks: in 1979, when Miami was in the grips of a cocaine craze fed by the Colombian cartels, the Miami branch of the Federal Reserve reported a US$5 billion surplus—more than the entire rest of the US Federal Reserve banks combined.[42] Recent scandals at Wachovia and HSBC banks illustrate this point.

MONEY LAUNDERING 101

It was the Watergate scandal in 1973 that brought us the first known use of the term "money laundering"; it first appeared in a court decision nine years later, in 1982.[43] The UN Office on Drugs and Crime estimates that the amount of money laundered globally in one year is 2 to 5 percent of global GDP, or $800 billion to $2 trillion in current US dollars. Given what we know about the size of the proceeds of crime, the UNODC estimate is likely low. Money laundering threatens legitimate business and the clean economy, making honest businesses uncompetitive, generating unemployment, and providing richer pickings for the criminals and terrorists to gain supporters and collaborators. It disguises the proceeds of crime and integrates them into the legitimate financial system, creating a link between the legal and the underground economies.

Money laundering not only robs governments of tax revenue and generates corruption, bending the loyalties of public servants to their new private masters, but has significant second-order effects on legitimate business as well. Money laundering distorts the competitive environment. Businesses whose primary purpose is to be a money-laundering vehicle do not need to make a profit through their ongoing operations. They are therefore able to undercut their competitors, causing clean businesses to fail. When clean businesses go under, the unemployed examine their options and turn to the dirty businesses or the crime syndicates themselves, thus further eroding law and order and improving the black market operating environment. This then accelerates the downward spiral: economies become weaker, and more people are unemployed and turn to the black markets of illicit trade and criminality.

According to the Financial Crimes Enforcement Network of the US Treasury Department (known as FinCEN): "Money laundering is the process of making illegally-gained proceeds (i.e. 'dirty money') appear legal (i.e. 'clean')."[44] The dirty money—the proceeds from a crime, such as prostitution, or the sales of narcotics, weapons, or counterfeit goods—is laundered in three steps,[45] whose detailed mechanisms can vary.

The first step is placement: putting the money, furtively, into the financial system. The easiest way to do this is to go through a financial institution or through the broker of another commodity who can transform the cash into a less identifiable and more discreet tradable good or monetary instrument, such as traveler's checks, bearer bonds, a foreign currency, diamonds, gold, or even cigarettes. Gambling the money and having it be paid back in winnings is a popular method, too.

When cash is first deposited into a financial institution, two more tricks are used to avoid triggering a currency transaction report from the teller that can prompt a suspicious-activity report, prompting investigation by federal authorities. Under US law, a currency transaction report must be filed anytime an account receives more than $10,000 in a day—even if the deposits are made by different people at different branches. Therefore, one must "structure" the deposits, limiting them to $9,000 a day per account; but one can deposit $9,000 into each of several accounts, all with the same "beneficial owner" (a legal term whereby specific property rights—"use and title"—in equity belong to a person even though legal title of the property belongs to another person).

In addition to structuring, depositors can engage in "smurfing": using runners to make the deposits for them, in case the bank demands identification and also so the criminal's face does not appear on closed-circuit video surveillance. These runners are referred to as "smurfs," like the little blue cartoon people.

The second step has a number of names: "layering," "dispersion," "stacking," or "conversion." The goal is to move money around (by wiring or transferring it through numerous accounts) to create confusion as to its origin and owner. It gets separated from its source by using anonymous shell companies and multiplying their financial transactions. The use of false invoices is a growing trend in what is known as trade-based money laundering (known affectionately as "TBML" to the security wonks), because trade-based money laundering is harder to capture in suspicious-activities reports. (Since 1996, the Banking Secrecy Act has required banks and other financial institutions to report transactions they suspect may be laundering money or financing terrorism within 30 days of the transaction to FinCEN. Other countries have similar requirements for reporting to their financial intelligence units.)

Another classic move is to secure loans equivalent to the amount in the bank's coffers: loan repayments do not trigger currency transaction reports—and if you're really clever, you use the loan as a tax deduction on other income.

Finally, the money is integrated into the financial system through additional transactions until the "dirty money" appears "clean" and is returned to the criminal from a legitimate-looking source. This is also known as "recycling," and it completes the money-laundering process: the money is reinvested in the legal economy. To maximize efficiency, "bundlers" will take money from several different criminal groups for joint laundering operations, such as buying buildings and other large property developments. It is so prevalent that in February 2017, FinCEN renewed Geographical Targeting Orders[46] requiring heightened due diligence and reporting of large cash purchases of real estate in six US cities: New York, Miami, Los Angeles, San Francisco, San Antonio, and San Diego. Bundling money will increase the rate of return on investments, buy more corrupt complicity, and make the beneficial owners harder to identify.

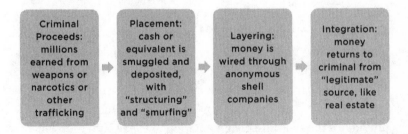

Nearly all the major banks are in on it: the money is too big for them not to be. HSBC admitted to violating the Bank Secrecy Act by failing to monitor more than $670 billion in wire transfers and more than $9.4 billion in purchases of US currency from HSBC Mexico,[47] thereby allowing money laundering, prosecutors said. The bank also violated US economic sanctions against Iran, Libya, Sudan, Burma, and Cuba, according to criminal information filed in the case. US federal and state authorities secured a $1.92 billion payment from HSBC (the self-proclaimed "world's local bank") in December 2012 to settle charges that the banking giant transferred billions of dollars for nations under US sanctions, enabled Mexican drug cartels to launder tainted money through the American financial system, and worked closely with Saudi Arabian banks linked to terrorist organizations. HSBC was also forced to pay the US Office of the Comptroller of the Currency $500 million and the Federal Reserve $165 million in civil penalties.

Speaking on the case, Manhattan district attorney Cyrus R. Vance said, "New York is a center of international finance, and those who use our banks as a vehicle for international crime will not be tolerated."[48] While $1.92 billion may be a hefty penalty for one bank, it is a tiny penalty when compared with the entirety of the illicit banking system. Recent anti-money-laundering settlements indicate that the practice is widespread and tremendously valuable—otherwise the banks would not be so quick to settle with such enormous sums in order to prevent further investigations of their accounts.

It is not hard: money-laundering services are available to anyone with a few million dollars to stash. Guatemalan banks offer excellent money-laundering services to drug traffickers: for 17 percent of deposits of $3 million and above, the banks will provide not just money management and safeguarding, but will also provide all the requisite documentation to evade law enforcement prosecution: business registries, receipts, and falsified tax returns for three previous years.[49]

Two more recent US law enforcement cases illustrate the extent to which dirty money enters global financial and capital markets. In March 2010, Wachovia Bank, which was one of the largest banks in the United States, entered into a deferred prosecution agreement with the Department of Justice. Wachovia was charged with willfully failing to maintain an anti-money-laundering program from May 2003 through June 2008, in violation of the Bank Secrecy Act. During this time, it failed to effectively monitor for potential money-laundering activity involving more than $420 billion in cross-border transactions with high-risk Mexican currency exchange houses, including millions of dollars used to purchase airplanes for drug cartels.

As part of the agreement, Wachovia agreed to forfeit to the United States $110 million, representing some of the proceeds of illegal narcotics sales that were laundered through the bank. FinCEN also assessed a $110 million civil penalty. In another recent case, MoneyGram International Inc.—a global money services business—entered into a deferred prosecution agreement with the Justice Department and consented to forfeit $100 million. MoneyGram admitted to criminally aiding and abetting wire fraud and failing to maintain an effective anti-money-laundering program.

The French bank BNP Paribas SA is so far the largest known offender: in late June 2014, US prosecutors reached a deal in which the bank would pay $8.9 billion as punishment for hiding $30 billion of financial transactions that violated US sanctions. The transactions were conducted on behalf of Sudanese and Iranian officials and companies. They are known to have involved oil deals, and are suspected to have involved weapons trafficking—at a time when Sudan was committing full-blown genocide.[50]

The bankers knew they had blood on their hands. To avoid detection by the "OFAC filter" (the Office of Foreign Asset Control is the body within the Treasury Department that publishes and enforces the list of sanctioned entities), BNP Paribas used a network of banks in East Africa, the Middle East, and Europe, while "stripping" such red-flag information as the codes that identify the sender or recipient of the funds as being in a sanctioned country. The process was simple enough for any lackey to do it: information fields were simply left blank, or filled in with a single period or an internal code that indicated the transaction involved a bank branch somewhere else, such as London or Paris.

The shame of it is that these penalties are a pittance compared with the amount of money these financial institutions made processing the vast sums of dirty money they probably really laundered. While BNP Paribas's settlement is a record penalty for a sanctions violation, it is literally pennies on the dollar for Paribas: the penalties represent 27 to 30 cents for every dollar in illegal financial transactions. According to US law, the bank could have been liable for $2 for every dollar in illegal financial transactions—in other words, $60 billion. But even the US authorities (the Treasury and Justice departments) agree that such a staggering sum would have been "unreasonable and uncollectable."

"Unreasonable" by whose measure? Authorities found $100 billion in suspicious financial transactions, but could only prove malfeasance for $30 billion. By this standard, Royal Bank of Scotland got a bad deal: in 2013, it paid $100 million in penalties on $32 million of illegal transactions; that is $3.13 in penalty for every $1 of alleged violations. So the outer limit of what BNP Paribas could have faced is $313 billion in penalties. No wonder it settled for $8.9 billion! For BNP Paribas, it is the cost of doing business. What would really hurt the bank in the settlement? A one-year ban on transacting in US dollars that started in January 2015.

Had any of these financial enterprises abided by anti-money-laundering and know-your-customer legislation (or simply not been corrupt), those criminals and terrorist networks would have been significantly hampered in their efforts to move billions globally to finance their crimes, including genocide.

Corruption is a key entry point in the strategy to capture the state and make it a more hospitable environment for criminal operations, and money laundering hampers clean business. The dark, hidden money of corruption and illicit trade always ends up in jurisdictions with banking secrecy and a strong rule of law protecting property—precisely because criminals and terrorists want their assets protected from the hands of those who might overthrow or kill them. As corrupt officials steal the money and stash it overseas, physical infrastructure and political institutions crumble. Some theorists consider capital flight to be a bigger problem than corruption: if the corrupt officials reinvested in housing, energy, and farms, the country would end up with a true oligarchy—where the political power is held by those with economic power—but at least there would be development.

Too many countries trap their citizens between violence and corruption. What almost no one offers is what we as rational citizens want, the third option: a clean government that is not corrupt, where rule of law is strong and violence is low—a system where everyone has equal access to an education and economic participation, the tools to lead a life they have reason to value. But once the downward spiral of corruption and violence and fear sets in, it is phenomenally difficult to eradicate.

STARVING THE BEAST

The global threat of crime-terror pipelines grows at the pace of global business. While the multilayered complexity and rapid adaptability present challenges to traditional single-approach interdiction, the cross-border activities and their role in threat finance can also be used to build a multipronged approach that has a proven record of success: a counterterrorism tactic commonly referred to as a "multiagency swarm."

This means that if the network is properly mapped and its vulnerabilities are properly identified, you can tackle it in various ways at once: customs and tax agencies can seize the smuggled consumer goods while drug enforcement agencies pursue the drug trafficking element, local law enforcement liberates the slaves, and bank accounts are frozen and assets seized. Closing in with these multiple prongs at once is a far more effective strategy to bring down a transnational criminal enterprise than just tackling one criminal activity with one enforcement authority at a time, which allows the networks to move and reconstitute, as we have seen them do. As the criminals and terrorists collude and share activities, so must military and law enforcement, ever more.

These are multibillion-dollar transnational businesses and should be treated as such. We have to understand their supply chains and examine the networks for vulnerabilities that we can attack to degrade, disrupt, and destroy these hybrid threat networks. Some of this has already been occurring: since 9/11, US Code Title 10 and Title 50 authorities have synchronized in the counterterrorism environment, forcing the US Department of Defense to interact with the broader intelligence community.[51] The coordinated initiatives can be everything from kinetic military operations to combating the manufacture of counterfeit goods and intellectual property theft, which is a great source of income for criminals and, increasingly, for terrorists. The goal is to "starve the beast," thereby reducing the need for and boosting the effectiveness of targeted kinetic operations—in other words, takedowns and killings.

The good news is that the corrupted entities that are the principal facilitators of the illicit financial flows that produce these multiple harms are also the greatest threat to the criminals themselves. They can become the key strategic nodes for disrupting, dismantling, and destroying the networks. Some of the more effective solutions are not complicated: businesses can increase their compliance, strengthen internal controls, and undertake due diligence to verify beneficial owners when establishing a business relationship with their customers. By expanding its corporate social responsibility to protect against illicit actors that abuse its services and damage the integrity of the global financial system, the private sector can significantly restrict the operational environment for the criminals and terrorists. It is therefore highly effective to focus law enforcement efforts on these fixers and facilitators.

Public and private actors can partner together to improve the overall governance climate, shut down the illegal economy and crime-terror pipelines, and build tomorrow's new markets and investment frontiers, in which communities in the US, Europe, Latin America, Africa, and Asia can improve their futures, anchored in the rule of law, democratic governance, and integrity in markets and public institutions. Failure is not an option, for failure is a world set ablaze with kidnapped schoolgirls, modern slaves, spreading caliphates, and perpetual war coming to your hometown—with no one to run to for redress.

Ultimately, we must accept that our personal choices as consumers have global impact with serious repercussions. Drug cartels exist because people consume drugs. Slavery exists because people want cheap clothes and cheap handbags and cheap labor in mines or in their homes, and because they want cheap prostitutes. The illicit trade in tobacco products exists because people want to smoke and either do not want to or cannot pay full price for the taxes on legal cigarettes. So much of the deepest suffering and so many of the greatest harms are a consequence of our avaricious or intemperate desires. We could easily ameliorate global tragedies with only moderate adjustments to our choices as consumers. If we fail to act on this moral duty and continue to profit from the suffering of our fellow men and women, their blood will not easily wash from our hands.

Crime and Terror Converge

There are some individuals who are the very convergent threat we have considered. Dawood Ibrahim, the Indian crime lord based in Pakistan, built up a smuggling network in Southeast Asia and the Middle East, but he began his empire by stealing Bollywood film copyrights and selling bootlegged movies on the streets of India. From selling pirated DVDs in Mumbai, Ibrahim moved into narcotics, and his organization started controlling an informal money transfer system popular in the Muslim world: *hawala*. His organization became known as "D-Company."

After becoming one of India's most notorious crime bosses, Ibrahim also became a supporter and financial facilitator for the Lashkar-e-Taiba (LeT) and Al Qaeda terrorist groups, and had direct ties to Osama bin Laden. D-Company ordered and organized the twelve simultaneous bombings that racked Bombay (as Mumbai was then known) on March 12, 1993, following which Ibrahim became a US Treasury–designated terrorist. When the dramatic attacks in Mumbai occurred in November 2008, Ibrahim's name headed the Indian government's request for extradition by the

Pakistanis.[1] He is suspected of dividing his time between Pakistan (a well-known harbor for Islamist terrorists, including Osama bin Laden, who was found and killed there) and the United Arab Emirates (a well-known hub of illicit trade): an unsurprising combination for a man of his background. D-Company epitomizes the modern crime-terror pipeline in which major terrorists start as salesmen of pirated movies.

How and why did this convergent threat of illicit trade in consumer goods and terrorism emerge? There are two main causes: globalization and the collapse of the Soviet Union. Since the fall of the Berlin Wall, international smuggling has exploded, deepening and accelerating the collaboration of transnational organized crime and terrorist groups, for several reasons.

The first reason is that the financial support of governments driven by the ideological Cold War agenda of East-versus-West, communism-versus-capitalism has shrunk (though by no means been eliminated) for the shadow wars carried out by proxies, such as the American-backed mujahideen in Afghanistan or Russian-backed Marxist guerrillas in Latin America or Africa. With their Cold War–related support drying up, these groups had to go into business to support themselves, usually with narcotics smuggling, kidnapping, or extortion.

Second, the borders of the Iron Curtain collapsed, opening up a whole new world to the reach of trade, in both directions: from the former Soviet Union out into the rest of the world, and from the rest of the world into Russia, Central Asia, and Eastern Europe. Furthermore, free trade zones were specifically set up to be a bulwark against a return to socialism or fascism, on the premise that countries behave like people and their interest in economic stability and growth would trump belligerence: the European Economic Area (EEA) is a prime example of this thinking.

Third, most of the former Soviet Union's scientists and intelligence agents (who know a thing or two about moving things covertly), and goods and service providers to the USSR, were suddenly left with no steady income, but terrific skill sets. So they found illicit sources of income.

Fourth, giant regional trade pacts established huge lagoons where goods would move swiftly and freely, and also created new borders around those vast new free trade zones, where penetrating those borders becomes a profitable opportunity for arbitrage: exploiting the price differentials on the same goods in different markets. The borders around the EEA and NAFTA are prime examples. Penetrate those outer borders and you have a variety of profitable markets from which to choose, with little hassle or additional cost.

Fifth, digital and information technology stunningly accelerated access to know-how, money, goods, and services—both legal and not.

Studies by the UN Office on Drugs and Crime and the Organisation for Economic Cooperation and Development estimate the illicit economy at around 10 percent of the global economy. Higher estimates[2] likely double-count criminal revenues and their laundering, and also include income from legitimate businesses owned by bad guys. The illicit goods and money flow the same way the goods and money of the rest of the global trade economy do: transnationally. Criminology professor Jay Albanese parses "transnational crime"—"violations of law that involve more than one country in their planning, execution or impact"[3]—into three broad categories: the provision of illicit goods (drug trafficking, stolen property, counterfeiting), illicit services (human trafficking, cyber-crime and fraud, commercial vices such as prostitution and pornography), and the infiltration of business or government (extortion and racketeering, money laundering, corruption).[4]

The lesson gleaned from the 9/11 attacks, contained in 2002's *National Security Strategy of the United States of America*, was that whereas "enemies in the past needed great armies and great industrial capabilities to endanger America, now shadowy networks of individuals can bring great chaos and suffering to our shores for less than it costs to purchase a single tank."[5] Because of the convergence of criminals and terrorists, whereby a small gang can threaten a country, Professor Robert Mandel considers that asymmetric threat "unprecedented since the emergence of the nation-state."[6] According to 2011's *White House Strategy to Combat Transnational Organized Crime*, "Criminal networks are not only expanding their operations, but they are also diversifying their activities, resulting in a convergence of transnational threats that has evolved to become more complex, volatile and destabilizing."[7] Combating transnational criminals is now viewed as critical to cutting the funding of terrorist operations.

This is because, increasingly, terrorists and criminals are colluding. The net effect of the growing criminal-terrorist collusion is an accelerating subversion of good governance and law and order. They collude most frequently in wealthy countries, where profits are highest and law enforcement capabilities are strongest, because that is where they need each other the most.[8] Criminals and terrorists share at least one overarching desire: an alternative space of governance in which they are the predominant force, whether this is achieved visibly through a violent overthrow (the means of jihadists and insurgents) or invisibly through insidious corruption and intimidation (the means of the classic criminal archetype). In both cases, the intermediate step to attaining their goals is not an empty, ungoverned space—it is a governable yet criminalized space, where the terrorist or criminal organization, rather than the elected (or otherwise official) government, is the controlling force.[9]

Keeping a government structure is key, for without it there would be no effective delivery system to allow them to carry out daily criminal activity—namely, the infrastructures of transportation, communications, and finance, as well as access to the markets to which the criminals want to sell and access to the goods they want to buy. Personal security and the ability to protect private property are prime reasons why major transnational and terrorist facilitators run their operations from wealthy, First World countries, which are dependent on a strong state structure with (ironically) a strong rule of law.

Generally speaking, the World Bank and International Monetary Fund consider that a state has been "captured" when there is corruption on such a grand scale that the state's decision-making processes are predictably skewed in favor of private interests through nonobvious means. Others prefer to talk about "the criminalization of a state"[10] rather than its "capture." In both cases, government institutions stop defending the rights of the average citizen. The increasing lawlessness creates fertile ground for criminals and the disaffected, who turn to violence and insurgency. Both state capture and criminalization usually begin with corruption.

Corruption and violence are complementary tools. Key government officials are often given a very clear choice: *plata o plomo*— "silver or lead," money or a bullet. Those who don't accept the silver get the lead, and are hung out to dry—in the most literal sense—as an example to the next person facing the choice. "Following the money" is the path not just to finding corruption, but to finding the connections between criminals and terrorists. If you follow the money, though, it gets messy: instead of the crime you were tracking, you get a whole network of interconnected crimes pursued by competing authorities struggling to cross jurisdictions.

You also get our complicity: the money starts with each of us, as consumer or supporter. Much of the financing of illicit trade comes from the small everyday choices consumers make: buying that counterfeit handbag on the street, buying drugs or ten minutes of a live-performing stripper on the Internet. So, consumer tolerance is high, the penalties are small, and the profit margins are big, in all cases—the counterfeit handbag, for example, is a more profitable item than heroin.[11]

Boundaries and borders are the reasons for the profit margins;

as licit business seeks competitive advantage by developing supply and distribution chains efficiently, so with illicit business— production is handled in areas where costs are low, and product is shipped to places where prices are high, with enforcement risk priced in.

Following the money leads to the money launderers, one of the key points of convergence between terrorist and criminal organizations. Their service, in the world's great financial institutions, is one of the prime reasons that illicit superconnectors are more prevalent in wealthy First World countries than in poor countries.

A Defense Department study conducted by Dr. Scott Helfstein during his time at the Combating Terrorism Center at West Point[12] reveals just how intertwined transnational smugglers are with terrorists. Examining 40 individuals who were known transnational smugglers, Helfstein's team found that all of them were in regular contact with 754 others. Of those 754 people, 221 were involved in narcotics, while 86 were involved in terrorism. By the time the network analysis reached the second degree of separation from the starting group, terrorists outnumbered drug traffickers: of the 1,942 individuals identified at this level, 392 were involved in narcotics, while 404 were terrorists. The rapid intertwining of criminals and terrorists poses dangers of both the criminal and terrorist varieties in one network. This is the convergent threat of the crime-terror pipeline, and is unique for two reasons.

First, the threat is adaptive. Both criminal and terrorist organizations have broken down their networks into small, separate cells to thwart the effectiveness of law enforcement, military, and intelligence services. This microstructure design is calculated on the premise that if only one or a few cells are taken down, the chance of collateral damage being inflicted on the greater organization is minimized. Intelligence agencies function the same way: it's called "compartmentalization."

The head of each of these cells can manage only the activities of his or her cell members, not beyond. Also, the cell head usually receives management and direction from someone at a higher level whom he or she knows only by a code name and through telecommunications devices that are changed out every few days. That way, if law enforcement captures the cell head, he or she cannot give up a superior or disrupt the rest of the organization, either under interrogation or as part of some plea agreement. Because of this miniaturization of the cells, organizations such as terrorist groups and drug trafficking organizations have the ability to quickly rejuvenate. Even if government succeeds in taking down a number of cells simultaneously, the remaining cells shift and realign, quickly morphing into something that neither looks nor acts like what government security forces were focused on just a few months earlier.

Battling crime-terror networks is a real-life war game: while we work to disrupt and degrade their operating environment, the criminal and terrorist groups engage in actions to either restore their original operating environment or alter it to something more beneficial to them. While we try to exploit their vulnerabilities, they simultaneously try to exploit ours—and we are at a terrible disadvantage.

The United States has far more exploitable seams than the criminal organizations: while we are stymied by borders and authorities, they use these borders to play hide-and-seek with law enforcement authorities. Miami was once the main entry point for cocaine in the US; when we increased security in that part of the Caribbean, the smugglers rerouted into Central America and through Mexico to get to the US. We increase security on the Southwest-Mexico border, they shift to boats and small submarines to evade detection. Cocaine use goes down and marijuana becomes increasingly legalized, the cartels increase the push of methamphetamines and opiates, whether fentanyl or heroin. Europe increases security on its eastern border, smugglers come in through the southern border, particularly Greece. Europe increases security in Greece, smugglers shift and enter via Italy and Spain from North Africa. Our foes in the criminal universe use a much more open playbook than we do: they are unconstrained by law and order or procedural and institutional checks and balances, such as getting warrants and due process.

This is what international relations professor Jakub Grygiel calls "the power of statelessness": the "power without the responsibility of governing."[13] In other words, transnational bad guys embrace their lack of national ties as an asset, because it increases their organization's chances of survival. Organizations that are substate or (even worse) transnational are far more difficult to target, enclose, or sanction. In short, both criminals and terrorists want to exploit state infrastructure, but they do not want to be as vulnerable to attack as the state structure they have subverted.

Second, the links between different illicit trades are blurring: narcotics and weapons smugglers are also smuggling tobacco and people. While this approach complicates investigations by possibly getting different agencies entangled if handled incorrectly, it presents an opportunity for law enforcement: it means multiple law enforcement agencies can tackle a single network as part of their core duty. The Central Intelligence Agency, the Federal Bureau of Investigation, and Special Operations Command tackle terrorism; the Drug Enforcement Administration, narcotics; for the financing of any threat, a panoply of authorities can be activated, from the US Treasury's FinCEN to the Financial Action Task Force. A transnational organized crime network, depending on its tentacles, can be investigated by the Drug Enforcement Administration, the Federal Bureau of Investigation, the Department of Homeland Security, Interpol, Europol, the UK's National Crime Agency, and the Central Intelligence Agency and its counterparts in other countries. This is the "multiagency swarm" tactic: like hornets simultaneously attacking the same victim.

Each of these law enforcement and military organizations with the authority to act against their corresponding bad actors is collaterally affected by illicit trade. Each one therefore requires valuable and actionable information about the illicit trade in which these criminal and terrorist pipeline organizations are involved. This is what Asymmetrica has specialized in: pulling the thread on private sector information regarding illicit trade to find the intelligence on threats of interest to government.

It is not easy work. Criminal organizations tend to expand from one illicit enterprise into another and to spread their tentacles across borders and into government. Mexico's drug trafficking Gulf cartel (based in the border city of Matamoros, Tamaulipas) actually arose in the bootlegging era of the 1920s. It expanded as a prime drug trafficker in the 1980s—uncoincidentally, at a time that cocaine was all the rage in the US—when its leader, Juan García Abrego, established business relationships with both Colombia's Cali cartel and the Mexican federal police.[14] Like Los Zetas, the Gulf cartel's cells fragmented and got into other forms of illicit trade, including extortion and fuel theft. Los Zetas had such territorial control, the government had to dispatch federal troops in May 2014 to reimpose government authority in the oil-rich state of Tamaulipas.

WHEN IS CONVERGENCE REAL?

There are two different views regarding the convergence of criminals and terrorists in a pipeline of money. One is that the data bears out great organizational convergence: two groups actually working together for mutual benefit over an extended period of time. The second is that there is sometimes tactical convergence, also known as "activity appropriation," in which groups borrow each other's tactics in order to achieve a particular objective. The two scenarios are very different.

Organizational convergence involves two groups working together, not the unilateral appropriation of one group's set of tactics by the other. Activity appropriation may be short-lived, but convergence among groups is generally long term, lasting well beyond a single illegal narcotics transaction or arms deal. Examples of organizational convergence include: the Haqqani network's relationship with Al Qaeda; D-Company's relationship with Lashkar-e-Taiba; the protection provided by the former Irish Republican Army (IRA) and the Ulster Defense Association (UDA) for smuggling and prostitution enterprises in Northern Ireland run by Italians, Serbians, and Chinese triads; and the Venezuelan vice president Tareck El Aissami's drug trafficking in support not only of his own enrichment but of Lebanese Hezbollah.[15]

On the other hand, the activity appropriation of the more superficial tactical convergence is pretty horrific. Los Zetas (who were formerly Mexican Special Forces) have committed acts of terrorism, the most renowned of which is the 2011 firebombing of a casino in Monterrey that killed 53 people, as well as the torture and mass execution in 2011 of 193 migrants who were traveling through northern Mexico by bus, but had not paid their extortion fees.[16]

These acts should not be mistaken for an organizational convergence: they are merely examples of one group temporarily employing the tactics of another to achieve particular ends. Splinter drug trafficking organizations *Los Rojos* ("The Red Ones") and *Guerreros Unidos* ("United Warriors," or "United People of Guerrero," the state in which they are based) have expanded into kidnapping and extortion. The *Guerreros Unidos* are responsible for the disappearance and murder of forty-three Mexican teacher trainees (students) who'd been handed over to them by corrupt local authorities in Iguala, Guerrero.[17]

In some Latin American countries where I have worked, the threat to state government from the collusion of transnational organized criminals with terrorist groups is less than the threat presented by collusion among private armies or paramilitaries, which creates the conditions for insurgency, usurping the state. Criminals (including narcos) collude with insurgents and paramilitary groups because doing so maximizes their power. They collude to create the "permissive environment" security analysts are so fond of discussing. They each bring important components for a strategy of asymmetric war—also known as "total war."

In fact, the problem is not so much that the environments themselves are permissive but that the effective presence of either group produces what economists term a "positive externality": a by-product of one group's activity that benefits the other, like a bacterium whose presence changes the alkalinity of the liquid in which it lives, making it easier for other bacteria to grow.

Criminals want more than just profit—they want sanctuary: a space where they can operate with minimal pressure from law enforcement and other government agencies. Criminals do not want to exercise "positive political control" by governing; they want to exercise "negative political control" by denying others the ability to govern effectively. And the best group at challenging a government and making it more difficult for that government to assert political control? Terrorists.[18] Thus, criminals and terrorists benefit from a symbiotic destabilization of government. When terrorists attack the government with brutal violence, the criminals benefit; when criminals destabilize the government through physical attacks or well-planned corruption campaigns, terrorists benefit just as much as organized crime.[19] The crime-terror pipeline represents the best way to weaken and exhaust the state.

The initial basis for criminal and terrorist collusion is practical efficiency. Drug traffickers and other transnational criminals have ample money and lines of transportation and communication. Insurgents and paramilitaries have organization, discipline, and leadership over a constituency of motivated followers. These components allow organized criminals (particularly narcos) to project their power within and across countries, enabling them to protect their substantial assets. Insurgents and paramilitaries need the financial, logistical, and communications support that transnational criminals have.

When transnational criminals, terrorists, paramilitaries, and insurgents collaborate in some combination, their power to challenge the state increases drastically. "Whether the insurgents are reformers or criminals is irrelevant, for their avowed objective is to take direct control of the government and state."[20] Indeed, criminal violence can resemble political violence in more than just its brutality: it shifts control and authority from the state to "violent nonstate actors." Successful criminal organizations resemble insurgencies: they rival the state for control of territory, people, and resources; their commercial motivations comprise an implicit political agenda.[21]

All of this crime-terror intersection accelerates learning for both groups. Over time (a very brief time), they adopt each other's more efficient techniques, resulting in activity appropriation. A case in point is the use of vehicle-borne improvised explosive devices (VBIEDs, also known as car bombs), at which Hezbollah is an expert. Recent incidents involving the use of car bombs in Mexico marked a significant change in tactics employed by drug trafficking organizations and conjure images more typical of the Middle East. While no specific and irrefutable connection has been made, Hezbollah's extensive use of car bombs raises strong suspicion concerning a possible connection to Mexico's drug cartels.

In the summer of 2012, the Juárez drug cartel used a remote-controlled car bomb that killed four and wounded twenty others in Ciudad Juárez, Mexico's murder capital, creating a massive blast within walking distance of downtown El Paso, Texas. A second car bomb exploded outside a police station in Ciudad Victoria. With $19 to $35 billion a year in income, these groups are also well equipped with military-grade weaponry and powerful enough to challenge government agencies. The weapons are mainly procured from the US: cars and trucks bring drugs into the United States and money and weapons down into Mexico. Cartels hire teenage kids to be "straw buyers" of weapons inside the United States, paying them $100 for every weapon they buy.

This is why in every US-Mexico conversation about the Southwest border, while the US carps about the drugs and the illegal immigrants, Mexico retorts that it is US drug users who demand the drugs and pay for them, US banks that launder the proceeds, and the US itself that sells the weapons that fuel the violence in Mexico and Central America that causes migrants to flood the US-Mexico border. Unsurprisingly, Mexico wants the US to tighten its gun laws.

The cartels are armed not only with automatic weapons, but also rocket-propelled grenades, machine guns, and .50-caliber antiaircraft guns, enabling them to engage in direct firefights with Mexican marines and soldiers. They also have a demonstrated ability to abduct squad-sized units of the army and federal police, torture them to death, decapitate them, and then leave their bodies (or just their heads) as a message to the broader community.[22] They would not be so bold if they were not so well armed. Civilians flee the violence by crossing into the US.

WHEN TERRORISTS SUBCONTRACT TO CARTELS: THE ARBABSIAR PLOT

The famous Saudi ambassador plot is an excellent example of the complex and deadly operations that can result from criminal and terrorist interconnections. Mansor Arbabsiar, a naturalized US citizen, pled guilty on October 17, 2012, in federal court in New York to his part in a scheme with members of the Iranian government to recruit a Mexican drug cartel, Los Zetas, to kill Saudi Arabia's ambassador to the United States by bombing a Washington, D.C., restaurant. Arbabsiar, fifty-eight, a former used car salesman from Corpus Christi, Texas, admitted to arranging a $1.5 million payment from Iran to kill Saudi ambassador Adel al-Jubeir, describing as "no big deal" the fact that others, including US senators, could die in the bombing.

The veracity and seriousness of the plot, as well as the involvement of Iran, was ascertained when Arbabsiar was called overseas to arrange wire transfers totaling approximately $100,000 to be sent in early August 2011 to two FBI undercover accounts as a down payment for an undercover operative to carry out the assassination. When on September 20, 2011, the undercover DEA agent told Arbabsiar that the operation was ready and requested that he pay half of the agreed-upon price of $1.5 million for the murder or that Arbabsiar himself go to Mexico as collateral for the final payment of the fee, Arbabsiar agreed to travel to Mexico, which he did on September 28, 2011. After his capture, Arbabsiar made phone calls to his Quds Force contact, Gholam Shakuri, at the behest of and under the monitoring of US law enforcement, wherein Shakuri pressed Arbabsiar to execute the plot as soon as possible. That provided all the confirmation US law enforcement needed that Iran was indeed behind the plot.[23]

Had the plot succeeded, it could have started a war. The Arbabsiar plot was the most serious Iranian-attempted act of terror against the United States since the Khobar Towers bombing in 1996; it likely would have compelled the United States and Saudi Arabia to retaliate against Iran with military force.[24] Precisely because of the possibly dire consequences, a lot of security analysts have questioned the plot's veracity. True, Iran has a long history of assassinating its dissidents even while they are overseas, but Iran experts have struggled to understand "why Iran would suddenly choose a Mexican drug cartel over trusted and financially dependent proxies such as Hezbollah and pro-Iranian Muslim militias."[25] Subcontracting poses risks.

Besides, Iran has refined its covert action tradecraft since the

US introduced more draconian counterterrorism measures after 9/11. Nonattribution and plausible deniability are thought to have been the key motivators in this choice. The consequences of the operation would have been severe for the United States, not only because of the number of dead, but geopolitically.

Iran is not alone, either; Somali terrorist group Al Shabaab is also smuggling its operatives into the United States over the US-Mexico border. Joan Neuhaus Schaan, an expert on homeland security and terrorism, considers Al Shabaab "certainly a real threat to US security and an increasing threat to US security,"[26] because of the ability of Somali nationals to gain access to the United States through Mexico.

In May 2010 an indictment was unsealed in Texas federal court that revealed that a Somali man, Ahmed Muhammed Dhakane, led a human smuggling ring that brought East Africans, including Somalis with ties to terror groups, via Brazil and across the Mexican border and into Texas. The indictment also alleged that Dhakane was associated with Al-Barakat, a Somalia-based company that is involved in the transfer of money to Somalia. The US government claims that Al-Barakat is involved in funding terrorist groups and has designated the company a terrorist entity. Diaspora Somalis transfer a great deal of legitimate money to family members back in Somalia through organizations such as Al-Barakat because there is no official banking system in the country, and Somali militant groups like Al Shabaab use this flow of money as camouflage for their own financial transactions,[27] the process of "layering," "stacking," and "dispersion."

Somalia's Al Shabaab attempted to conduct operations against the US Embassy in Mexico City.[28] On June 9, 2010, after the plot was discovered, Mexican marines raided the house of a suspected Al Shabaab operative in the middle-class Mexico City neighborhood of Roma—less than a mile from the US Embassy—and found 22.7 kilos of explosive material and detonators.

LEGITIMACY AND SECURITY

The defense of territory is one of the key functions of a state, but it can be co-opted by nonstate actors. At the outbreak of World War I, German economist and sociologist Max Weber defined the state as a human community that successfully claims a monopoly on the legitimate use of physical force within a given territory.[29] The ability to provide security is one of the key tests of legitimacy for a government leader. I saw it in Colombia: the insurgents took over terrain with little government presence (but high coca crop presence), and then the paramilitaries stepped in to provide private self-defense against them, unleashing brutality that nearly collapsed the Colombian state. In Venezuela, in response to the collapse of the state's ability to provide security, private security firms have skyrocketed in both number of companies and number of personnel. The privatization of security is one of the hallmarks of a state's downward spiral, its loss of power vis-à-vis nonstate actors.

Furthermore, a deep concern about or urgent need for security provides a good justification for the erosion or removal of the standard citizen rights of constitutional liberal democracy, including elections themselves. The first major modern text—and the locus classicus—of this might-makes-right argument was published during the English Civil War of the seventeenth century: Thomas Hobbes's *Leviathan*. As the Roundheads (fighting for the rising merchant class, who wanted parliamentary representation) battled the Cavaliers (fighting to defend the aristocratic feudalism of landlords and parliamentary representation limited to their class), Hobbes (himself supported by an aristocrat he tutored) argued that people should support the king, who could best defend them and impose order in the territory.

Leviathan is generally considered the first modern text of political theory. Following Hobbes's argument to its natural conclusion, however, if the one who can best provide security and access to food and jobs is a cartel capo, Lebanese Hezbollah, or the Italian Mafia, then supporting that entity is not an unreasonable choice. This is not merely theoretical. There are areas of Mexico where the Mexican military dare not land a helicopter; in Ciudad Juárez, residents were grateful when the Mexican military capitulated and ceded control to the Sinaloa cartel, for the gruesome killings decreased dramatically. The problem is that such power—holding a monopoly on violence in a given territory—provides legitimacy over time. Russian president Vladimir Putin understands this; it is a core reason he has advocated freezing the Ukrainian conflict[30] with his proxy soldiers ("Little Green Men"), who've been in place for more than a year—after their occupation ends, they will be accepted as legitimate.

There are a number of proposals to tackle the US-Mexico border problem. Some would tackle it right at the border, while others would go to the source—deeper into Central America. One proposal is to increase the number of people running US border patrols to forty-five thousand. This proposal is considered a minimum, given that forty-five thousand was the high-water figure of the NYPD and its civilian component, who protected eight million New Yorkers. Many find it unreasonable, then, to expect fewer officers to protect five thousand miles of the Canadian frontier, a couple of thousand miles of Mexican border, the Virgin Islands, Puerto Rico, and the Gulf Coast states.[31]

The real solution, though, lies in building law enforcement capacity in Latin America, ending the corruption that alienates government officials from the people they are supposed to serve, and ending the flow of drugs and weapons—which means ending US drug consumption and US weapons sales. There will be no solution until the region exhausts itself and the people produce a merchant and political class with the will to turn their countries around, as they have in Colombia. That is an internal evolutionary process that will take a lot of time and be largely outside US control.

In short, the real solution to the convergent threat is multi-pronged: stop funding and arming bad guys, and reinforce state legitimacy through security that comes from rule of law. Only long-term security plus anticorruption measures plus social justice will ultimately keep us safe from the growing convergent threat of the crime-terror pipeline.

The Stories We Tell

OUR YOUTH: AT THE CROSSFIRE OF THE INFORMATION WARS

To maintain and add membership, both terrorists and cartels inculcate the young into their narratives and manipulate their emotions to join their ranks. Drug cartels use *narcocultura,* the culture of drug trafficking. *Narcocultura* is pervasive: it encompasses every media and cultural outlet there is, from music to journalism to graffiti. The music video for *El Movimiento Alterado—Carteles Unidos, Volume 5* has had almost 3.7 million views on YouTube;[1] it celebrates the violence of the Sinaloa cartel (*El Chapo* Gúzman's cartel)—describing beheadings, for example—while insisting that "the united cartels fight to protect your land." It means protection from the government: in other words, the *Carteles Unidos* position themselves as an insurgency. *Los Tucanes de Tijuana,* the local cartel's official narco band, won a Latin Grammy; you can follow them on tour and buy their music on iTunes.

In response, the Mexican government has been producing *anti-narcocorridos,* songs that denounce the violence of the cartels and the corruption of the kingpin lifestyle. With more modern styles and heavy synthesizing, they sound more urban and Americanized than the *narcocorridos*. You can tell from the start what the message will be; thus are the two sides of the war taking to the streets with their music.

Adding to the narco musical menu is *narco-rap*. Similar to the underground gangsta-rap scene that emerged on the East and West Coasts of the United States in the late 1980s, narco-rap has a more urban tone; rather than celebrate the exploits of the cartels, it deals more with the realities of living in the streets of Tamaulipas, on the border with Texas, under the cloud of the violent turf war between the Zetas and Gulf cartels and the watchful eye of *halcones* ("hawks"), the cartel spies who are the lookouts for the cartel convoys in the streets, guarding against the intrusion of government agents.

This influence operation (as intelligence agencies call it—"IO" for short) extends to the written word, too, both in its standard and in its rather more gruesome forms. *Narcomensajes* are messages left on dead bodies, often explaining who committed the murder and why. A body will often exhibit signs of torture (such as the victim having been burned by fire or acid while alive) and is sometimes decapitated as well. Decapitation is a narco signal that someone did not do as he or she was ordered, or was a traitor, playing both sides of the fence.

The narcos also post banners (*narcomantas*) with threatening messages to rival organizations. The Knights Templar, *La Familia Michoacana*, and the *Cartel Jalisco Nueva Generación* (known as CJNG) have all used them. The latter group announced its arrival on the scene with a gruesome twist: in 2011, it hung the bodies of thirty-five Zeta members on prominent display with signs proclaiming itself the "Zeta Killers." Later, in 2013, CJNG hung more *narcomantas,* announcements that it was fighting to rid Mexico of its "bad actors" (who also happened to be its rivals) and promising the people a cleansing of the kidnappers and extortionists.[2]

When leaders of *La Familia Michoacana* and the Knights Templar were caught, *Jalisco Nueva Generación* grew and claimed its old terrain. In February 2014, Los Zetas hung *narcomantas* celebrating the capture of *El Chapo* Guzmán, the head of their rival Sinaloa cartel. On February 6, 2016, new *narcomantas* appeared, proclaiming that the presence of *La Nueva Familia* (the offshoot of the old *Familia*) would cleanse the area of the presence of *Jalisco Nueva Generación*. The next day, yet another *narcomanta* appeared, in the township of Lázaro Cárdenas, posted by a criminal group calling themselves *Los Justicieros*—"The Justice Men"—and announcing their "ownership" of the central square. All of these messages are about establishing territorial control. The cartels are purporting to act as protostates. They are vying with each other, but also against the state.

Prior to his recapture in January 2016, *El Chapo* Guzmán would hang *narcomantas* denouncing the "abuses" of the state for the actions of the Mexican marines, who eventually recaptured him. He positioned himself as a protector of the people from the evil state, particularly President Enrique Peña Nieto, who some of his *narcomantas* would call out by name. Mexicans consumed the message: a Mexican friend in New York told me she and her friends would wear *El Chapo* T-shirts, celebrating him as a hero, like some people wear T-shirts of Che Guevara. I wondered if she saw the parallel between the T-shirts and the *narcomensajes* left on the bodies of the thirty-four thousand people[3] for whose deaths he is responsible. Probably not: she told me she had no idea what a murderous thug *El Chapo* was until I gave her a book on him.

The manipulation narrative to justify the seizure of territory and the recruitment of its residents extends into the journalistic and cyber-worlds. Not only do the cartels kidnap, torture, and murder so many journalists that many publications (even in the US) now self-censor to avoid these dangers, but the cartels also issue their own press releases, recruit reporters they can control, or even outright buy their own newspapers. They are, after all, flush with cash and always in the market for good money-laundering opportunities. Digital media (their publications and their social media profiles) accelerates their spread of disinformation about the government or their own beneficence and also issues threats—and given the cartels' reputation for following through with swift brutality, these warnings are very effective.

Since narcos know the government watches their digital world, they hire *narcohackers* to conduct counterintelligence operations against the government—i.e., to stop government infiltration of their networks. Everyone knows the consequences if narcohackers flip and go to work for the other side—in September 2011, Los Zetas hung two bodies from a bridge with the *narcomensaje* "Internet snitches"; they were known bloggers telling the truth about cartel brutality. However, when the police are cooperative, the cartels will advocate (or even write themselves) positive stories about the corrupt and compliant cops. That way the public will be driven to trust the police officers who are working for the cartels.

There are counterpropaganda efforts, too. Web sites like *El Blog del Narco*, *Mundo Narco*, and *Diario del Narco* sought to expose the truth about narco techniques and brutality, but they were shut down by narco threats. The cyber-hacker group Anonymous launched an effort to expose the names of cartel members and supporters, but the project ended. No one is quite sure why, but fear of brutal retribution was likely the cause. You tangle with the US government, they send prosecutors after you; you tangle with the cartels, they torture you to death—and your spouse, children, parents, and siblings, too.

Like terrorists, drug traffickers tap deep into the cultural psyche. Malverde beer, popular in Sinaloa, is named after Jesús Malverde,[4] a Sinaloa criminal revered as a Robin Hood who is alleged to have been executed under Mexican dictator Porfirio Diáz (though there are many different versions of the story of his death) in Sinaloa, on May 3, 1909. According to legend, he was denied a proper burial, and his body was left to rot in public as an example—like the cartels do now. Jesús Malverde is today revered as the patron saint of drug trafficking.

The sanctification of the criminal cause is taken to its pinnacle by members of the Knights Templar cartel, who present themselves as protectors of the people against the evil and corrupt state, and even more so against the violent Los Zetas. Their members carry with them a "code of conduct" booklet with Knights Templar holding swords on the cover. Allegedly the booklet tells them that they are to fight poverty, injustice, and tyranny, protect women and children, and be loyal to their families and country. The Knights Templar also hand out and post flyers that denounce the federal authorities and that contain Bible verses and quotes, and give free T-shirts with antipolice slogans to each participant in protests in favor of the cartels (*narcomanifestaciones*). (Hugo Chávez would do the same thing: gather massive crowds with the promise of free beer and give each person a red T-shirt so there would be a sea of red for the TV cameras.)

Just prior to the Pope's visit in 2011, the Knights Templar publicly placed the bodies of eight people they had murdered along with *narcomensajes* warning other cartels to stay out of their territory while the Pope visited. Hearts and minds, indeed. For the cartels, these tactics are particularly effective in areas where violence is high, police protection is lacking, and government resources are low: they encroach on the space left by government and pry it wider open.

The propaganda that criminal organizations use is similar to that of insurgencies and terrorist groups who position themselves as freedom fighters. Their terror tactics are designed to scare people—both civilian citizens and government or law enforcement officials. They're also aimed at spreading the glorification of their lifestyle so that they can gain control of those upper factions of society that are most prized: the highly educated and well connected—those who can move money, influence policy, and run for political office, extending the criminal pipeline deep into our government and long into the future. The bad guys plan a whole generation ahead.

Entry-level recruitment is usually subtle: asking kids to be straw buyers of weapons, usually inside the United States. The cartels also place ads in classified sections of newspapers offering to pay $500 for a drive to a destination in the US; the driver will be unaware that the car is packed with drugs. Or, more simply, they place ads offering $500 a week for "entry-level positions"; that is a lot of money to a sixteen-year-old in Mexico, but these kids are as cheap and expendable to the cartels as they are to Daesh. The US government has also paid for ads in these classified sections, warning readers that such offers are criminal acts of recruitment into the cartels and to stay away.

The objective of recruitment is clear: get power to control the money flows. Los Zetas, the cartel that was born of former Special Ops, trains these "entry-level" kids in paramilitary operations in a program akin to a boot camp. They are trained in surveillance and assassination tactics, including weaponry, martial arts, hand-to-hand combat, aggressive driving, and even SERE: survival, evasion, resistance, and escape.

The more genteel and longer-term offerings for the particularly bright ones are college scholarships for those who want to study law and criminal justice, so that they may enter law enforcement or become judges with lifetime loyalty to the cartels. That is the kind of long-term strategic thinking law enforcement needs to confront. The cartels' highest-value targets for recruitment are American police officers and border agents, precisely because they are trusted by law enforcement and know the vulnerabilities within the system, and can thus help the cartels to circumvent interdiction. An added bonus: the officers may even be trained in weaponry and torture techniques.

As in Colombia's reintegration program, the Mexican government has joined the narrative battle space and reached out to its youth with anti-narco comics and songs directed at kids.[5] The Mexican government sponsored a ten-episode comic series depicting the heroics of federal agents and cops. This is not unlike the comic strips and TV shows glorifying the US G-Men (the FBI) during Prohibition in the US, when mobsters such as Al Capone or outlaws like Bonnie and Clyde, John Dillinger, "Pretty Boy" Floyd, and "Baby Face" Nelson were admired by Depression-era impoverished and desperate Americans. The bad guys and the media platforms may have changed, but the battle for the "hearts and minds" of supporters has been going on for centuries—certainly since the time of Christ.

THE JIHADI NEW WAVE: FOREIGN FIGHTERS AND "LONE WOLVES"

Few people know more about how bad guys recruit good guys than Sri Lankan de-radicalization expert Professor Rohan Gunaratna. We met while working together at the Asymmetric Warfare Group, where his expertise in manipulating identity narratives (in his case: turning the bad guys back to good) was useful. When I was in Singapore in March 2013 for other reasons, I went to visit him at his home and brought another friend who had been involved in the Global War on Terror. We three chatted for several hours.

Gunaratna finds a predictable pattern of radicalization. First, there is some event in the teenage years that triggers a search for self-identity. The crisis can be personal (heartbreak in romance, death of a loved one), economic (layoff, lack of advancement), social (racism or discrimination), or political (feeling that an event in another place affects him or her, like attacks on Muslims elsewhere). The young person feels he or she will never psychologically recover, begins to question his or her worldview or place in life, and goes in search of group with a set of beliefs that might give him or her a sense of purpose.

Then the person searches for institutions that will provide answers, a way to understand and process the trauma of the crisis. These institutions become "incubators,"[6] where the process of radicalization starts. They are everywhere, and as varied as the stories that drive people to radicalize: mosques and Islamic centers, prisons, coffee shops, bookstores, student associations, *shisha* smoking bars, halal butcher stores—or, more simply, the Internet.

When that person has a confrontation with other members or leaders of a moderate mosque and then leaves to find a more radical Salafi mosque (practicing the ultra-conservative branch of Sunni Islam that developed in Arabia as a reaction to colonialism in the early eighteenth century) more suited to the anger he or she is feeling, that is a pretty good sign we could have a blossoming jihadist on our hands. Assessing whether an individual poses a risk of becoming a jihadist is not easy. The person's behavior has to be assessed holistically, considering a number of factors and relationships in context. While adoption of a jihadist Salafi interpretation of Islam (*Salafiyyah jihadiyah*) is the final step in Sunni radicalization, there are other signs: alienation from old social groups in favor of other Salafis, quitting drinking alcohol or smoking, growing a beard, adopting traditional Islamic dress, and assuming voluntary duties inside the Salafi community.

Back to the point of context and holistic assessment: I have plenty of Brooklyn hipster friends who are bearded, teetotaling vegans but are in no way Islamist radicals. When radicalization is under way, the radical cell seeks a role model, a spiritual and operational mentor who has street credibility as a jihadist, having fought in Afghanistan, Bosnia, Kashmir, or any other jihad arena.[7] This is their revolutionary hero, whom they will seek to emulate, in order to belong, by becoming a good fellow revolutionary Muslim. (In its mechanism, not its goal, this is not dissimilar to the *Chavistas* and their purported Bolivarian Revolution.)

In the jihadist cell, total group thinking takes over and each individual assumes his or her personal responsibility for jihad. There can be a variety of tasks: operational training, perhaps by traveling to seek military training; renting safe houses; making explosives; identifying targets.[8] A bit before they are ready to execute a terrorist attack, the radicalized youth revert to Western dress and behavior in order to evade surveillance and capture before the attack is carried out. You might think they have re-entered the Western liberal community, but they are actually just blending in so they can get close to their targets.

As criminals like to recruit law enforcement, jihadists like to recruit Westerners, and Daesh has improved the operational model that was first formulated by Al Qaeda. All but one of the terrorist attacks (plotted or carried out) in the West by the different elements of the Global Jihad Movement since 9/11 were perpetrated by home-grown cells: the terrorists were born, resided, and were educated for a substantial and significant time in the United States, Canada, Western European countries, or Australia.

While the organizational affiliation behind the attack or plot will vary, the homegrown cells are highly prized by jihadists as a key operational asset: ready-made individuals who speak Western languages, are familiar with the Western mentality and lifestyle, and in most cases hold genuine documentation, like passports and driver's licenses. Among the "Abbotabad papers" (found during the raid that killed Osama bin Laden) was an instruction from bin Laden to Abu Bassir al-Yamani, leader of Al Qaeda in the Arabian Peninsula (AQAP), to "[c]oncentrate on the Yemeni emigrants who come back to visit Yemen and have American visas or citizenship and would be able to conduct operation inside America."[9]

I attended a UN Security Council briefing on November 24, 2015, discussing the recruitment and possible de-radicalization of fighters from the West who had gone to fight alongside Daesh in Syria and Iraq. Analyzing the social network is essential. Three-quarters of foreign fighters join through friends; one-fifth join through family. Often those who live with them are not aware they have a jihadist-in-the-making under their roof: the prospective jihadists hook up and connect online in secret. Eighty percent of youth who radicalize do not have a religious background, but radicalize through contact with other active and prospective jihadists on social media sites.

The consensus at the UN Security Council was that we shouldn't just focus on socioeconomic factors, but also on how those factors connect with grievances. Therefore, counterterrorism strategies that violate human rights are counterproductive. Approaches should be family-based and culturally literate. Children are not necessarily looking for religion, but rather something to belong to.

To the terrorist groups (as to the criminal groups), these kids are little more than cannon fodder. When and if they do travel to Iraq or Syria to get Daesh training, they sometimes do not make it any farther than Turkey. In border terrain, they are trained minimally in how to handle an automatic weapon and a suicide vest. They are given little combat experience for a reason: they are used for suicide missions. However, they are indoctrinated to believe that they are not allowed to become martyrs until they pass on their knowledge to at least five people, growing Daesh terrorist ranks exponentially.

Two factors determine whether people are willing to fight and die. First, there must be fusion with their group; and second, the fusion must be great enough that they come to perceive themselves as physically strong and invincible, to believe they possess superhuman powers, thus driving them to identify further with the group, in a self-reinforcing cycle.

To activate this willingness to fight to the death, Daesh needs the ultimate enemy fighting on its terrain: it needs Western forces in the Middle East. It is in a hadith (hadiths are the collection of traditions containing sayings of the Prophet Muhammad that, along with accounts of his daily practice, constitute the major source of guidance for Muslims apart from the Koran) that when an army with black flags (like Daesh uses) rises from Khorasan (a region in modern-day Afghanistan), it prepares the terrain for the arrival of Imam Mahdi, the Twelfth, or "Hidden," imam, who will rule over the caliphate that will bring "The Hour," the End of Days, the Apocalypse. In other words, Daesh thinks it is bringing forth the Apocalypse. Since Daesh took over the Khorasan region in

Afghanistan, the recruitment of foreign terrorist fighters from Central Asia has become more acute: more fighters travel to die.

One of their main recruitment tools is their glossy magazine, *Dabiq*, named for a town in rural Aleppo, Syria, that is featured in an old hadith about the "The Hour," the apocalyptic battle. *Dabiq*'s headlining motto, with which it opens every issue, is: "The spark has been lit here in Iraq and its heat will continue to intensify, by Allah's permission, until it burns the crusader army in Dabiq." The motto is also featured in Daesh videos featuring Al-Zarqawi (the former leader of Al Qaeda in Iraq, who then founded Daesh), marching in slow motion, holding up the Daesh black flag.[10] Daesh's public actions are designed to presage The Hour, "including the blowing up of shrines and the tossing of homosexuals from rooftops."[11] Even the sexual enslavement of women is part of this. "According to a hadith, the apocalypse will come when a 'slave gives birth to her master.'"[12]

Daesh's "jihadist pornography" has been stunningly effective. Films of gun-toting fighters out on patrol, calling themselves *Rafidah* Hunters (*"rafidah"* is a pejorative term Sunnis use to refer to Shia; in Arabic it means "the rejectors," because the Shia reject the "true" lineage from the Prophet Muhammad), often culminate in personalized and graphic beheadings. "Don't hear about us, hear from us," say the Daesh recruits.[13] Their messages of brutality with purpose are targeted, whether by Twitter or YouTube, in *Dabiq*, or in the encrypted audio file-sharing app Zello, where followers can tune in to ISIS sermons.

The current trend of the Global Jihad Movement's activating local citizens in Western countries was officially espoused as military doctrine in a 2004 publication by Mustafa Satmariam Nasser (better known by his nom de guerre, Abu Musab al-Suri), *The Call to Global Islamic Resistance*. This text is so familiar to scholars of violent extremism that they refer to it simply by its initials, *GIR*. Al-Suri wrote the *GIR* while on the run in the aftermath of 9/11, when America was aggressively hunting Al Qaeda terrorists. His purpose was suited to those circumstances: to greatly reduce Al Qaeda's vulnerability to disruption by transforming it from a hierarchical organization to a decentralized one[14]—in other words, a flat and adaptive network.

In the *GIR*, al-Suri advocates constant and independent jihadi activity at the level of individual or small, isolated Al Qaeda cells, all over the world, against Western interests and targets. This would lead to an unprecedented number of attacks,[15] many more than one centrally commanded organization could ever achieve. The attacks would appear random but be continual, creating psychological terror and making life untenable in Western countries. This decentralized global jihad would give the impression of a bourgeoning global movement and inspire more Muslims all over the world to join the cause. Al Qaeda commanders Ayman Al-Zawahiri and Anwar al-Awlaki recognized the brilliance of al-Suri's argument and adopted the *GIR* as Al Qaeda's official warfare doctrine. Thus Al-Suri's "death by a thousand cuts" military strategy became Al Qaeda's Global Jihad Movement.

Global Jihad Movement ideology radicalizes and mobilizes using mechanisms that are remarkably similar to those in "the GIR." In al-Suri's work and subsequent derivative texts, America is a "disease," the "cure" for which is jihad. America, the Soviet East, and the Crusader West (sometimes referred to by the ancient term *"Al-Room,"* to further the impression of historical legitimacy) are destined for decline because such is the will of God, who is on the side of the jihadists.

The worldview is simple and binary. This future superior *ummah* (Muslim community) will be led by the jihadists, who are in effect precursors and the vanguard of the rest of the (purified) Muslim *ummah*. As in conquest ideology, the jihadist revolutionary will purify himself and his entire community through his struggles.[16] (Similar arguments were used by the conquistadors of South America in the late fifteenth and early sixteenth centuries.)

Although carried out in the name of Daesh, the terrorist attacks in Paris in early November 2015 were *GIR* strategy perfectly executed by French nationals and native speakers living in the *banlieues* (suburbs), where francophone North African Muslims feel angry, warehoused in public housing projects. With some direction from overseas and minimal training, several attacks were carried out at once, terrifying the whole city. Furthermore, the bombs that would have gone off inside the Stade de France would have forced tens of thousands of people out specific exits and onto the streets in predictable patterns, where more suicide bombers would have killed them at strategic nodes, generating even more pandemonium.

Daesh is well funded by the same thing that funds the repressive *Chavista* government in Venezuela: oil. Colombia's FARC and the Mexican cartels also extort oil companies or simply punch holes in the pipelines and steal oil. For Daesh, it is even easier, as it controls territory in two oil-rich countries: Iraq and Syria. In Syria, while it controls the territory, it controls the supply to the locals, to the truckers, to the hospitals in enemy territory, and even to the Assad regime, whom it fights. In 2015, Daesh was making $1.5 million a day from the oil sold at the wellheads in the territory under its control.[17] Thus, the Syrian dictatorship has to buy diesel fuel and oil from the insurgent terrorist group it is fighting.

So Daesh is not only the most sophisticated manipulator of narratives on the Internet and other platforms, but the sophistication is funded by vast coffers: it is the "world's richest terrorist organization,"[18] benefiting from a vast black market. In Iraq, in addition to the oil, it overran Iraq's Central Bank and stole $420 million from its vaults. It extorts local businesses, sells women into prostitution, and coerces local government officials so that it benefits at the expense of Iraqi taxpayers. Like all terrorist groups, it also gets donations from wealthy donors and charities.

The form of illicit trade in which the Western consumer is most complicit is the trade in antiquities. Modern-day Iraq is the cradle of civilization: Mesopotamia thrived in the Indus Valley between the Tigris and Euphrates rivers. Syria's and Iraq's antiquities predate Rome, Greece, and even Egypt—and are highly coveted by museums and collectors. The fog of war has facilitated looting and the corruption of customs officials, and many antiquities have been reaching dealers in Vienna, Munich, London, and New York. Daesh profits from the international art market. (The need for applying banking-level due diligence standards to the international art market was discussed at a UN Security Council meeting on terrorist finance in December 2016.)

WHY IDENTITY NARRATIVES WORK

Yet regardless of how much a terrorist group may have "sold out" to the profit motive by funding itself mainly through the business of illicit trade, grievance is a good fund-raiser. A good grievance is still the best tool to raise donations, recruit fighters, and motivate the diaspora. Groups use the classic manipulations of subversive identity politics: to be one of us, you will support our cause; to be a good citizen, you need to be a good supporter of our revolutionary cause: you will fund it; you will advocate it, and you will enjoin others to do so, too. In the context of terror, the shortest route to pride is making others fear you. Fear is power.

The violence we see across our television screens at night is at least as much about getting and keeping power as it is about Christians or Jews or Muslims. If you strip away the Daesh rhetoric on religion, the scenario is the same: thugs inspiring fear to consolidate their power. Religion is their excuse, fear their method. Daesh and the Mexican cartels operate much the same way: they control territory, kill their enemies, videotape beheadings to intimidate those who would challenge them, and use pervasive propaganda to recruit. The Mexican cartels also use religious insignia to mark their territory and legitimize their power.

Nationalism and national identity are always necessary fictions with a symbiotic relationship to their consumers: the citizenry create national identity, but that identity also creates the citizenry, who get a part of their personal identity from it. In asserting "I am American" or "I am Czech" or "I am Venezuelan," I assert my identity, or at least that part of it as it relates to a collectivity in contradistinction to others; think of Marx, for whom nationality is nothing more than the outward assertion in foreign relations of an organized state.[19] But I am only any of these things insofar as I accept and partake in the mythology of that nationality.

These myths are not irrelevant. "Myths which are believed in tend to become true, because they set up a type or 'persona,' which the average person will do his best to resemble."[20] A change in the myth, then, will bring changes to the hearts of individuals, in two ways. First, it will shape what individual citizens will come to value as the virtues of citizenship in the nation to which they belong. Second, a change in the myth will result in a change in the individual's relation to the group, to the collectivity, changing the way the individual sees him- or herself reflected in the gaze of fellow citizens.

The public realm has, therefore, a fundamental and symbiotic role in connecting the personal to the political. British-American-Ghanaian philosopher Kwame Appiah makes the point cogently: "Once labels are applied to people, ideas about people who fit the label come to have social and psychological effects. In particular, these ideas shape the ways people conceive of themselves and their projects . . . I shape my life by the thought that something is an appropriate aim or an appropriate way of acting for an American, a black man, a philosopher."[21]

IDENTITIES IN CRISIS

Group identities that result in political violence or simply an erosion of justice are evident in the terrorist and criminal groups I have seen firsthand. Hezbollah, the Mafia, drug cartels: they all in one way or another identify themselves in contradistinction to the government they are challenging. For Hezbollah, the cause is allegedly religious: to redress the oppression of the Shia, as well as defend Lebanon against Israel. For the others, their cause might be more avowedly financial, but they too use religious iconography: cartels have patron saints and modern-day troubadours who sing of their exploits in *narcocorridos*. They all move us to participate in challenging the rule of law and the government institutions that (were they well functioning and not corrupt) would protect our rights and leave us a way out, with the levers of power in our hands, so we could change or reform those who govern us when we decide we have had enough.

So how do we tell the good guys from the bad? How do we know whether the group we believe in and its leader, who purports to fight for our interests, is liberating or oppressing us? After all, "One man's terrorist is another man's freedom fighter" goes the common refrain. How can we tell the difference between self-identifying groups fighting for better justice and equality and political inclusion and those groups whose identities are being hijacked by demagogues whose intent is to manipulate the groups' emotions into a broad base of support for his or her sinister quest for power—which will ultimately oppress the people the demagogue claims to be liberating?

What we as autonomous citizens want is not just freedom from interference—to be left alone to get on with our lives and our plans—but freedom from tyranny. Freedom from tyranny means that the rules (laws) cannot suddenly be changed without our consent, that we cannot suddenly wake up and find ourselves oppressed. Freedom from tyranny is what we philosophers call positive freedom: it is freedom with power.

It is not my project here to destroy identities completely, as cages from which we, as intelligent beings, must escape in order to attain our ultimate individualistic and rational apotheosis—though that position does have some arguable cogency and inherent elegance. Rather, the point is to examine numerous instances where rational citizens seeking a better life through identifying with a group have been cajoled into sacrificing their long-term goals for short-term stability. Authoritarian regimes are particularly adept at this manipulation, particularly when they utilize political parties to mobilize support and indemnify political labor through the game theory economics of stable (if corrupted) political institutions.[22] One way to tell the power-hungry demagogue from a justice-loving revolutionary is through their actions: over time, their actions will reveal their motives. In all institutional reform to governance structures, the Devil is in the details.

To use one example, people in Mexico generally choose the relative stability of life under the shadow of the drug cartels over being caught in the crossfire of the violent clashes of the war on drugs waged by the Mexican government. For example, as noted, "Calderón's War" led to Felipe Calderón's leaving the presidency in 2012 with an 8 percent approval rating. However, what citizens would truly prefer is what would be behind the nonexistent Door #3: life under a just, inclusive, liberal democratic system where politicians are honest, law-abiding, and responsive to the needs of their citizens and drug cartels and terrorist attacks do not exist.

But since criminal and terrorist organizations benefit from each other's exploitation of state weakness or failure for their advantage, they both have a vested interest in corrupting good governance. It is not just because such degradation is the short path to their achieving their smuggling and money-laundering aims, but because the expansion of their activities requires broad-based popular support: the bad guys need good guys to sign on. In order to achieve this, they need to restrict the options of good, rational citizens. They can restrict the options either by taking real actions to limit them (such as changing the constitution or governing institutions) or by psychologically manipulating fear, resentment, or other emotions of nationalism or group identity. In this way, citizens become the pawns of criminals and terrorists and tools in their own oppression.

In fact, a properly functioning governmental institution is as strong a basis as any for a sense of community belonging. The United States is an example of this. A country founded on the premise of being a "melting pot" has come together behind the unifying political principles of its Constitution and Bill of Rights and its judicial system. Whether these principles are always observed in the country's institutions is another question. The fact is that they are ingrained in the American psyche as a unifying factor behind what it means to be American (to wit, Superman's pledge to protect "truth, justice, and the American way"). Even when groups run afoul of each other (as is arguably the case with the current polarization in America along various fault lines), they all claim their stake in that unifying principle.

Properly functioning governmental institutions will reinforce community ties; effective political ties will engender organic ones over time. A governmental institution that functions properly will lead to a community and a "state" that will cohere and peacefully reinforce the political and legal structure that unites its citizens, who will participate politically and seek to reform it if necessary, rather than to revolt, secede, and found a new nation-state or an alternate (perhaps criminal) system of governance. People who have had to cohabitate and share a territory and an extended history will naturally form bonds that unite them.

Perhaps the problem with revolution and insurgency, secession and balkanization, is not the arbitrary drawing of geographical boundaries, but rather the breakdown of the legal and political infrastructure in such a way that it does not represent the interests or the will of one or more segments of the population.

Government institutions are supposed to further human autonomy and dignity. When they no longer do so—when they, in fact, even *quash* autonomy and dignity—they have contradicted their purpose and become illegitimate. It has always been my view that it is not legitimate for a fearful citizenry to surrender the power and rights of current or future generations by allowing a charismatic demagogue to centralize power: some rights are simply inalienable. They are so intertwined with the notions of human rights, political equality, and the very purpose of government that they simply cannot be taken away.

The negation of future free choice that occurs with an elected dictatorship (e.g., Venezuelans giving Chávez the power to rule by decree) or when there is support of a criminalized governance certainly seems to imply that there are deep flaws in that country's fundamental social and/or political conditions—conditions such as desperation, hunger, fear, ignorance, and intense propaganda (with possible censoring of differing views). The very conditions that led to the antidemocratic choice, though, are usually exacerbated, not alleviated, by that very choice—a prime reason for retaining electoral control and supporting good governance, anticorruption measures, and the rule of law.

LIGHTS OUT

Mid-2016, I was in New York on a video call with one of my sources in Caracas, Venezuela, when the screen went dark. A minute later, I got a text on the encrypted app we used to protect us from surveillance by the regime, which had imprisoned a lot of people for less than what we were discussing.

Sorry. The lights went out. FML.

The electrical grid was failing due to a lack of maintenance, mainly because corrupt government officials had just plundered government coffers and sent the money into bank accounts in Panama, Andorra, and Switzerland. The country's collapse was accelerating; food was becoming scarcer with every passing day. By early 2017, riots for food were commonplace, with hungry protesters shouting at soldiers to shoot them because they were hungry. Friends of mine were hospitalized and dying because they could not find common medications.

The government refused to grant a referendum on holding a

midterm presidential election that had been overwhelmingly demanded by the desperate citizenry; it had canceled the December 2016 local elections and instead appointed the sanctioned drug trafficker and renowned terrorist supporter Tareck El Aissami as vice president, virtually ensuring that no one would overthrow President Nicolás Maduro, because El Aissami would be worse.

In February 2017, my buddy Joe Humire, with whom I had done the asymmetric warfare seminar in Guatemala, was briefing the US Congress that Venezuela posed a threat to the US homeland, through its selling of passports to known terrorists. By that time, the wealthy people I knew in Caracas had dropped an average of 8 kilograms (17.5 pounds) because of food shortages; the poor were starving, with malnutrition rampant among children.

FML? I texted back.

Fuck My Life. It's what we young people say.

If we are to build a better future, with more equality and less violence, we need to understand how interconnected we are. We must accept responsibility for how the choices we make impact the lives of others—and then come back to haunt us as humanitarian or refugee crises or acts of terrorism. When we tolerate corruption, we increase inequality, needed infrastructure does not get properly built, and people become stuck in a system that does not care about them. When we pay for narcotics or prostitution or counterfeit goods or that rare antiquity, when we fuel our cars with gasoline produced by corrupt dictators, we give money to criminals and terrorists. When we buy into their stories that they are doing criminal or terrorist acts for some greater cause, we enable them to recruit our young and add to their ranks, and we give away our power as citizens and our human dignity. All we need to do is think before we buy: what is really happening with this transaction? Money may not buy happiness, but it need not pay for misery.

SELECTED BIBLIOGRAPHY

107th Congress of the United States of America. H.R. 3162 ("Patriot Act"). Washington, D.C.: Government Publishing Office, 2001.

Albanese, Jay S. *Transnational Crime and the 21st Century: Criminal Enterprise, Corruption and Opportunity.* New York: Oxford UP, 2011.

Asher, David and Scott Modell. *Pushback: Countering the Iran Action Network.* Washington, D.C.: Center for a New American Security, September 2013.

Bartell, Dawn L. "Hezbollah and Al Shabaab in Mexico and the Terrorist Threat to the United States." In *Global Security Studies* 3, number 4 (Fall 2012).

BASCAP and UNICRI. *Confiscation of the Proceeds of IP Crime: A Modern Tool for Deterring Counterfeiting and Piracy.*

Bate, Roger. *Phake: The Deadly World of Falsified and Substandard Medicines.* Washington, D.C.: American Enterprise Institute Press, 2012.

Beittel, June S. *Mexico: Organized Crime and Drug Trafficking Organizations.* Congressional report, Washington, D.C.: Congressional Research Service, July 22, 2015.

Berlin, Isaiah. "Two Concepts of Liberty." In *Four Essays on Liberty*, pp. 133–34. New York: Oxford UP, 1969.

Blackstone, Erwin A., Joseph P. Fuhr, and Steve Pociask. "The Health and Economic Effects of Counterfeit Drugs." In *American Health & Drug Benefits* 7, number 4 (2014), pp. 216–24.

Brown, Jon Murray and Rob Minto. "Tennis Match-Fixing: Djokovic Approached in 2007 to Throw Match." In *Financial Times*, January 18, 2016. http://

www.ft.com/intl/cms/s/0/0ae03b0a-bdd0-11e5-846f-79b0e3d20eaf
.html#axzz3z8oWcllv

Calderón Hinojosa, Felipe. Private briefing with Felipe Calderón Hinojosa, Former President of Mexico. New York: Instituto Cervantes, November 9, 2015.

"Canadian Soccer League Rife with Match Fixing, According to Report." In *The Star,* October 15, 2015, p. 15. http://www.thestar.com/sports/soccer /2015/10/15/canadian-soccer-league-rife-with-match-fixing-according -to-report.html

Cardash, Sharon L., Frank J. Cilluffo, and Bert B. Tussing. "Mexico and the Triple Threat." In *The Hybrid Threat: Crime, Terrorism and Insurgency in Mexico,* pp. 16–18. Washington, D.C.: Center for Strategic Leadership, December 2011.

Chayes, Sarah. *Thieves of State: Why Corruption Threatens Global Security.* New York: Norton, 2015.

Financial Action Task Force. *Vulnerabilities of Casinos and Gaming Sector.* Paris: FATF/OECD, March 2009.

Forrest, Brett. *The Big Fix: The Hunt for the Match-Fixers Bringing Down Soccer.* New York: William Morrow, 2014.

Gambling Commission. *The Prevention of Money Laundering and Combating the Financing of Terrorism: Guidance for Remote and Non-Remote Casinos* (2nd ed.). Birmingham, UK: Gambling Commission, July 2013.

Gunaratna, Rohan, and Aviv Oreg. *The Global Jihad Movement.* New York: Rowman & Littlefield, 2015.

Grygiel, Jakub. "The Power of Statelessness." In *Policy Review,* Hoover Institution, April and May 2009, pp. 35–50.

Habermas, Jürgen. *Between Facts and Norms: Contributions to a Discourse Theory of Law and Democracy,* translated by William Rehg. Cambridge, Mass.: MIT Press, 1996.

Hassan, Hassan, and Michael Weiss. *ISIS: Inside the Army of Terror.* New York: Regan Arts, 2015.

Helfstein, Scott, and John Solomo. *Risky Business: The Global Threat Network and the Politics of Contraband.* Washington, D.C.: US Department of Defense's Combating Terrorism Center at West Point, May 2014.

Her Majesty's Ministry of Justice. *The Bribery Act 2010: Guidance.* London: Ministry of Justice, March 2011.

International Chamber of Commerce. *Controlling the Zone: Balancing Facilitation and Control to Combat Illicit Trade in the World's Free Trade Zones.* May 2013.

LaCapra, Dominick. "Experience and Identity." In *Identity Politics Reconsidered,* edited by Linda Martin Alcoff, Michael Hames-García, Satya P. Mohanty, and Paula M. L. Moya. New York: Palgrave Macmillan, 2006, p. 232.

Law Enforcement Alliance of America. "Controlling Key Inputs to Starve Illicit Trade," January 2014.

Liberty Asia and The Freedom Fund. *Modern Slavery and Corruption.* New York: Freedom Fund, 2015.

Loret de Mola, Carlos. *The Evolving Economics of Mexico's Drug Cartels.* New York: Americas Society/Council of the Americas, November 23, 2015.

Marx, Karl. "The German Ideology." In *The Marx-Engels Reader,* edited by Robert C. Tucker. Princeton, NJ: Princeton UP, 1978, p. 163.

McCaffrey, Gen. Barry R. "Mexico: Drugs, Crime and the Rule of Law." In *Hybrid Threat: Crime, Terrorism and Insurgency in Mexico,* Washington, D.C.: HPSI, December 2011, pp. 7–8.

Miller, David. *On Nationality.* New York: Oxford UP, 1999.

Moore, Malcolm. "Chinese Rail Crash Scandal: 'Official Steals $2.8 Billion.'" In *The Telegraph,* August 1, 2011.

Moore, Malcolm and Ralph Atkins. "FIFA: The Fall of the House of Blatter." In *Financial Times,* November 22, 2015.

Moreau, Jean-Luc. "Coartem: Une Tragédie en Trois Actes." In *Crime Pharmaceutique: Une Épidémie Silencieuse,* in *Défis,* number 5, a publication of Institut National des Hautes Études de la Securité et de la Justice (INHESJ). Paris: INHESJ, Juin 2015.

Moreau, Jean-Luc. "Counterfeit Drugs: Fighting Illegal Supply Chains," statement before the Subcommittee on Oversight and Investigations House Energy and Commerce Committee, February 27, 2014.

Moreau, Jean-Luc. "L'industrie pharmaceutique: le délit de contrefaçon est devenu un crime." In *Défis,* number 3, a publication of Institut National des Hautes Études de la Securité et de la Justice (INHESJ). Paris: INHESJ, 2014.

Neumann, Vanessa. *The Autonomy and Legitimacy of States: A Critical Approach to Foreign Intervention.* New York: Columbia University, 2004.

Neumann, Vanessa. "The Global Convergence of the Crime-Terror Threat." In *Orbis* 57, number 2 (Spring 2013).

Neumann, Vanessa. "Never Mind the Metrics: Disrupting Human Trafficking by Alternate Means." In *Journal of International Affairs* 68, number 2 (Spring 2015), pp. 39–53.

Neumann, Vanessa. "The New Nexus of Narcoterrorism: Hezbollah and Venezuela." *E-Notes,* Foreign Policy Research Institute, December 2011.

Neumann, Vanessa. "Of Chinese Snakeheads and Mexican Coyotes: The Globalization of Crime-Terror Pipelines." *E-Notes,* Foreign Policy Research Institute, August 2012.

Neumann, Vanessa. "Radicalization of Diaspora Networks." In *Stratagem* (newsletter for the Asymmetric Operations Warfare Group) 7, number 1 (June 2012).

Ocando, Casto. *Chavistas en el Imperio: Secretos, Tácticas y Escándalos de la Revolución Bolivariana en Estados Unidos.* Miami: Plaza Editorial, 2014.

Ogorodnev, Igor. "Road Rage: Russians Up in Arms over Corrupt, Incompetent Road Builders," *RT,* December 12, 2012. https://www.rt.com/news/ekaterinburg-road-city-manager-855/

O'Hare, Bernadette, Innocent Makuta, Naor Bar-Zeev, Levison Chiwaula and Alex Cobham, "The Effect of Illicit Financial Flows on Time to Reach the Fourth Millenium Development Goal in Sub-Saharan Africa: A Quantitative Analysis," *Journal of the Royal Society of Medicine* 107, number 4 (2014), 148–156.

Organisation for Economic Co-operation and Development. *CleanGovBiz: Integrity in Practice (Background Brief).* Paris: Organisation for Economic Co-operation and Development, 2014.

Organisation for Economic Co-operation and Development. *Illicit Trade: Converging Criminal Networks.* Paris: Organisation for Economic Co-operation and Development, 2015.

Organisation for Economic Co-operation and Development and European Union Intellectual Property Office. *Trade in Counterfeit and Pirated Goods: Mapping the Economic Impact.* Paris: Organisation for Economic Co-operation and Development, 2016.

Pufendorf, Samuel. *On the Duty of Man and Citizen According to Natural Law.* Edited by James Tully and translated by Michael Silverthorne. New York: Cambridge UP, 1991.

Rawls, John. *The Law of Peoples.* Cambridge, Mass.: Harvard UP, 1999.

Rawls, John. *Political Liberalism.* New York: Columbia UP, 1996.

Rawls, John. *A Theory of Justice.* Cambridge, Mass.: Harvard UP, 1971.

Realuyo, Celina B. *The Future Evolution of Transnational Criminal Organizations and the Threat to U.S. National Security.* Washington, D.C.: William J. Perry Center for Hemispheric Defense Studies at National Defense University, July 2015.

Rosaldo, Renato. "Identity Politics: An Ethnography by a Participant." In *Identity Politics Reconsidered*, edited by Linda Martin Alcoff, Michael Hames-García, Satya P. Mohanty and Paula M. L. Moya. New York: Palgrave Macmillan, 2006, p. 124.

Roth, Brad R. *Governmental Illegitimacy in International Law.* New York: Oxford UP, 2000.

Rumsby, Ben. "Revealed: Entire 'Rogue League Corrupted by Match Fixing.'" In *The Telegraph*, October 14, 2015. http://www.telegraph.co.uk/psrot/football/11932437/Revealed-Entire-rogue-league-corrupted-by-match-fixing.html

Stephens, Brett. "From Tehran to Tijuana." In *The Wall Street Journal*, October 19, 2011. http://professional.wsj.com/article/SB10001424052970204346104576636802670463380.html?mg=id-wsj&mg=reno64-wsj

Stewart, Scott. "Al Shabaab Threats Against the United States?" June 3, 2010. https://www.stratfor.com/weekly/20100602_al_shabaab_threats_united_states#ixzz2JftT48U5

Svolik, Milan. *The Politics of Authoritarian Rule.* Cambridge: Cambridge UP, 2012.

Thompson, Ginger. "Trafficking in Terror." In *The New Yorker.* December 14, 2015.

Union des Fabricants (UNIFAB). *Counterfeiting and Terrorism,* report, 2016.

United Nations Office on Drugs and Crime (UNODC). *United Nations Convention Against Transnational Organized Crime and the Protocols Thereto.* New York: United Nations, 2004.

United States Department of Justice. *DEA 1990–1994.* Department History, Drug Enforcement Administration. Washington, D.C.: Drug Enforcement Administration.

United States Department of Justice, Drug Enforcement Administration. *2016 National Drug Threat Assessment Summary.* Washington, D.C.: Drug Enforcement Administration, November 2016.

United States Department of Justice and Securities and Exchange Commission. *FCPA: A Resource Guide to the US Foreign Corrupt Practices Act.* Washington, D.C.: DOJ and SEC, November 14, 2012.

United States Department of State. *International Narcotics Control Strategy Report, Volume I: Drug and Chemical Control.* Washington, D.C.: United States Department of State, Bureau of International Narcotics and Law Enforcement Affairs, March 2015.

United States House Committee on Homeland Security, Subcommittee on Oversight, Investigations and Management. *A Line in the Sand: Countering Crime, Violence and Terror at the Southwest Border.* Washington, D.C.: US House of Representatives, November 2012.

Verité and the Freedom Fund. *An Exploratory Study on the Role of Corruption in International Labor Migration.* London: Verité, January 2016.

Williams, Sharon A. "The Double Criminality Rule and Extradition: A Comparative Analysis." In *Nova Law Review* 15, number 2 (1991), pp. 581–624.

Winslow, Don. "El Chapo and the Secret History of the Heroin Crisis." In *Esquire,* August 9, 2016. http://www.esquire.com/news-politics/a46918/heroin-mexico-el-chapo-cartels-don-winslow/?curator=MediaREDEF

Winter, Jana. "Feds Issue Terror Watch for the Texas/Mexico Border." Fox News, February 24, 2012. http://www.foxnews.com/us/2010/05/26/terror-alert-mexican-border

World Economic Forum. *Building Foundations Against Corruption.* Geneva: World Economic Forum, 2015.

World Economic Forum. *Learnings from the Field: Cases on Corruption in the Infrastructure and Urban Development Industries.* Geneva: World Economic Forum, 2015.

Zackie, M. W. "An Analysis of Abu Mus-ab al-Suri's 'Call to Global Islamic Resistance.'" In *Journal of Strategic Security* 6, number 1 (2013), pp. 1–18.

NOTES

PREFACE

1. Approximate, as of January 2017, when the Bolívar Fuerte (Bs.F.) was trading at about Bs.F. 2,200=US$1 in the black market. Because of runaway inflation, the Bolívar Fuerte (Bs.F.) replaced the Bs. (Bolívar) on January 1, 2008. Bs.F. 1=Bs. 1,000.

CHAPTER 1

1. This anecdote is a fictional amalgamation of facts.
2. http://www.unodc.org/toc/en/crimes/migrant-smuggling.html
3. http://www.harpersbazaar.com/culture/features/a359/the-fight-against -fakes-0109/
4. https://www.cbp.gov/newsroom/national-media-release/cbp-ice-hsi -report-12-billion-counterfeit-seizures-2014
5. Excerpt from Dana Thomas, "Deluxe: How Luxury Lost Its Luster," in http://www.harpersbazaar.com/culture/features/a359/the-fight-against -fakes-0109/
6. Organisation for Economic Co-operation and Development and European Union Intellectual Property Office (2016), *Trade in Counterfeit and Pirated Goods: Mapping the Economic Impact*, p. 11.
7. Ibid., p. 5.
8. http://www.telegraph.co.uk/finance/newsbysector/retailandconsumer /7969335/Fake-goods-are-fine-says-EU-study.html

9. http://www.nytimes.com/2007/08/30/opinion/30thomas.html?_r=1

10. Union des Fabricants (UNIFAB), "Counterfeiting and Terrorism," report 2016, p. 14.

11. David S. Wall and Joanna Large, "Jailhouse Frocks: Locating the Public Interest in Policing Counterfeit Luxury Fashion Goods," *British Journal of Criminology* 50, number 6 (July 2010), pp. 8–9.

12. On eBay in the first half of 2006. http://www.harpersbazaar.com/culture/features/a359/the-fight-against-fakes-0109/

13. http://newsfeed.time.com/2012/11/06/how-to-make-a-rotten-egg/

14. Michael A. Braun, "Iran, Hezbollah and the Threat to the Homeland," Statement for the record before the US House of Representatives, Committee on Homeland Security, March 21, 2012. http://homeland.house.gov/sites/homeland.house.gov/files/Testimony-Braun.pdf

15. James J. F. Forest, Ph.D. "Crime-Terror Interactions and Threat Convergence: Comments Prepared for Trans-Atlantic Dialogue on Combating Crime-Terror Pipelines Session I," The Crime-Terror Panorama: New Paradigms, June 25, 2012, National Defense University, Fort McNair, Washington, D.C.

16. Robert Mandel, *Dark Logic: Transnational Criminal Tactics and Global Security* (Stanford, CA: Stanford UP, 2011), p. 73.

17. United States House Committee on Homeland Security Subcommittee on Oversight, Investigations and Management, *A Line in the Sand: Countering Crime, Violence and Terror at the Southwest Border,* 112th Congress, 2nd Session, November 2012, p. 13.

18. Braun, p. 11.

19. Mandel, p. 9.

20. According to a 2011 research report by the United Nations Office on Drugs and Crime (UNODC), *Estimating Illicit Financial Flows Resulting from Drug Trafficking and Other Transnational Organized Crimes* (October 2011), p. 5.

21. Vanessa Neumann, "Political Bullshit and the Stoic Story of Self," in *Bullshit and Philosophy,* edited by Gary A. Hardcastle and George A. Reisch (New York: Open Court, 2006).

22. Osama bin Laden videotape of December 2001, transcript available at: http://www.npr.org/news/specials/response/investigation/011213.binladen.transcript.html

23. Lee Smith made this point cogently in his book *The Strong Horse: Power, Politics and the Clash of Arab Civilizations* (New York: Anchor, 2011).

24. The discussion of the religious semiotics of the transmutation from the "noble savage" to the "good revolutionary" is heavily drawn from an essay of mine: Vanessa Neumann, "Not Noble, Not Savage," *Varsity,* October 23, 2009.

CHAPTER 2

1. "All 107 Aboard Killed as Colombian Jet Explodes," *New York Times*, November 28, 1989. http://www.nytimes.com/1989/11/28/world/all-107-aboard-killed-as-colombian-jet-explodes.html

2. Daniel Hellinger, "Nationalism, Globalization and Chavismo," Webster University, Paper prepared for delivery at the 2001 meeting of the Latin American Studies Association, Washington, D.C., September 2–8, 2001, p. 4.

CHAPTER 3

1. John Otis, *The FARC and Colombia's Illegal Drug Trade* (Washington, D.C.: Wilson Center, November 2014), p. 5.

2. https://travel.state.gov/content/passports/en/alertswarnings/colombia-travel-warning.html

3. Joe Parkin Daniels, "Helping Columbia's Landmine Survivors," *Lancet,* May 21, 2016, pp. 2079–2080. http://www.thelancet.com/journals/lancet/article/PIIS0140-6736%2816%2930597-9/abstract

4. Otis, p. 8.

5. Ibid., p. 3.

6. Ibid., p. 6.

7. Ibid., p. 7.

8. Ibid., 2014, p. 9.

9. Ibid., p. 10.

10. Ibid., pp. 10–11.

11. Jorge Enrique Botero, *La Vida No Es Fácil, Papi: La Holandesa de las FARC* (Bogotá, Colombia: Ediciones B, 2011), pp. 57–58.

12. http://www.insightcrime.org/news-briefs/leader-colombia-farc-announces-halt-to-extortion

13. Otis, p. 19.

14. https://www.pwc.com/gx/en/oil-gas-energy/publications/assets/pwc-colombia-oil-gas-industry-2014.pdf

15. http://www.insightcrime.org/news-briefs/guerrilla-oil-pipeline-attacks-surge-amid-colombias-slow-peace-talks

16. Congressional Research Service, *Colombia: Issues for Congress*, March 8, 2011, p. 15.

CHAPTER 4

1. Much of the agglomerated network mapping of the *Chavistas*'s global ties is pulled together in the book by Miami-based Venezuelan investigative

reporter Casto Ocando, *Chavistas en el Imperio: Secretos, Tácticas y Escándalos de la Revolución Bolivariana en Estados Unidos,* pp. 686–87.

2. Iran's theocratic government mixes religious leadership, business, and the diplomatic and security services in ways that are far more intertwined than any of the Western liberal democracies. Excellent work on analyzing its funding streams has been by Dr. David Asher, a former US State Department and Special Operations Command adviser on threat finance. This quote comes from David Asher and Scott Modell, *Pushback: Countering the Iran Action Network* (Washington, D.C.: Center for a New American Security, September 2013), p. 9.

3. The tactics of asymmetric warfare are the same as those of an insurgency, and involve a small force fighting a standing army. They consist of taking advantage of what might be considered points of weakness and turning them into strengths: small size enables quick mobility; insurgents can attack the expensive infrastructure of a state (pipelines, electrical grids, government buildings), while the insurgents themselves are not vulnerable to such attacks. Insurgents can hide within the civilian population, and turn others who dislike the state into supporters. They can cross borders for shelter easier than can a standing army, for whom that would qualify as an invasion.

4. "Iran's Quds Force in Venezuela, Latin America: Pentagon," AFP, April 22, 2010. http://www.google.com/gwt/n?u=en.infoanda.com/link.php%3Flh%3DUFQFUQANUAwA

5. Joel Hirst, *The ALBA: Inside Venezuela's Bolivarian Alliance* (Washington, D.C.: Interamerican Institute for Democracy), 2012, p. 214.

6. Founded in 2004 by then-president of Venezuela Hugo Chávez, ALBA is a free trade zone whose members are Antigua and Barbuda, Bolivia, Cuba, Dominica, Ecuador, Grenada, Nicaragua, St. Kitts and Nevis, St. Lucia, St. Vincent and the Grenadines, and Suriname. Haiti, Iran, and Syria have observer status.

7. "US General Voices Concern over Iran Venezuela ties," AFP, April 5, 2011. http://www.google.com/hostednews/afp/article/ALeqM5gMdmJ9NnlROhzcDjs457Jwn0gBEg?docId=CNG.692381365d745fc505df40c97673c9ec.861

8. United Nations Office on Drugs and Crime (UNODC), *World Drug Report 2011* (New York: United Nations, 2011), p. 107.

9. Hirst, p. 234.

10. Jo Becker, "Beirut Bank Seen as a Hub of Hezbollah's Financing," *New York Times,* December 13, 2011. http://www.nytimes.com/2011/12/14/world/middleeast/beirut-bank-seen-as-a-hub-of-hezbollahs-financing.html?

11. https://www.fbi.gov/newyork/press-releases/2011/civil-suit-seeks-more

-than-480-million-from-entities-that-facilitated-Hezbollah-related
-money-laundering-scheme

12. Sections of what follows were previously published as Vanessa Neumann, "The New Nexus of Narcoterrorism: Hezbollah and Venezuela."

13. https://mltoday.com/article/760-continental-bolivarian-movement-significance-for-socialists/47

CHAPTER 5

1. Neumann, "The New Nexus."

2. While Hezbollah blamed the killing on Mossad (Israel's intelligence service), it has since emerged that it was the CIA that built the bomb, tested it twenty-five times before taking it to Damascus, and were the on-the-ground spotters for agents back in Mossad's headquarters in Tel Aviv, according to The Washington Post: https://www.washingtonpost.com/world/national-security/cia-and-mossad-killed-senior-hezbollah-figure-in-car-bombing/2015/01/30/ebb88682-968a-11e4-8005-1924ede3e54a_story.html

3. https://data.unhcr.org/syrianrefugees/country.php?id=122 and https://www.cia.gov/library/publications/the-world-factbook/geos/le.html

4. "Hadith" comes from the Arabic meaning a "report," "account," or "narrative." It is allegedly based on reports of the Prophet Muhammad's words, actions, or habits.

5. Jo Becker, "Beirut Bank Seen as a Hub of Hezbollah's Financing," New York Times, December 13, 2011. http://www.nytimes.com/2011/12/14/world/middleeast/beirut-bank-seen-as-a-hub-of-hezbollahs-financing.html?

6. Asher and Modell, p. 26.

7. Juval Aviv, Interfor Report (intelligence report on PanAm 103) (New York: Interfor, 1989), p. 11.

8. Scott Helfstein and John Solomo, Risky Business: The Global Threat Network and the Politics of Contraband (Washington, D.C.: US Department of Defense's Combating Terrorism Center at West Point, May 2014), pp. 49–50.

CHAPTER 6

1. Max Manwaring, "Gangs and Cartels in Coalition and Conflict: The Insurgency Phenomenon in Mexico," in The Hybrid Threat: Crime, Terrorism and Insurgency in Mexico, HPSI Issue Brief (Washington, D.C. and Carlisle, PA: George Washington University and US Army War College, December 2011), p. 131.

2. Ibid., pp. 131–32.

3. Ibid., p. 132.
4. Ibid., p. 113.
5. Ibid., p. 23.
6. Operation Martillo ("hammer" in Spanish) is a multinational detection, monitoring, and interdiction operation focused on the activities of transnational criminal and terrorist organizations. It is a critical component of the US government's coordinated interagency regional security strategy in support of the White House Strategy to Combat Transnational Organized Crime and the US Central America Regional Security Initiative. As of 2012, fourteen countries were participating: Belize, Canada, Colombia, Costa Rica, El Salvador, France, Guatemala, Honduras, the Netherlands, Nicaragua, Panama, Spain, United Kingdom, and the United States; Chile had also given help. The US contribution includes US Navy and Coast Guard vessels, aircraft from US federal law enforcement agencies, and military and law enforcement units from various nations working together to deny transnational criminal organizations the ability to exploit these transshipment routes for the movement of narcotics, precursor chemicals, bulk cash, and weapons along Central American shipping routes. http://www.southcom.mil/Media/Special-Coverage/Operation-Martillo/
7. CIA, *The World Factbook*, Guatemala, Transnational Issues. https://www.cia.gov/library/publications/the-world-factbook/geos/gt.html
8. *International Narcotics Control Strategy Report, Volume I: Drug and Chemical Control* (Washington, D.C.: United States Department of State, Bureau of International Narcotics and Law Enforcement Affairs, March 2015), p. 10.
9. http://www.mcclatchydc.com/2011/08/11/120336/violent-mexican-drug-gang-taking.html#storylink=cpy
10. Neumann, "Never Mind the Metrics."
11. Manwaring, p. 24.
12. Ibid., p. 27.
13. Ibid., p. 26.
14. Barry R. McCaffrey, General, USA (Retired), "Mexico: Drugs, Crime and the Rule of Law," in *The Hybrid Threat: Crime, Terrorism and Insurgency in Mexico*, p. 6.
15. DEA assistant administrator and chief of intelligence Rodney G Benson, in his testimony before the Western Hemisphere Subcommittee, Committee on Foreign Affairs, and the Oversight, Investigations and Management Subcommittee, at the House Committee on Homeland Security, in the House of Representatives. Sharon L. Cardash, Frank J. Cilluffo, and Bert B. Tussing, "Mexico and the Triple Threat," in *The Hybrid Threat: Crime, Terrorism and Insurgency in Mexico*, p. 11.

16. McCaffrey, p. 6.
17. June Beittel, *Mexico: Organized Crime and Drug Trafficking Organizations,* Congressional report (Washington, D.C.: Congressional Research Service, July 22, 2015), p. 5.
18. United States Department of Justice, Drug Enforcement Administration, *2016 National Drug Threat Assessment Summary* (Washington, D.C.: Drug Enforcement Administration, November 2016), pp. 6–8.
19. Ibid., p. 22.
20. United States House Committee on Homeland Security Subcommittee on Oversight, Investigations, and Management, *A Line in the Sand: Countering Crime, Violence and Terror at the Southwest Border,* 112th Congress, 2nd Session, November 2012.
21. http://www.washingtontimes.com/news/2004/sep/28/20040928-123346 -3928r/
22. http://www.washingtontimes.com/news/2009/mar/27/Hezbollah-uses -mexican-drug-routes-into-us/#ixzz2JIMNOgPK
23. http://www.dtic.mil/cgi-bin/GetTRDoc?Location=U2&doc=GetTRDoc .pdf&AD=ADA514191
24. http://www.washingtontimes.com/news/2004/oct/5/20041005-013052 -7047r/ and http://www.washingtontimes.com/news/2004/sep/28/20040928 -123346-3928r/#ixzz2HPE4HFYt

CHAPTER 7

1. "Chinggis Khaan" is Mongolia's preferred local spelling for "Genghis Khan."
2. Stephen Mihm, "No Ordinary Counterfeit," *New York Times,* July 23, 2006.
3. Organisation for Economic Co-operation and Development and European Union Intellectual Property Office, *Trade in Counterfeit and Pirated Goods: Mapping the Economic Impact* (Paris: OECD, 2016), p. 12.
4. https://ustr.gov/sites/default/files/Notorious%20Markets.pdf
5. http://www.toptechnews.com/article/index.php?story_id=120003R5FKXC
6. Klaus von Lampe, Marin K. Kurti, Anqi Shen, and Georgios A. Antonopoulos, "The Changing Role of China in the Global Illegal Cigarette Trade," *International Criminal Justice Review* 22, number 1 (2012), pp. 43–67, 49–50.
7. Ibid., p. 51.
8. Ibid., pp. 58–59.
9. Ibid., p. 54.
10. 18 US Code § 798.
11. 18 US Code Chapter 115.

CHAPTER 8

1. http://www.state.gov/r/pa/prs/ps/2013/218880.htm
2. Jaime Doward, "How Cigarette Smuggling Fuels Africa's Islamist Violence," *The Guardian*, January 26, 2013. http://www.theguardian.com /world/2013/jan/27/cigarette-smuggling-mokhtar-belmokhtar-terrorism
3. Wolfram Lacher, "Organized Crime and Conflict in the Sahel-Sahara Region," Carnegie Endowment for International Peace, September 2012. http://carnegieendowment.org/files/sahel_sahara.pdf
4. Ibid.
5. Sabbagh was later replaced by Gen. Jesús Manuel Zambrano, who was named the new president of the CVG Ferrominera Orinoco C.A., according to the national decree *Gaceta Oficial # 40241*, dated Monday, September 2, 2013. http://www.el-nacional.com/economia/Designan-presidente -CVG-Ferrominera-Orinoco_0_257374300.html
6. Chris Rawley, "Terrorists, Tyrants and Tobacco: How the Illicit Cigarette Trade Fuels Instability in the Middle East," Center for International Maritime Security (CIMSEC), August 20, 2014. http://cimsec.org/terrorists -tyrants-tobacco-illicit-cigarette-trade-fuels-instability-middle-east/12623
7. Ibid.
8. Ibid.
9. *Federal Register,* Friday, February 15, 2008, Executive Order 13460. https:// www.treasury.gov/resource-center/sanctions/Documents/13460.pdf
10. Greg B. Smith and Oren Yaniv, "Terrorists May Get Money from Regional, Cheap Cigarette Ring: Ray Kelly," *Daily News,* May 16, 2013. http://www .nydailynews.com/new-york/terrorists-money-regional-cigarette -smugglers-ray-kelly-article-1.1346120#ixzz2ebDJWWLV
11. Sari Horwitz, "Cigarette Smuggling Linked to Terrorism," *Washington Post,* June 8, 2004. http://www.washingtonpost.com/wp-dyn/articles /A23384-2004Jun7.html
12. Against Organized Crime, INTERPOL Trafficking and Counterfeiting Casebook, 2014.
13. www.INTERPOL.org
14. Ibid.
15. Elizabeth Allen, *The Illicit Trade in Tobacco Products and How to Tackle It,* 2nd ed. (London: International Trade and Investment Center 2013), p. 5.
16. "Memorandum Submitted by the Serious Organized Crime Agency (SOCA)," Parliament, June 2009. http://www.publications.parliament.uk /pa/cm200910/cmselect/cmhaff/74/74we15.htm
17. www.acetateweb.com
18. GAMA's Web site, http://acetateweb.com/kyc-program/, accessed February 6, 2016.
19. Ibid.

CHAPTER 9

1. Name has been changed.
2. "'Money-Launderer' Nidal Waked Arrested in Colombia," BBC, May 7, 2016. http://www.bbc.com/news/world-latin-america-36218993
3. Malcolm Moore and Ralph Atkins, "FIFA: The Fall of the House of Blatter," *Financial Times,* November 22, 2015. http://www.ft.com/intl/cms/s/0/64573fc6-8df6-11e5-a549-b89a1dfede9b.html#axzz3xb9k3IqL
4. http://www.telegraph.co.uk/sport/football/fifa/11680400/Swiss-investigation-into-Fifa-corruption-and-awarding-of-World-Cups-to-Russia-and-Qatar-could-take-years.html
5. http://www.independent.co.uk/news/world/europe/fifa-corruption-arrests-how-chuck-blazer-rinsed-money-from-the-beautiful-game-10279922.html#gallery
6. Organisation for Economic Co-operation and Development, *Illicit Trade Converging Criminal Networks*, pp. 240–41.
7. Ibid., pp. 241–42.
8. http://www.thesportster.com/entertainment/top-15-craziest-sports-bets-of-all-time/?view=all
9. OECD, Illicit Trade, pp. 243–47.
10. Ibid., p. 246.
11. http://www.telegraph.co.uk/sport/football/fifa/11680400/Swiss-investigation-into-Fifa-corruption-and-awarding-of-World-Cups-to-Russia-and-Qatar-could-take-years.html
12. International Center for Sport Security (ICSS), Match-Fixing/Sport Betting—Background Fact Sheet.
13. OECD, *Illicit Trade*, p. 249.
14. Ibid., p. 251.
15. Ibid., p. 252.
16. Brett Forrest, *The Big Fix: The Hunt for the Match-Fixers Bringing Down Soccer* (New York: William Morrow, 2014), pp. 208–09.
17. Ibid., p. 182.
18. Ibid., pp. 52–53.
19. http://guardian.ng/business-services/communication/how-and-why-online-betting-fund-terrorism/
20. Forrest, p. 151.
21. http://www.thesportster.com/entertainment/top-15-craziest-sports-bets-of-all-time/?view=all
22. Vice Sports gives an example of a Belarussian Premier League match on February 3, 2014, where FC Slutsk beat the heavily favored Shakhter Soligorsk 2-1 with two late goals. bet365 and SBOBET took bets (SBOBET even confirmed the results with the victorious team) and paid out winnings.

The match never took place. Betfair has similarly paid out winnings on matches that never happened, including the "friendly" exhibition match between Portugal's Freamunde and Spain's Ponferradina in August 2014. Betfair offered live betting.

23. http://www.nytimes.com/2015/10/03/sports/soccer/sepp-blatter-coca-cola-mcdonalds-fifa-resign.html?_r=0
24. http://www.coca-colacompany.com/press-center/company-statements/open-letter-to-the-fifa-executive-committee/

CHAPTER 10

1. Jean-Luc Moreau, "Coartem: Une Tragédie en Trois Actes," *Crime Pharmaceutique: Une Épidémie Silencieuse, Défis* 5 (June 2015), pp. 7–12.
2. Ibid., pp. 7–10.
3. http://news.bbc.co.uk/2/hi/africa/8512195.stm
4. Moreau, Coartem, pp. 18–19.
5. This is according to the Global Fund's Web site: http://www.theglobalfund.org/en/financials/
6. Sarah Chayes, *Thieves of State: Why Corruption Threatens Global Security* (New York: Norton, 2015), p. 194.
7. OECD, *Illicit Trade,* p. 80.
8. Moreau, "L'industrie," p. 17.
9. Roger Bate, *Phake: The Deadly World of Falsified and Substandard Medicines* (Washington, D.C.: American Enterprise Institute Press, 2012), p. 362.
10. Ibid., 369, and OECD, *Illicit Trade,* p. 78.
11. OECD, *Illicit Trade,* p. 78.
12. Newton (2012) in OECD, *Illicit Trade,* p. 79.
13. Moreau, "L'industrie," p. 17.
14. Erwin A. Blackstone, Joseph P. Fuhr, and Steve Pociask, "The Health and Economic Effects of Counterfeit Drugs," *American Health & Drug Benefits* 7, number 4 (2014), pp. 216–24.
15. Ibid., p. 217.
16. Bate, p. 398.
17. Jean-Luc Moreau, "Counterfeit Drugs: Fighting Illegal Supply Chains," statement before the Subcommittee on Oversight and Investigations House Energy and Commerce Committee, February 27, 2014.
18. Bate, pp. 360–61.
19. Moreau, "Counterfeit Drugs."
20. Ibid.
21. Bate, p. 359.
22. Ibid., p. 361.

23. Ibid., p. 358.

24. OECD, *Illicit Trade,* p. 86.

25. Bate, p. 376.

26. http://definitions.uslegal.com/h/hostis-humani-generis/

27. https://www.youtube.com/watch?v=X6Y9nT71lFI

28. Elizabeth Allen, *The Illicit Trade in Tobacco Products and How to Tackle It,* 2nd ed. (London: International Trade and Investment Center, 2013), p. 12.

29. Ibid.

30. International Chamber of Commerce, *Controlling the Zone: Balancing Facilitation and Control to Combat Illicit Trade in the World's Free Trade Zones.* May 2013, p. 12.

31. http://www.bloomberg.com/news/articles/2016-04-04/ethiopia -somaliland-sign-accord-to-boost-use-of-berbera-port

32. The press release: http://www.africanews.com/2016/06/01/somaliland -secures-442m-deal-to-revamp-berbera-port/

33. http://www.transparency.org/news/feature/corruption_perceptions _index_2016

CHAPTER 11

1. https://panamapapers.icij.org/the_power_players/

2. http://www.miaminewtimes.com/news/kilo-cocaine-made-miami-part -1-6366058

3. June S. Beittel, *Mexico: Organized Crime and Drug Trafficking Organizations,* Congressional report (Washington, D.C.: Congressional Research Service, July 22, 2015), pp. 7–9.

4. Ibid., p. 14.

5. According to famed Mexican journalist Carlos Loret de Mola, at a talk at the Americas Society in New York.

6. Based on chart from LSE Expert Group on the Economics of Drug Policy, "Ending the Drug Wars" (London: London School of Economics, May 2014), p. 19.

7. According to Loret.

8. Beittel, p. 29.

9. Don Winslow, "El Chapo and the Secret History of the Heroin Crisis," *Esquire,* August 9, 2016. http://www.esquire.com/news-politics/a46918 /heroin-mexico-el-chapo-cartels-don-winslow/?curator=MediaREDEF

10. Beittel, p. 16.

11. Ibid., p. 24.

12. Max Manwaring, "Gangs and Cartels in Coalition and Conflict: The Insurgency Phenomenon in Mexico" in *The Hybrid Threat: Crime, Terrorism*

and Insurgency in Mexico, HPSI Issue Brief (Washington, D.C. and Carlisle, PA: George Washington University and US Army War College, December 2011), p. 128.

13. Beittel, p. 8.
14. Ibid., citing Steven Dudley, "Police Use Brute Force to Break Crime's Hold on Juárez," *InSight Crime: Organized Crime in the Americas,* February 13, 2013, p.17. Mexican newspapers such as *El Diario* reported more than three hundred homicides a month in 2010, when the violence peaked.
15. Doug Farah, "Central America's Dangerous Actors: The Convergence of Transnational Organized Crime, Terrorism and Extra-Regional Actors" (IBI Consultants: September 2013), p. 10.
16. Cardash, Cilluffo, and Tussing, p. 18.
17. DEA, *Drug Enforcement Administration: 1990–1994* (Washington, D.C.: Drug Enforcement Administration Museum), p. 77
18. Beittel, p. 28.
19. Helfstein and Solomo.
20. Ibid., p. 80.
21. Jay S. Albanese, *Transnational Crime and the 21ˢᵗ Century: Criminal Enterprise, Corruption and Opportunity* (New York: Oxford UP, 2011), p. 137.
22. Chayes, p. 24.
23. Ibid., p. 40.
24. Gupta et al. (2011), cited in Organisation for Economic Co-operation and Development, *CleanGovBiz: Integrity in Practice (Background Brief)* (Paris: OECD, 2014), p. 3.
25. OECD, *CleanGovBiz*, p. 3.
26. Bernadette O'Hare, Innocent Makuta, Naor Bar-Zeev, Levison Chiwaula, and Alex Cobham, "The Effect of Illicit Financial Flows on Time to Reach the Fourth Millenium Development Goal in Sub-Saharan Africa: A Quantitative Analysis," *Journal of the Royal Society of Medicine* 107, number 4 (2014), p. 151.
27. Albanese, p. 133.
28. I thank Prof. Thomas Pogge for this insight, in emailed communications.
29. OECD, *CleanGovBiz,* p. 3.
30. Chayes, p. 41.
31. Ibid., p. 69.
32. Ibid., p. 43.
33. Ibid., pp. 184–85.
34. Ibid., p. 63.
35. Ibid., p. 62.
36. According to Loret at his Americas Society talk. In his first eighteen months in office, Peña Nieto also managed to reform education, the tele-

communications sector (much to the consternation of Carlos Slim, the world's wealthiest man), and energy, and imprisoned *El Chapo* Guzmán (though his subsequent escape via a vast tunnel has hurt Peña Nieto's credibility) and the head of the teachers' union.

37. To date, the biggest security program pertaining to the threat coming from Central America is the Mérida Initiative, which has cost approximately $1.3 billion over the last three years. While the program was originally designed to provide specific equipment and training to the government of Mexico and assist it in developing the tools to confront the cartels, the partnership has evolved, such that the program is now guided by a strategy that aims to: "1) disrupt the capacity of organized crime to operate; 2) institutionalize reforms to sustain rule of law; 3) create a 21st century border structure; and 4) build strong and resilient communities." http://www.centerforhuman rights.org/PFS_Petition/Ex56_MeridaOverview-Jul15.pdf

38. Beittel, p. 7.

39. Ibid., p. 1.

40. Ibid., p. 25.

41. http://www.cnn.com/2012/11/10/opinion/bergen-petraeus-legacy/

42. Jonathan Weil, "Cocaine Cowboys Know Best Places to Bank," Bloomberg, August 2, 2012.

43. Albanese, p. 108.

44. http://www.fincen.gov/news_room/aml_history.html

45. OECD, *Illicit Trade*, p. 248.

46. https://www.fincen.gov/news/news-releases/fincen-renews-real-estate-geographic-targeting-orders-identify-high-end-cash

47. http://www.bloomberg.com/news/articles/2013-07-02/hsbc-judge-approves-1-9b-drug-money-laundering-accord

48. Jessica Silver-Greenberg, "HSBC to Pay Record Fine to Settle Money-Laundering Charges," *New York Times,* December 11, 2012. http://dealbook.nytimes.com/2012/12/11/hsbc-to-pay-record-fine-to-settle-money-laundering-charges/

49. Farah, p. 9.

50. Devlin Barrett and Christopher M. Matthews, "BNP News Settlement with US for up to $9 Billion," *The Wall Street Journal,* June 23, 2014.

51. Cardash et al., in *Hybrid Threat,* p. 21.

CHAPTER 12

1. Cardash et al., *Hybrid Threat,* p. 48.

2. Helfstein and Solomo, pp. 83–84.

3. Albanese, p. 2.

4. Ibid., p. 3.

5. National Security Strategy of the United States of America (2002), p. 3. https://www.state.gov/documents/organization/63562.pdf.

6. Robert Mandel, *Dark Logic: Transnational Criminal Tactics and Global Security* (Stanford, CA: Stanford UP, 2011), p. 26.

7. Strategy to Combat Transnational Organized Crime: Letter from the President, July 19, 2011. http://www.whitehouse.gov/administration/eop /nsc/transnational-crime/letter

8. Helfstein and Solomo, pp. 64, 73–77.

9. Ibid., 61.

10. Doug Farah, "Transnational Organized Crime, Terrorism, and Criminalized States in Latin America: An Emerging Tier-One National Security Priority," US Army War College, August 2012.

11. Albanese, p. 46.

12. Helfstein and Solomo, p. 89.

13. Jakub Grygiel, "The Power of Statelessness," *Policy Review*, Hoover Institution, April and May 2009, p. 36.

14. Beittel, pp. 18–19.

15. Helfstein and Solomo, pp. 19–20

16. Beittel, p. 20.

17. Ibid., p. 22.

18. Helfstein and Solomo, p. 12.

19. United States House Committee on Homeland Security Subcommittee on Oversight, Investigations and Management, *A Line in the Sand: Countering Crime, Violence and Terror at the Southwest Border,* 112th Congress, 2nd Session, November 2012, p. 13.

20. Max Manwaring, *Gangs, Pseudo-Militaries and Other Modern Mercenaries: New Dynamics in Uncomfortable Wars* (Norman: University of Oklahoma Press, 2010), p. 65.

21. Ibid., pp. 26–27.

22. McCaffrey, p. 5.

23. US Department of Justice press release, October 11, 2011, www.justice.gov.

24. Asher and Modell, p. 9.

25. Ibid., p. 22.

26. http://www.khou.com/story/news/2014/07/11/11315838/

27. http://www.stratfor.com/weekly/20100602_al_shabaab_threats_united _states#ixzz2JftT48U5

28. Dawn L. Bartell and David H. Gray, "Hezbollah and Al Shabaab in Mexico and the Terrorist Threat to the United States," *Global Security Studies* 3, number 4 (Fall 2012), p. 109.

29. Max Weber, "Politics as a Vocation," in *From Max Weber: Essays in Sociology*, translated and edited by H. H. Gerth and C. Wright Mills, pp. 77–128 (New York: Oxford UP, 1946), p. 77.

30. https://www.bloomberg.com/view/articles/2015-05-15/putin-tries-to-freeze-the-ukraine-conflict
31. McCaffrey, pp. 7–8.

CHAPTER 13

1. https://www.youtube.com/watch?v=YfC1MqzoO7w, accessed on March 8, 2017.
2. Beittel, p. 26.
3. http://time.com/3954802/joaquin-el-chapo-guzman-escape/
4. http://www.azcentral.com/news/articles/2008/08/26/20080826narc obeer0823.html
5. https://en.wikipedia.org/wiki/Propaganda_in_the_Mexican_Drug_War
6. Rohan Gunaratna and Aviv Oreg, *The Global Jihad Movement* (New York: Rowman & Littlefield, 2015), pp. 394–95.
7. Ibid., p. 399.
8. Ibid., pp. 401–03.
9. Ibid., pp. 408–09.
10. Hassan Hassan and Michael Weiss, *ISIS: Inside the Army of Terror* (New York: Regan Arts, 2015), pp. 174–75.
11. Ibid., p. 177.
12. Ibid., p. 176.
13. Ibid., p. 170.
14. M. W. Zackie, "An Analysis of Abu Musab al-Suri's 'Call to Global Islamic Resistance,'" *Journal of Strategic Security* 6, number 1 (2013), p. 1.
15. Gunaratna and Oreg, pp. 386–87.
16. Zackie, p. 9.
17. https://www.ft.com/content/b8234932-719b-11e5-ad6d-f4ed76f0900a
18. http://www.foxnews.com/politics/2015/02/16/isis-empire-smuggling -shakedowns-donations-feed-swelling-terror-budget.html
19. Karl Marx, "The German Ideology" in *The Marx-Engels Reader*, 2nd ed. edited by Robert C. Tucker (Princeton: Princeton UP, 1978), p. 163.
20. George Orwell in David Miller, *On Nationality* (New York: Oxford UP, 1999), p. 37.
21. Kwame Anthony Appiah, *The Ethics of Identity* (Princeton, NJ: Princeton University Press, 2005), p. 66.
22. Milan Svolik's *The Politics of Authoritarian Rule* (Cambridge: Cambridge UP, 2012) is the locus classicus for this theory.

INDEX

Abbotabad papers (found during Osama bin Laden raid), 264
Abdel-Rahman, Omar, 155
Abdulla, Miskal Al, 154
Abu Dhabi, 13, 139, 144
Acebes, Angel, 12
Achille Lauro hijacking, 97
Acosta Carles, Luis Felipe, 72
Aeroterror ("Terror Air"), 69
Aeterni Regis (*King Eternal*, papal bull), 25–26
Afghanistan, 84, 122, 43, 214, 222
    and Daesh, 265–66
    and drug trade, 51, 95, 124, 214
    and jihadism, 140–41, 143, 265–66
    and land mines, 50
    mujahideen, 104, 140, 239
    Taliban, 143
    US invasion of, 145
Ahmad, Nazem Said, 93
Ahmadinejad, Mahmoud, 68–69
AK-47, 155, 204, *205*
Al-Amine, Ali, 92
Al Qaeda, 7, 12, 17, 71, 104, 108–9, 115–17, 153, 219, 238, 247, 266–67
Al Qaeda in Iraq, 266
Al Qaeda in the Arabian Peninsula (AQAP), 264

Al Qaeda in the Islamic Maghreb (AQIM), 7, 10, 140–41
Al Shabaab, 10, 204, 252
Albanese, Jay, 240
Algeria, 139–40, 142–43, 223
Angola, 186, 222
anti-narcocorrido (song that denounces violence and corruption of drug cartels), 256. See also *narcocorrido*
Aponte Aponte, Eladio, 73
Appiah, Kwame, 270
Apple, 54, 133
Arab Spring, 84
Araujo, Álvaro, 59
Araujo, Maria Consuelo, 59
Arbabsiar plot, 250–55
arepa (corn patties), 149–50
Argentina, 53, 66, 183
    AMIA bombing (Buenos Aires, 1994), 66
    Israeli embassy attack (Buenos Aires, 1992), 28, 66, 83
Argentine-Israeli Mutual Association, 28
arms dealing, 10, 97, 204–5, 247
arms smuggling, 97
arms trafficking, 18, 22, 107

Arria, Diego, 38–39
Assad, Bashar, al-, 68, 87, 153
Assad, Hafez al-, 87, 97
Assad regime (Syria), 87, 153–54, 268
assassination, 16, 33, 49, 85, 89, 219
    and Arbabsiar plot, 251
    and Los Zetas, 261
    of Rafic Hariri, 87
asymmetric (fourth generation)
    warfare, 102–4, 111
Asymmetric Warfare Group (US
    Army), 99–100, 262
Asymmetrica (Neumann's company),
    5, 131–132, 143–146, 152, 160,
    162, 176, 207, 220, 246
AUC. See Colombia: United
    Colombian Self-Defense Forces
    (AUC)
avian flu. See H1N1 (avian flu)
Awlaki, Anwar al-, 267
Azerbaijan, 122, 124
Aznar, José Maria, 104–5

bacrim (criminal gangs), 17–18,
    36, 52
Baghdadi, Abu Bakr Al, 10
Bank Secrecy Act, 231, 233
Bassiur, Matthew, 133
Bate, Roger, 200, 202
beheadings, 16, 19, 24–25, 256, 266,
    269
Belmokhtar, Mokhtar
    ("Mr. Marlboro"), 139–42
Benedict XVI, Pope, 260
Betancourt, Ingrid, 47
Bin Hammam, Mohamed, 183
bin Laden, Osama, 24, 70, 115, 141,
    238–39, 264
Birkin bags, 128–31
Blatter, Sepp, 177–78, 187
Blazer, Chuck, 178–79
BNP Paribas SA, 233–34
Boko Haram, 10, 185
Bolívar, Simón, 40, 69
Bolivia, 34, 64, 92, 215
Bonilla Orozco, Maximiliano, 70–71
Botero, Fernando, 36
Bout, Viktor, 97–98
Bouterse, Dino, 166
Brazil, 53, 63, 66, 182, 183, 201, 252

Bruck, Bill, 177–78
Burberry, 12
Bush, George W., 29, 84, 177–78

Cabezas, Hugo, 71–72
Café de la Reconciliación, El
    (Reconciliation Coffee), 47–48
Calderón, Felipe, 213, 216–18, 220,
    224–28, 272
"Calderón's War," 217, 224–25, 272
Cali (cartel), 17, 33–34, 45, 58–59,
    246
Call to Global Islamic Resistance, The
    (GIR), 266–67
Campbell, Naomi, 29
Canadadrugs.com, 199
Cano, Alfonso, 75
capital flight (money leaving a
    country), 210, 235
Cárdenas Guillén, Mario ("El
    Gordo"), 213
Cartel Jalisco Nueva Generación
    (CJNG), 220, 257–58
Cartel of the Suns, 71
cartelitos (minicartels), 18
cartels, 17–19, 24, 27–28, 33–34, 36,
    109–110
    Arbabsiar plot, 250–55
    and convergence of crime-terror
        pipeline, 246–50
    "big four," 110–11
    and fourth-generation warfare, 103
    economics of, 211–17
    and gangs, 114–15
    and identity, 268–72
    recruitment, 256–61
    and smuggling, 53, 110
    See also specific cartels
Carvajal, Hugo, 71, 73
Cash, Bill (Neumann's former
    father-in-law), 4
Cash, William (Neumann's
    ex-husband), 4
Castro, Fidel, 75
Catholicism, 66, 79, 164, 169
Center for a Secure Free Society, 101
Central Intelligence Agency (CIA), 66,
    96–97, 100, 107, 146, 170, 219,
    226, 251, 286n2
Chanel, 6–7, 9–11, 208

Chávez, Hugo, 64, 220, 260
    1992 coup attempt by, 2–3, 26, 32,
        40, 74
    1998 presidential election, 3
    2002 coup against, 71
    2004 recall referendum, 72
    2007 constitutional referendum, 4
    2009 constitutional referendum, 4,
        30, 41
    and ALBA, 285n6
    and anti-semitism, 166
    and celebrities, 29–30
    Chavismo (ideology of Chávez), 3,
        69, 72
    Chavistas (Chávez supporters),
        27–28, 36–40, 63–67, 69, 73–74,
        147–49, 165, 263
    and corruption, 36
    death of, 146, 148
    and elected dictatorship, 274
    and elections, 31–32
    and FARC, 27, 33, 35, 82
    and Hezbollah, 82, 85
    and ideology and power, 64
    and International Rebellion, 74–75
    and Iran, 64, 68
    and jihadism, 67
    La Chavera (family estate), 75
    por ahora (for now) motto, 2–4
    and trade and terrorism, 67–74
Chayes, Sarah, 194, 220–22
Chelsea Holdings, 176
China
    Alibaba, 128, 132–33
    Beijing, 120–21, 126–30, 135
    "China, Inc." 119
    and counterfeit goods, 8–9, 12, 110,
        128–35, 195, 197–98, 206
    Great Leap Forward, 127
    Guangzhou, 9, 200
    hutongs (old neighborhoods with
        narrow streets), 127
    and Mongolia, 119, 122–24
    Olympics (2008), 127
    People's Liberation Army (PLA),
        119, 121, 134
    Silk Road market, 128–30
    triads (criminal networks), 9, 13,
        110, 127–33, 181, 184, 247
cigarettes. *See* tobacco

Citgo Petroleum Corporation, 36, 68
Coartem (antimalarial drug), 190–92,
    194, 197
Coca Growers of Putumayo, 34
cocaine, 33, 45, 114
    and Escobar, 34, 53
    and FARC, 51–52, 70, 73–74
    and Guatemala, 105, 107
    and Hezbollah, 14, 16, 27–28, 73, 82,
        93–94
    and Mexico, 52, 74, 114, 213, 216,
        246
    and Miami, 210, 228, 244
    and money laundering, 210–16
    retail markup, 13, 155, 212
    and United Kingdom, 137, 158
    and Venezuela, 41, 70, 72–74
    White Triangle of, 33–34, 215
Coffee Growers Federation, 48
coffee industry, 45, 47–48, 50, 212
Cold War, 87, 239
Collins, Jeffrey, 116
Colombia
    Armenia, 45
    Bogotá, 33–34, 36, 44–45, 49, 57,
        164
    and drug trade, 27–28, 32–36,
        42–53
    False Positives scandal, 57–58
    and flattening of terrorist networks,
        17–18
    Heroes and Martyrs of Guática, 48
    Justice and Peace Law, 44, 46–48,
        61
    Law 002 ("war tax" law), 53
    Medellín (cartel), 17, 33–36, 74, 94
    Medellín (city), 21, 34–36, 45
    Parapolitical Scandal, 59–60
    peace process, 47–49, 63
    Radio Caracol, 34, 55–56
    United Colombian Self-Defense
        Forces (AUC), 33, 44, 48, 56, 59
    and violence, 42–49, 53, 59, 63
    See also Revolutionary Armed
        Forces of Colombia (FARC)
Columbus, Christopher, 26
Committee on Foreign Investment in
    the United States (CFIUS), 68
communism, 3, 39, 90, 105, 119, 127,
    134, 239

compartmentalization, 243–44
Confrérie des Mourides (Mouride Brotherhood), 192
Corimon (Neumann family business), 1–2
counterfeiting, 6–9, 11–14, 22, 128–30, 132, 144, 171, 189, 242
and China, 119, 127–35
and money laundering, 229
and North Korea, 124
pharmaceuticals, 194–203
tobacco products, 155, 158
and transnational crime, 240
counterinsurgency, 43, 53, 226
Creative Associates International, 83
crime-terror pipeline (CTP), 12, 14, 17, 26–28, 78, 137
and convergence, 13–20, 74, 97, 109, 151–52, 211, 238–55
and multiagency swarm, 235–37
and smuggling, 110–114
and the state, 20–21
Crino, Scott, 100
Cuba, 39, 74–75, 232
cyber-crime, 119, 135, 240, 259

D-Company, 238–39, 247
Daesh (Arabic name for ISIL/ISIS), 10, 55, 104, 153, 177
beheadings, 24
Dabiq (magazine), 266
funding, 16, 153, 268–69
and Hezbollah, 79, 90
jihadist pornography, 266
origins of, 84
recruitment, 261, 264–66
in Syria, 15
Daily Journal, The (Neumann family newspaper, later *The Latin American Herald Tribune*), 2
DDR (demobilization, disarmament, and reintegration), 42, 143, 225
del Rosario Fuentes, Ramón Antonio ("Toño Leña"), 70
Dhakane, Ahmed Muhammed, 252
Diallo, Amadou, 183
diamonds, 54, 93–94, 120, 229
Díaz, Porfirio, 259
document forging, 15, 18, 107

Dodd-Frank Act (US), 54
Drug Enforcement Administration (DEA), US, 18, 34, 95, 112, 164, 213, 215, 217–18, 228, 245, 251
Dubai, 8, 10, 13, 22, 138–39, 143–44, 162, 167, 195, 198–99, 205–6
Burj Khalifa, 143
Jebel Ali Free Zone Area (JAFZA), 8, 13, 205–6

Eaton, Chris, 184–85
Ecuador, 8, 27, 52, 92
Eder, Alejandro, 46
Egypt, 25, 79, 154–55, 205, 269
Ejército de Liberación Nacional (ELN), 33, 47, 57, 60–61, 70
El Aissami Maddah, Tareck Zaidan, 70, 247, 275
El Salvador, 105, 111–12, 117
el-Shukrijumah, Adnan, 116–17
ELN. *See* Ejército de Liberación Nacional (ELN)
Empresas Polar, 149–50
Escobar, Pablo, 21, 34–35, 53, 69, 72, 214–15, 217
bombing of Avianca Airlines Flight 203, 34–35
Los Pepes (people persecuted by Pablo Escobar), 34
European Economic Area (EEA), 239–40
extortion, 16, 44, 49, 53–56, 213–15, 227, 239–40, 246–47, 257, 268
Extraditables, Los (The Extraditables), 34–35
extradition, 34–35, 54, 178, 201, 238–39

Farah, Doug, 216
FARC. *See* Revolutionary Armed Forces of Colombia (FARC)
Federal Bureau of Investigation (FBI), 179, 193, 245, 251, 261–62
Ferreira, Marcos, 71
FIFA. *See* International Federation of Association Football (FIFA)
Financial Crimes Enforcement Network (FinCEN), US Treasury, 229–31, 245
Foley, James, 24–25
Foreign Corrupt Practices Act, 175

Fox, Vicente, 224–25
France, 140–41, 152
  Direction Générale de Securité
    Exterieure (DGSE), 190
  Paris attacks (2015), 268
Franco, Carlos, 58, 60
Fraser, Douglas, 69
Free Shia movement, 84
free trade
  ALBA, 69, 285n6
  Colón (Panama), 160, 163–173
  free trade zones, 8, 13, 53, 132, 160,
    163–73, 202, 205–6
  Jebel Ali Free Zone Area (JAFZA),
    8, 13, 205–6
  NAFTA, 220, 240

Gambia, Republic of The, 7
Gates, Robert, 67
Gemayel, Bachir, 96
Global Acetate Manufacturers
  Association (GAMA), 157–59
global financial crisis, 21
Global War on Terror, 104, 157, 222,
  262
globalization, 13, 61, 180, 239
Glover, Danny, 29
Gómez, Servando ("La Tuta"), 215
gray economy, 22
Grygiel, Jakub, 245
Guardian, The, 28–30
Guatemala, 101, 105–7, 111, 119–20l,
  136, 232, 275
Gucci, 12
Guerreros Unidos ("United Warriors"
  or "United People of Guerrero"),
  247
Guinea-Bissau, 7
Gulf (cartel), 110, 115, 213, 246, 257
Gulf War, 140
Gunaratna, Rohan, 262
Guzmán, "El Chapo," 29, 213–14, 218,
  256, 258, 293–94n36

H1N1 (avian flu), 12, 36–37
Hamas, 71, 154, 165
Hammoud, Mohamad, 155
handbags, counterfeit, 6–9, 12, 13,
  128–30, 132, 242
Hariri, Rafic, 85, 87

hawala (informal money transfer
  system), 238
Helfstein, Scott, 243
Hermès, 85, 128–31
heroin, 7, 9–10, 13, 16, 45, 51, 96, 107,
  124, 195, 211–14, 242, 244
Hezbollah, 10, 12, 14–16, 78, 88–92,
  108, 115–16, 151, 254
  and car bombs, 249
  and cigarette smuggling, 155
  and cocaine, 14, 16, 27–28, 73, 82,
    93–94
  and identity, 271
  and Iran, 28, 64, 74, 77, 82, 85–87,
    90, 251
  and money laundering, 93–94
  and Syria, 87
  and trade, 64–66, 71–74
Hobbes, Thomas, 253
Homeland Security, US, 17, 109, 115,
  117, 245
Honduras, 105, 111, 117, 166
Hong Kong, 9, 132, 134, 184, 198
hostis humani generis ("enemy of
  humankind"), 203
Howard, Chris, 160–61, 175–78,
  187–89, 204–7
HSBC, 228, 231–32
human smuggling, 15, 17, 107–9, 113,
  116, 213, 223, 252
human trafficking, 7–9, 16, 18, 20, 22,
  223, 240
Humire, Joe, 101, 106, 275
Hussein, Saddam, 70, 84

Ibrahim, Dawood, 238
identity narratives, 269–71
illicit trade in tobacco products
  (ITTP), 16, 139–42, 155–57, 175,
  201, 237. *See also* tobacco
immigrants, illegal, 8–9, 17, 111, 114, 250
immigration and customs
  enforcement (ICE), 108
India, 201, 238
intellectual property, 8, 130–35, 196,
  201–2, 206, 236
International Anti-Counterfeiting
  Coalition, 12
International Center for Sport
  Security (ICSS), 152, 183–84

International Federation of
   Association Football (FIFA), 152,
   177–79, 182–84, 187
International Institute of Strategic
   Studies (IISS), 3–4
International Monetary Fund, 162,
   242
International Rebellion, 74–76
Interpol, 66, 156–57, 184, 192, 245
Iran, 14, 74, 232–33
   and Arbabsiar plot, 250–52
   Farsi, 67, 87, 92
   and Hezbollah, 28, 64, 74, 77, 82,
      85–87, 90, 251
   Islamic Revolution, 67, 87, 165
   nuclear program, 64, 83
   Qom, 66
   Quds Force, 66–67, 251
   and Venezuela, 65–69, 150–51, 165
Iran-Contra affair, 97
Iran-Iraq War, 84
Iranian Revolutionary Guard Corps
   (IRGC), 66–68, 82, 86–87, 165
Iraq, 10, 14, 24–25, 70, 188, 193, 205,
   206, 226, 264–66, 268–69
   Al Mahdi Army, 82
   Ba'ath Party, 70, 84
   US invasion of, 84, 102, 104–5
Isa Conde, Narciso, 75
Islam
   abaya (full-body robe), 144, 167, 169
   burqa (full head and body robes), 85
   de-radicalization, 262–64
   hadith, 89, 265–66, 286n4
   hijab (head scarf), 85, 88, 144–45,
      167
   Koran, 89–90, 265
   Muhammad (the Prophet), 84, 91,
      265–66, 286n4
   niqab (black veil that covers entire
      face, leaving only slit for eyes), 10
   Ramadan, 167–69
   Sharia (Islamic law), 16, 141, 153
Islamic Caliphate, 10. See also Daesh
Islamic State of Iraq and the Levant/
   Syria (ISIL/S). See Daesh (Arabic
   name for ISIL/ISIS)
Islamism, militant, 239
   and counterfeit sporting goods, 14
   and Daesh, 15

   growth of, 25
   and illicit trade, 191–92, 204–208
   militant, 66, 85, 139–40, 140–41,
      160–63, 166
   radicalization, 14, 66, 71, 166,
      262–65, 267
Israel, 25, 28, 49, 60, 77, 83, 85, 89–91,
   97, 166, 204, 271, 286n2

Jafar, Khalid, 96
Jeishy, Hassan, 91
jihadism, 15, 52, 66–67, 91, 113, 116,
   139–41, 167, 241, 263–67
Jiménez, Aref Richany, 64
Jiménez, Timoleón (alias
   "Timochenko"), 54
Jokan, Mandhai, 116
Joumaa, Ayman, 74, 93–94
Juárez (cartel), 110, 249
Jubeir, Adel al-, 251

Kabboul, Fadi, 64
Kan'an, Fawzi, 64–65
Kangas, Roger, 125
Kassar, Monser al-, 97
Kazakhstan, 124
keffiyeh (sheikh's headdress), 80
Kelly, Ray, 154–55
Khamenei, Sayyid Ali Hosseini, 85
Khans (Mongolian emperors), 120–25
   Chinggis (Genghis) Khan, 120,
      122–23
   Kublai Khan, 120, 122
kidnapping, 16, 33, 43–47, 49, 51,
   55–59, 90, 113, 139, 148–49, 171,
   213–15, 228, 237, 239, 247, 257–58
Kingpin Strategy, 217–19
Knights Templar (cartel), 115, 215,
   257, 260
Kourani, Mahmoud Youssef, 116
Kuwait, 91

La Familia Michoacana (cartel), 257
La Nueva Familia (cartel), 258
Lashkar-e-Taiba (LeT), 238, 247
latifundios (rural estates), 33, 46
Lebanese Canadian Bank (LBC), 92–94
Lebanon, 24, 64–65, 74, 77–96
   Baalbek, 86, 95
   Beirut, 28, 76, 77–78, 81, 83–84

Lebanon (*continued*)
 Beirut bombing (2013), 28, 83
 Beqaa Valley, 83, 86, 94–96
 Christian Phalange Party, 95
 Dahieh, 90
 Now Lebanon (online publication),
  88
 See also Hezbollah
Leviathan (Hobbes), 253
Liberia, 49
Libya, 14, 25, 139, 142, 205, 232
lithium, 64
"lone wolves," 15, 262–69
Lord, Fred, 152, 160, 175
Loret de Mola, Carlos, 212, 214, 220,
  225
Los Zetas (Mexican cartel), 17, 74,
  93–94, 110–13, 115, 216–17,
  246–47, 250, 257–61
Louis Vuitton, 6, 12, 128–29, 131
Louverture, Toussaint, 29
Luna, David, 137–38, 147, 160, 174–76
LVMH, 12

M-4, 204, *205*
M-16, 45, 49, 161, 204, *205*
Ma'arouf, Jamal, 154
Machado, Maria Corina, 40–41
Madrid bombings (2004), 12, 104
Maduro, Nicolás, 148, 220, 275
Mafia, 270
 California Mexican, 114
 Israeli, 166
 Italian, 21, 254
 Japanese, 21
 and loyalty, 223
 and RICO, 178
 Texas Mexican, 115
Magda, Yunus, 167
Mahdi, Imam, 265
Mahdi Army, Al, 82
Makhlouf, Rami, 153
Makled, Walid, 72–73
Malverde, Jesús, 259
Mandel, Robert, 241
Manwaring, Max, 101, 105–6
Mara Salvatrucha (MS-13), 111–113,
  117
marijuana, 7, 51, 211–14, 244
Maronite Catholics, 79, 164

Marquéz, Iván, 75
Marxism, 16, 32, 41, 46, 66, 69–70,
  74–75, 165, 239
Marzouk, Mousa Abu, 154
May, Theresa, 137
MBR-200. *See* Bolivarian
  Revolutionary Movement 200
  (MBR-200)
Medellín (Colombian cartel), 17,
  33–36, 74, 94
Medina, Pablo, 74
Melzer, Susan, 174–76
Mendoza, Lorenzo, 150
mens rea (intention to commit a
  crime), 196, 203
methamphetamine, 9, 114, 213, 244
Mexico
 Ciudad Juárez, 216, 219, 249, 254
 Justice in Mexico Project, 225
 Mérida Initiative, 225, 294n37
 Tamaulipas, 219–20, 225, 246, 257
 "Tortilla Riots," 224
Miami, Florida, 210–11, 228, 244
militarization, 217, 225
Milne, Sevmag, 28
Moncada, Samuel, 31–32
money laundering, 9, 13, 18, 21–22,
  54, 65, 68, 74, 107, 109–10,
  210–11
 definition of, 229
 and Hezbollah, 93–94
 process of, 228–35
 and sport corruption, 160, 162,
  164–66, 177–79, 181–88
 and travel agencies, 65
MoneyGram International Inc., 233
Mongolia, 119–26, 136
Moore, Michael, 29
Morales, Evo, 64
Morales, Treviño, 16–17
Moreau, Jean-Luc, 190–93, 208
Morocco, 142–43
Morris, Erik, 59
Mossack Fonseca (law firm), 163, 210
Mouawad, Robert, 93
Mouride Brotherhood (*Confrérie des
  Mourides*), 192
Moyo, Dambisa, 194
MS-13. *See* Mara Salvatrucha (MS-13)
Mughniyah, Imad, 83

multiagency swarm (counterterrorism tactic), 235–36, 245
Muslim Brotherhood, 167

narcocorrido (song that glorifies drug cartels), 33–34, 256–57, 271
narcocultura (criminal culture of drug cartels), 33–34, 256
narcohackers, 259
narcomanifestaciones (protests in favor of cartels), 260
narcomantas (banners with threatening messages), 257–58
narcomensaje (messages left on dead bodies), 257–60
narco-rap, 257
narcoterrorism, 3, 27, 35, 66, 82, 88, 165
Nasr Al-Din, Ghazi, 64–66
Nasrallah, Hassan, 85, 89–91
Nasser, Mustafa Satmariam (nom de guerre, Abu Musab al-Suri), 266–67
natural disasters, 21
Nawabi, Shahla, 144–45
Neumann, Vanessa
    Asymmetrica, 5, 131–132, 143–146, 152, 160, 162, 176, 207, 220, 246
    Central Asia Counter Transnational Threats Symposium, 121–22
    family of, 1–3
    "Global Convergence of the Crime-Terror Threat, The" 151–52
    at International Institute of Strategic Studies (IISS), 3–4
    "my kids" (young Venezuelan university students), 148–49
    National Defense University, 136–38
    student at Columbia University, 2–3, 30
    teacher at Hunter College, 3
    Vanessa Neumann, Inc. (later Asymmetrica), 4, 144
Nijmeier, Tanja, 53
Noble, Ronald K., 12, 157
"noble savage" myth, 26, 283n24
Noguera, Jorge, 59
Norte del Valle (cartel), 18
North American Free Trade Agreement (NAFTA), 220, 240. *See also* free trade

North Coast (cartel), 18
North Korea, 82, 124–25
Northern Ireland, 12, 49, 92, 247
Northern Triangle, 105, 107
Notorious Markets List, 132–33
Novartis (pharmaceutical group), 177–78, 190–93, 197–99, 208
Núñez Fabrega, Fernando, 165

Obama, Barack, 105, 220
Odeh, Youssef, 155
OECD. *See* Organisation for Economic Development and Co-operation (OECD)
Office of Foreign Asset Control (OFAC), US Treasury, 64–65, 233
Organisation for Economic Development and Co-operation (OECD), 11, 130, 137–38, 147–48, 152, 157, 160–62, 174, 193, 195, 220
    Financial Action Task Force (FATF), 124, 162, 245
    Guidance on Conflict Minerals, 54
    Illicit Trade, 195
    Task Force on Charting Illicit Trade (later Countering Illicit Trade), 11, 147, 152, 157, 160, 180
Organization of the Petroleum Exporting Countries (OPEC), 68
Ould Kablia, Daho, 140

Padilla, José, 116
Pakistan, 122, 124, 233, 238–39
Palmer, Larry, 72
Pan Am Flight 103 bombing, 96–97
Panama, 14, 52–53, 116–17, 132, 160–68, 170–73, 183, 189
    Agua Dulce, 166
    Colón, 163–68, 170, 173
    Islamic Foundation of Panama, 166–67, 172
    mosques in, 166–67
    Panama City, 166, 172
Panama Canal, 165–66, 172
Panama Papers, 162–63, 210
Passports to Terror (CNN investigation), 72
Patriot Act (US), 94
Pax Mafiosa, 219–20, 217

PDVSA (Petroleum of Venezuela), 36, 64, 68, 74
Peña Nieto, Enrique, 225, 258, 293–94n36
Penn, Sean, 29
Pereira, Colin, 30
Pérez, Carlos Andrés, 40, 74
Pérez Henao, Diego (aka "Rastrojo"), 70
Peru, 34, 75, 215
Petkoff, Teodoro, 3, 39
Petraeus, David, 226
pharmaceuticals
    Coartem case, 190–192, 194, 197
    counterfeit, 194–203
    falsified medicines, 195–96, 198, 202, 207
    illicit trade, 158, 177, 190–93
Plan Colombia (counternarcotics program), 43, 215, 227
Plan Patriota (counterinsurgency program), 43
plata o plomo (silver/money or lead/bullet), 19, 108, 114, 242
populism, 28–29, 32
Porter, Michael, 2
positive externality, 248
poverty, 7, 32, 42, 61, 66, 117, 168, 194, 210, 221–22, 260
Putin, Vladimir, 69, 254

Qaddafi, Moammar, 69, 75, 166
Qatar, 91, 152, 182–83
Quinn Emanuel (law firm), 177–78

Rabbani, Mohsen, 66
Racketeer Influenced and Corrupt Organizations Act (RICO), 178
Rahbani, Ziad, 90
Rangel Silva, Henry, 73
Rawley, Chris, 153
refugees, 42, 45, 87–88, 98, 112, 275
resource curse (paradox of plenty), 120
Revolutionary Armed Forces of Colombia (FARC), 3–4, 10, 16–17, 27, 32, 35, 41–44, 47–48, 63, 66, 70, 73–75, 97, 165
    and "bomb necklaces," 140
FARC-EP, 61

funding, 51–57
and Hezbollah, 82
and human rights violations, 59
Law 002 ("war tax" law), 53
and money laundering, 93
and oil, 54–55, 268
Red Urbana Antonio Nariño (RUAN, Antonio Nariño Urban Network), 53
Reyes, Raúl, 27
Robin Hood narrative, 61, 214–15, 259
Rocket-propelled grenades (RPGs), 155, 204, *205*, 250
Rodríguez, Alí, 74
Rodríguez Chacín, Ramón, 71
Rodriguez Zapatero, José Luis, 105
Russia, 13–14, 68, 87, 120, 122–24, 135, 147, 183. 204, 239, 254. *See also* Soviet Union
Rx North, 199

Saba, Samira, 40–41
Sabbagh, Radwan, 64, 151, 289n5
Sadr, Moqtada Al, 82
Samper, Ernesto, 58–59
Santokhi, Chan, 166
Santos, Juan Manuel, 32–33, 52–53, 59
Sao Paulo Forum (1990), 74
Saudi Arabia, 14, 79, 87, 91, 117, 166, 168
    Arbabsiar plot, 250–55
    banks, 232
Schaan, Joan Neuhaus, 252
Secret Airstrip, 34
Securities and Exchange Commission (US), 54
Senegal, 6–7, 142, 191–92
September 11, 2001, 70, 77, 108, 117, 212, 236, 240, 252, 264, 266
shadow facilitators, 18–19
Shakuri, Gholam, 251
Sharia (Islamic law), 16, 141, 153
Sierra Leone, 54
Silk, Katie, 193
Sinaloa (cartel), 110, 112, 211–16, 218–19, 254, 256, 258–59
Singapore, 132, 211, 262
Sixtus IV, Pope, 25
slavery, 9, 10, 16, 17, 99, 109, 114, 117, 172, 203, 235–37, 266

Smith, Lee, 77–80, 88, 283n23
Snitch, The, 34
Société Generale Bank of Lebanon
    (SGBL), 94
Somalia, 97, 204–7
    Al-Barakat, 252
    Al Shabaab, 10, 204, 252
    Mogadishu, 204–6
    Mogadishu suicide bombings
        (July 2016), 205
Sotloff, Steven, 24–25
South of the Border (film), 29
Soviet Union, 1, 74, 87, 97, 104,
    120–23, 140–41, 149, 239. See also
    Russia
sport corruption
    and counterfeiting, 171, 189
    and economics, 183–86
    forms of, 179–83
    ghost matches, 186
    and International Federation of
        Association Football (FIFA), 152,
        177–79, 182–84, 187
    match-fixing, 181, 186–88
statelessness, power of, 245
Stone, Oliver, 29
Stratton, Richard, 94–96
Strempler, Andrew, 199
Strong Horse politics, 24
subject matter experts (SMEs), 100,
    136
Sudan, 42
Suriname, 166
Syria, 42, 64, 70–72, 79, 97, 117
    and cigarette smuggling, 14, 152–54
    and Daesh, 15, 25, 264–66, 268–69
    Damascus, 65, 69, 286n2
    Latakia, 153
    and Lebanon, 82–83, 87–88
    Raqqa, 15
    Treaty of Friendship and
        Cooperation, 87

Tajeddine, Ali, 93–94
Tal Cual ("Just So"; newspaper
    cofounded by Neumann's
    grandfather), 3, 39
Taliban, 70, 143
tax evasion, 181, 221
tax havens, 183, 210

taxation
    on cigarettes, 13, 136, 154–55,
        157–58, 205, 237
    and Daesh, 153, 268
    and FARC, 51–52, 54
    and money laundering, 229, 232
    and safe passage, 141–42
    "war tax" on drug crops, 51, 53–54
Thailand, 9
thawb (white robe-dress worn by
    men), 80
Tijuana (cartel), 111
tobacco
    British-American Tobacco, 134, 204
    cellulose acetate tow, 156–59
    Chinese black market, 134
    contraband cigarettes, 13–14, 16,
        22, 53, 124–25, 134, 139
    illicit trade in tobacco products
        (ITTP), 16, 139–42, 155–57, 175,
        201, 237
    illicit white cigarettes (smuggled
        but not counterfeit), 14, 158, 204–5
    and Mokhtar Belmokhtar
        ("Mr. Marlboro"), 139–42
    Operation Smokescreen, 155
    Philip Morris, 134, 204
    and taxation, 13, 136, 154–55,
        157–58, 205, 237
Todd, Brianne, 125
transnational crime, 240
Trump, Donald, 41, 178–79, 239
Turkey, 14, 25, 67, 153, 188, 265

Ukraine, 14, 204, 254
ummah (Muslim community), 267
United Arab Emirates, 13–14, 143–44,
    195, 199, 205–6, 239
    Abu Dhabi, 13, 16, 139, 144
    Sheikh Zayed Mosque, 144–45
    See also Dubai, United Arab Emirates
United Kingdom, 28, 31, 41, 148, 198–99
    and European Convention on
        Human Rights and Fundamental
        Freedoms, 204
    London Olympics (2012), 179
    National Crime Agency, 158, 245
    and National Defense University
        conference, 136–37
    National Health Service, 204

United Nations
  Convention Against Corruption, 124
  Global Fund, 190–91, 193
  Globalization of Crime, The, 109
United Nations Office on Drugs and
  Crime (UNODC), 70, 141–42, 228
United States Southern Command, 69
United States Trade Representative
  (USTR), 132–33
United States Visitor and Immigrant
  Status Indicator Technology
  (US-VISIT), 108
Urabeños (criminal gang), 52
Uribe, Alvaro, 32–34, 47, 58–59
Uribe, Mario, 59–60
Uruguay, 75
USAID, 83
Utopia, 72

Vance, Cyrus R., 232
vehicle-borne improvised explosive
  devices (VBIEDs, car bombs), 34,
  83, 205, 249
Venezuela
  Barinas, 76
  Biblos Travel Agency, 65
  Bolivarian Alliance for the Peoples
    of Our America (ALBA), 69
  Bolivarian Continental
    Coordinator, 75
  Bolivarian Continental Movement,
    75–76
  Bolivarian Liberation Forces, 72
  Bolivarian Revolution, 3–4, 28, 31,
    38–40, 66, 69, 148, 263
  Bolivarian Revolutionary
    Movement 200 (MBR-200), 39–40
  Caracas, 2, 29, 36–38, 40
  Caracas Country Club, 37–38
  CVG Ferrominera (state-owned
    mining company), 64, 151
  DISIP (intelligence service, later
    SEBIN), 71
  Hilal Travel Agency, 65
  International Development Bank
    (BID, Banco Internacional de
    Desarrollo), 68
  National Bolivarian Police (PNB), 70
  Orinoco Belt, 68
  Quds Force, 66–67
  Shia Islamic Center, 65
  See also Chávez, Hugo
Venezuelan Military Industries
  Company (CAVIM), 64
Verstrynge, Jorge, 67
Vietnam War, 43, 104
Villiger, Marco, 177
Violencia, La, 32
violent nonstate actors, 103, 249

Wachovia Bank, 228, 233
Wade, Abdoulaye, 192
Waked, Nidal, 164–65
Wall, David, 11–12
Waltz, Michael, 143–44
warfare, generations of, 101–6, 111
Warner, Jack, 178–79, 183
Watergate scandal, 228
Weber, Max, 253
Weekly Standard, The, 4, 63, 77
Werlen, Thomas, 177
Winslow, Don, 213
World Bank, 183, 221, 242
World Customs Organization, 130,
  147, 195
World Health Organization (WHO)
  definition of counterfeit medicine,
    195–96
  Framework Convention on
    Tobacco Control (FCTC),
    157–58, 203
  International Medical Products
    Anti-Counterfeiting Task Force
    (IMPACT), 203
  Protocol to Eliminate Illicit Trade,
    157–58
World Trade Center bombing (1993),
  12
World Trade Organization, 195, 201
World War I, 102, 253

Yakuza (Japanese crime syndicate), 21
Yamani, Abu Bassir al-, 164
Yemen, 223, 264
Yves Saint Laurent, 12

Zarqawi, Abu Musab al-, 266
Zawahiri, Ayman Al-, 267